OF
COUNSEL

OF COUNSEL

THE CHALLENGES OF THE MODI–JAITLEY ECONOMY

ARVIND SUBRAMANIAN

PENGUIN
VIKING

An imprint of Penguin Random House

VIKING

USA | Canada | UK | Ireland | Australia
New Zealand | India | South Africa | China

Viking is part of the Penguin Random House group of companies
whose addresses can be found at global.penguinrandomhouse.com

Published by Penguin Random House India Pvt. Ltd
7th Floor, Infinity Tower C, DLF Cyber City,
Gurgaon 122 002, Haryana, India

First published in Viking by Penguin Random House India 2018

Copyright © Arvind Subramanian 2018

ISBN 9780670092093

For sale in the Indian Subcontinent only

Typeset in Adobe Caslon Pro by Manipal Digital Systems, Manipal
Printed at Replika Press Pvt. Ltd, India

www.penguin.co.in

For

Bodhi, our new anchor and future
Tia, Karti, Maggie, Rohan, and Parul
Team CEA

Contents

Chapter 5: Agriculture

Chapter 6: The State's Relationship with the Individual

Chapter 7: Speaking Truth to Power

Chapter 8: What Do They Know of Economics Who Don't Know Globalization and Tennis?

Acknowledgements

This book is a repository of my writings and reflections since I was appointed Chief Economic Adviser (CEA) to the Government of India in October 2014. It is also a retrospective assessment of key events and policies. Because they are a collective product, I owe deep gratitude to all those who worked with me, whom I worked for, and who influenced me in that period. A comprehensive list would run into several pages. So with profuse apologies to those omitted—and acutely mindful of the dictum that the debts one owes vastly exceed those one acknowledges—let me thank a few.

As I have said many times, I had a dream boss, the Minister of Finance, Arun Jaitley. He gave me the freedom and support to be a hyperactive CEA while also being a shield, protecting me from the consequences of my overreach. Without him, my job, let alone this book, would not have been doable.

In the trenches were those who helped and contributed on a daily basis and without whom no consistently serious and quality output could have been produced. In the innermost circle was Team CEA, comprising members of the Indian Economic Service (IES), as well as outsiders who worked with me over the course of my tenure and many of whom were my family at work. I could write more about all their distinctive contributions but here I can only extend profound thanks to (in alphabetical order): Amrit Amirapu, Abhishek Anand, Shoumitro Chatterjee, Anthony Cyriac, Josh Felman, Siddharth George, Rangeet Ghosh, Siddharth Hari, Devesh Kapur, Parth Khare, Ananya Kotia, Rohit Lamba, Zubair Noqvi, Boban Paul, Dev Patel, Kapil Patidar, V.K. Premkumaran, Gayathri Ganesh, Siddharth Ravinutala, Sutirtha Roy, Justin Sandefur, Utkarsh Saxena, Kishan Shah, M.R. Sharan, Navneeraj Sharma, Aniket Singh, N. Srinivasan, and Tejaswi Velayudhan.

Counsellor, reader, editor, and muse Josh Felman expanded my bandwidth and that of Team CEA immeasurably. His contribution has been stupendous and I owe him gratitude beyond measure.

Nripendra Misra, the Principal Secretary to the Prime Minister (whose sense of humour, self-awareness and perspective were remarkable), and my close friend T.V. Somanathan, former Joint Secretary in the Prime Minister's Office and a jewel of the Indian bureaucracy, were two key interlocutors who kept me involved in a wide range of discussions and helped me navigate the rarefied world of policymaking. Hasmukh Adhia, Subhash Garg and Rajiv Mehrishi, my senior colleagues in the Ministry of Finance, as well as Simanchala Dash and Saurabh Shukla, with their openness, cooperation and warm embrace, allowed an outsider like me to work as an insider. Subhash Garg was also a rock of support in rough times.

I also owe thanks to a few people I turned to for help in understanding specific issues: the superb, public-spirited journalist, Harish Damodaran (agriculture); Sajjid Chinoy, the thoughtful analyst (macroeconomics and financial markets); Ashish Gupta, one of the few heroes of the Twin Balance Sheet (TBS) challenge (banking and corporate sectors); Arbind Modi, Alok Shukla and Amitabh Kumar, the amazingly knowledgeable and fine revenue service officers (tax); and Nandan Nilekani, the architect of one of the world's biggest efforts at building state capacity (JAM). My thanks to Madhav Khosla for suggesting the title of the book.

Meru Gokhale, my editor, was a calm and engaged presence, shepherding the book from conception to publication with the help of her terrific team at Penguin Random House.

Guides and anchors—Rukmini Banerji, Ramachandra Guha, Devesh Kapur, Udaya Kumar, Pratap Bhanu Mehta and Harsha Singh—kept me grounded in the quicksand that is the world of power and policy in Lutyens' Delhi.

I am blessed to have siblings—Anand, Mukund and Sunanda—who took unqualified pleasure in my work and its rewards. So too did my parents, my mother Girija, and my recently deceased father V.K. Subramanian, who probably had more influence on me than I gave them credit for.

I could have attempted nothing, much less accomplished anything, without my children, Tia, Karti and Rohan— inspirational activist, teacher-Buddha and joyful incandescence, respectively—and above all my unfailingly giving wife, Parul. They generously forgave me my desertion of them in order to be Chief Economic Adviser. This book owes everything to them.

Introduction

I was in Machu Picchu, the site of the spectacular, isolated ruins of the Incan civilization in Peru, when I first received an email in July 2014 asking if I'd be interested in the job of Chief Economic Adviser (CEA) to the Government of India. I was surprised, for I had no connections with anyone in the newly formed National Democratic Alliance (NDA) government. However, the prospect of working for a government with a decisive mandate, committed to reviving an economy wracked by slowing growth, rising macroeconomic troubles and corruption scandals, was unimaginably exciting.

I flew to Delhi a few days later and had encouraging meetings with Finance Minister Arun Jaitley, and Nripendra Misra, Principal Secretary to the Prime Minister. A few weeks later, the Indian media reported that I had been appointed the CEA; even the *New York Times* carried a long article on me. But from the government itself I heard nothing—for another two and a half months. I witnessed the media speculation silently, with as little real information as any of the speculators. I felt a bit like Mark Twain: 'The news of my death [read: appointment] has been greatly exaggerated.'

The delay, I was later told, arose partly because the nativist sections of the ruling party were opposing me, claiming I had indulged in anti-national activities. According to the Twitter trollers, my crime was that I had testified to the US Congress, inviting—even goading—the US to take action against India. The irony was that my testimony was actually aimed at protecting India, preventing the US from naming it as an offender on intellectual property issues. The bigger irony was that I had succeeded in my task, for which the then Indian ambassador in Washington, S. Jaishankar, duly thanked me. Eventually, I was appointed the CEA in October 2014, although the charge of being mentally un-Indian would come up occasionally during my tenure.

I left my job four years later in July 2018. My dream boss, Arun Jaitley, announced my departure while in quarantine after a major surgery, in a deeply moving Facebook post titled 'Thank you, Arvind'. Soon after, a number of my younger colleagues— Team CEA, as they called themselves—came with their spouses to New Delhi's Indira Gandhi International Airport, where they bid my wife and me a teary farewell.

Dramatic beginnings and emotional endings bookended my nearly four-year tenure as the CEA. It was the best, most exciting, challenging and fulfilling job I have ever had—and probably ever will.

~

One of the responsibilities of having been a privileged witness to history is the need to record for future historians the events and debates, actions and reforms of these years. In that way, I can also leave behind a record of my own contributions and failures. Accordingly, this book brings together my writings and reflections during (and since) my four years as the CEA.

I suspect that retrospective assessments of these years will accord demonetization an obsessive primacy. Fair enough. Posterity has its prerogatives that the present cannot pre-empt. But in economic policymaking terms, a lot more happened (and did not happen), which posterity should not be allowed to forget. It must have the full picture, the comprehensive inputs, or to quote Salman Rushdie, 'not a piece of blubber but the whole wretched whale'.

This volume, then, is an attempt to create such a record. Readers should be forewarned that the focus is squarely on policy debates. This is no kiss-and-tell memoir, no gossip-laden account of intrigue, backbiting, favour-trading and double-dealing, no tale of grand heroism and base betrayal. Not that the imperial spaces encompassed within Herbert Baker's awesomely symmetric domes of North and South Blocks, flanking Raisina Hill in Lutyens' New Delhi, don't lend themselves to these shadier pursuits. Perhaps they are the very stuff of power.

However, the theory of comparative advantage dictates that recounting these juicier tales is best left to others: gossip columnists, Twitter trollers and screaming TV anchors who holler to their multi-screen pundits: 'no more than two people [talking] at the same time'. Meanwhile, economists should focus on economics.

First, it might be useful to explain what a chief economic adviser actually does. In the public's eye, the role of the CEA is straightforward: it is, as the title suggests, giving the government economic advice. And this is indeed what I thought when I took office.

In fact, however, the CEA has no clear job description. The happy (or dirty) secret is that not much is actually required of him (unfortunately, there have been no women occupants of this job yet). The only requirement is to produce an annual economic survey reviewing the Indian economy—and that work can be delegated, should the CEA so wish.

Similarly, any involvement in policymaking is pretty much the result of the CEA's own temperament and inclinations, whims and idiosyncrasies, efforts and relationships. There is no real obligation on anyone, anywhere in government, to consult the CEA on any policy issue. As a result, the CEA is only as useful and effective as he makes himself, or is perceived or called upon to be by other key players in the system.

In my case, I had big ambitions for my job and role. I wanted to be involved in all aspects of economic policy within and outside government. I possess a manic energy, bordering on insanity, which makes me think (probably self-delusionally) that I can juggle many balls at the same time, contribute many ideas, and in the famous characterization of Isaiah Berlin, be both fox and hedgehog. I felt I had been given this one-time opportunity that I wanted to seize and not squander.

I also felt acutely aware of how much had to be done to address India's challenges: to transform a low-income economy into a prosperous middle-income country with all groups partaking of that prosperity in a way that would make the various divisions of caste, gender, religion, language, location and class melt away, or at least become less salient. And like all policymaking economists, I believed in Keynes's famous observation that it is 'ideas not interests' that shape the world, so it followed that the institution of the CEA was uniquely positioned to help in India's development transformation.

I also felt I needed to live up to the tradition of the office. Every Indian economist who has even a shred of policy pretension aspires to this job. Some covet it ferociously. I was lucky enough for my dream to be fulfilled, an interloper appended to a lineage of illustrious giants who built the foundations of India's economic policy framework, going back to I.G. Patel, V.K. Ramaswamy, Manmohan Singh, Ashok Mitra and Bimal Jalan.

In my old office room in North Block, squeezed between portraits of Rabindranath Tagore, Mahatma Gandhi and Jawaharlal Nehru, there is a board listing the names of my predecessors. Whenever I looked at it, I was reminded of the Patek Philippe advertisement: 'You never actually own a Patek Philippe. You merely look after it for the next generation.' As the CEA, I saw myself as the custodian of a sacred tradition. I felt responsible for upholding it honourably—and, at the same time, was petrified of debasing it.

This sense of tradition and continuity was reinforced strongly when Haseeb Drabu, the former finance minister of Jammu and Kashmir, informed me that the first Economic Survey was presented in Parliament by Pandit Jawaharlal Nehru. I felt blessed to be part of anything to do with one of India's nation builders, a figure of world history. I was not going to forgo my opportunity to occupy a place, even if only as a footnote, in India's economic history.

Having big ambitions for the job was one thing, but being able to deliver was an altogether different ballgame. I felt equipped for the technical demands of my job, having worked on macroeconomic issues, both at the country and international levels, as well as on macro-development issues such as economic growth and international trade. However, I had not lived or worked in India for thirty-three years. I had absolutely no experience of working in government or in leading large teams. In the previous decade, I had been a researcher and policy wonk in the insular Washington world of think tanks, universities and the International Monetary Fund (IMF), where I was accountable mainly to myself.

Transitioning to Indian public life and specifically to North Block, the seat of the Ministry of Finance, with politicians as bosses and entrenched government bureaucrats as colleagues, with my every move being watched and every utterance reported, was a radical leap that, at the time, I was not even aware I was making. Looking back, adjusting to it and then growing to love it seems a fairly low-probability outcome. How did it happen?

I realized that fulfilling my ambitious job description would require teamwork. Team CEA would need to be built with 'insiders' from the Indian Economic Service (IES, which I formally headed as CEA), but also supplemented with 'outsiders', bright students from foreign universities. The insiders would contribute their knowledge of the Indian economy, along with an understanding of ground realities, constraints and bureaucratic procedures. The outsiders would provide the latest skills and techniques, and possibly a freshness of perspective.

For this model to work, however, the outsiders could not carry a sense of being special because they were at universities like Harvard or Princeton; they had to be willing to work as equals with the insiders. I consequently chose my outsiders with a particular eye on their attitude and interpersonal skills, placing a high premium on humility. In turn, the insiders had to see value in learning about state-of-the-art skills, techniques and modes of thinking.

Even that wasn't enough; there also needed to be a balance. Too much reliance on outsiders and the CEA would become isolated and ineffective as the insiders would stymie them in ways that the CEA would not even realize. Too much reliance on insiders and the CEA's bandwidth would shrink because there simply wasn't enough skilled expertise to analyse all the 'Big Data', run the ten million regressions, produce the frequent PowerPoint presentations for senior policymakers, and ideate on the spectrum of issues that the rich Indian economy throws up.

I was fortunate in having young IES officers who bought into this ambitious, even risky, mission, and saw the outsiders as collaborative assets rather than threats. They were my bridge to the world of North Block's bureaucracy.

There was a Bengali, Rangeet Ghosh, deeply interested in economic theory and research, who was also able to educate me on Tagore, Satyajit Ray and Ramkinkar Baij. I think he only started taking me seriously when I began an op-ed on the importance of investment in the railways by recalling the famous scene in Ray's *Pather Panchali* where the young Apu espies an approaching train, billowing thick black smoke. The young bhadralok decided he had a boss with passable aesthetic qualifications.

There was Kapil Patidar, a farmer's son from Madhya Pradesh, who first encountered English as a medium of instruction only during his MPhil days and whose detailed knowledge of India's fiscal accounts, obsession with perfectionism, dedication, and much else still blows me away.

Zubair Noqvi, whose entire village in rural Uttar Pradesh turned out in celebration on hearing that he had passed the IES exam, deftly handled personnel and media matters and acted as the conscience of Team CEA.

Three very different people from very different walks of life. But they worked together so harmoniously and efficiently that I called them by one name: RKZ.

Finally, over and above these assets, I had my own personal chief economic adviser, the deeply thoughtful Josh Felman, a long-term collaborator and colleague from the IMF, who was my sounding board, reader and editor, who expanded my bandwidth immeasurably even as he worked seamlessly with Team CEA.

Wary of the unfamiliar high-stakes world I was entering, riddled with performance anxiety but imbued with a passionate sense of mission for the role of the CEA, I plunged myself into the job.

~

What is this book about and what ties it together? If there is a unifying theme, it is what I learnt about the Indian economy that I did not really know before I took up the job.

I had done a lot of academic and policy research on India throughout my career, compiled in my 2008 book, *India's Turn: Understanding the Economic Transformation*. My first influence as a researcher came in the late 1980s when India's trade negotiators picked up a study of mine. It documented and quantified the loss to India from the intellectual property rights negotiations in the Uruguay Round of trade negotiations (TRIPs). I was told that when the United States trade representative, Carla Hills, came to convince India that TRIPs would be in our interest, the then Indian commerce minister handed her my study as refutation of her argument. Other studies included my 2004 paper with Dani Rodrik, arguing that India's growth took off at least a decade before the reforms of 1991, and a 2006 paper on India's unusual pattern of development. I had always followed India's policy debates closely and wrote on India in my monthly columns in the *Business Standard*.

Even so, India and the Indian economy surprised me in many ways. Those surprises, and the new ideas and insights that they led to, form the essence of this book. Almost every section in this book was inspired by puzzles I encountered once I became CEA.

Chapter 1, for example, emphasizes that the Indian development model is unique, what I call Precocious Development, because India is doing what other countries did at a much later stage of development, when they were much richer. Politically, India became and sustained a democracy right from its inception; economically, it embarked on a services-led pattern of growth at a much earlier stage than other successful economies.

Both of these are achievements: we are rightly proud of our democracy and our information technology (IT) sector. But early democracy is also a burden because it forces the state to redistribute resources when it does not have the capacity to do so. Similarly, early reliance on services also represents a failure because it partly reflects inadequate industrialization, and over time, premature de-industrialization so that insufficient formal jobs are created for less skilled workers in, say, textiles, clothing, leather and footwear. How this happened and its implications for policy are developed in a conversation with a bright young professor, Karthik Muralidharan (Section 1.1).

Another aspect of the India model, which I had to face every day as the CEA, is that governments of all stripes have found it difficult to get out of bad policies (such as subsidies) or unwind inefficient enterprises, especially in the public sector. It seemed that India had gone from 'socialism with limited entry to capitalism without exit', a problem I termed the 'Chakravyuha Challenge' (referring to Arjuna's son, Abhimanyu, who entered a military formation, fought valiantly, but died because he did not know how to get out of it). I raised and discussed this issue in the Economic Survey of 2015–16, and Section 1.3 in this chapter summarizes the main ideas.

One of the reasons why reforms have often been stymied is that India went from 'crony socialism to stigmatized capitalism'. Others might say that the evolution was towards 'crony capitalism'. But I think 'stigmatized capitalism' is a better phrase, not least because it captures the fact that public scepticism and suspicion extend not just to the private sector but also to the state that is meant to be regulating it. It is the backdrop of stigmatized capitalism that explains the sting of the *suit-boot-ki-sarkar* taunt hurled by the Congress party leader, Rahul Gandhi, at the government.

Anti-corruption institutions have been given considerable leeway to investigate official actions precisely because the public has become sceptical of the state, and because corruption, resulting in favours to the private sector, is seen as a major problem. No less than four investigative institutions have been empowered:

the courts, the Comptroller and Auditor General (CAG), the Central Vigilance Commission (CVC) and the Central Bureau of Investigation (CBI). These 4Cs have pursued any exercise of discretion zealously, especially following a spate of corruption scandals in the early years of the new millennium, but even in cases where there was no whiff of malfeasance. In the United States, there is much talk about the Deep State. Sometimes I wonder whether the 4Cs embody the Indian Deep State.

This combination of stigmatized capitalism and the 4C problem has had major consequences for Indian policymaking. For example, it hinders any private-sector involvement in existing public-sector assets. So, privatization is difficult, and privatization involving selling land almost impossible: that is why I fear that privatization of hotels, which is an economic no-brainer, will be difficult to pull off. It also explains why public assets have been sold to other public-sector companies: the Oil and Natural Gas Corporation (ONGC), the upstream state oil company, has bought Hindustan Petroleum Corporation Limited (HPCL), one of the downstream oil companies; the Life Insurance Corporation (LIC) has bought stakes in the failing Industrial Development Bank of India (IDBI) and has been a major participant in the disinvestments that have taken place; and the State Bank of India (SBI), the largest public-sector bank, has bought other banks and is playing a role in the Infrastructure Leasing and Financial Services (IL&FS) scandal. Stigmatized capitalism has meant that the state is *back*!

However, the problems go far beyond the return of 'statism'. Indeed, it is not an exaggeration to say that stigmatized capitalism has led to paralysis in policymaking. The most salient example concerns the Twin Balance Sheet (TBS) problem, which was only seriously addressed some eight years after the first signs became evident. (I discuss this case in detail later.)

The paralysis extends far beyond the political class to officials, both in the government and in the public sector. We used to think of official discretion as the source of poor policies, because it led to favouritism and corruption. That was certainly true many years ago. Stigmatized capitalism and the 4C problem have led to the death of governmental discretion, giving us decades of indecision and inaction.

Even when decisions are made, stigmatized capitalism privileges a morality-play perspective that distorts policy outcomes. In the case of the TBS challenge, primacy has been accorded to going after the bad guys over allowing room for honest mistakes on the part of not-so-bad guys; sticks have been favoured over carrots; and the past has become an obsession at the expense of preventing the recurrence of future problems.

Finally, in thrall to stigmatized capitalism and fearful of the 4Cs, the executive has, over decades, ceded ground on decision making to the one organ that still retains strong public legitimacy, namely, the higher courts, especially the Supreme Court. Slowly, steadily and not costlessly, the judiciary has acquired a greater role in economic policymaking. In particular, it has shifted the balance of institutional power and authority away from the executive and legislature. Indeed, it seems at times that the only legitimate locus of decision making, even on major economic policies, is the Supreme Court. This situation is certainly better than a state of indecision. But it is not without costs.

The costs arise because economic policymaking requires balancing costs and benefits, harmonizing interests of different groups, and making trade-offs that often have profound political consequences. In contrast, judicial processes and verdicts favour blunt rules over calibrated policy instruments. Moreover, blunt rules can have inappropriate consequences: discretion should not be so circumscribed, spectrum should not always be auctioned, and eliminating corruption cannot be the overriding objective of policy because zero corruption will almost surely entail foregone development opportunities.

So that is where we are. A key long-term challenge will therefore be to re-equilibrate this institutional balance, so that the executive and legislature regain lost legitimacy and authority in decision making. In the meantime, we might say, 'The King is dead. Long live the Justices.' And sometimes: 'Long live the Unaccountable Regulators.'

~

When I first took up the CEA's job, I had the sense—which I articulated publicly two months into my tenure—that the corporate and banking sectors were both deeply stressed after the boom of the noughties. The problem turned out to be even more serious than I had originally understood, and my thinking on the strategy to address it evolved considerably. For example, I was initially in favour of creating a bad bank like many countries had done to solve the TBS problem. I still believe that a bad bank could have resolved the problem much more quickly, and hence at a lower cost to the taxpayer. However, I have accepted that a 'judicial strategy' was necessary, for the reasons that I have just mentioned, namely, that the government felt it lacked the legitimacy to deal with the problem directly.

This judicial strategy has made a good start, facilitated by one of the big achievements of the government, namely, the passage of a new bankruptcy code. Even so, the year 2018 has proved an annus horribilis for the financial system with a series of scandals beginning with Nirav Modi, extending to some senior private bankers, then spreading to India's non-bank financial companies such as IL&FS. The troubles in the NBFCs seem vaguely familiar; they resemble the problems in the US non-bank sector, which brought down its financial system in 2008. But in some sense it is no surprise that the US non-banks got into trouble, since these were 'shadow banks', outside the oversight of the regulator. NBFCs, in contrast, are 'sunshine' financial institutions (although some seem distinctly 'shady') in plain sight of the regulator, the Reserve Bank of India (RBI).

It cannot be emphasized enough that the origin of today's TBS problems goes back to the early years of the new millennium, the Original Sin being the reckless lending that occurred during the boom period in which private infrastructure projects were financed not by the capital market, not by private-sector financial institutions, but by public-sector banks (PSBs).

The government has had its share of complicity in these events, past and present. That the TBS problem has persisted for so long and that a series of scandals have erupted on its watch do not reflect very well on the regulator of the financial system, the RBI.

The RBI remains one of India's most trusted and trustworthy institutions and for good reason. It has implemented a new inflation-targeting framework and brought down inflation from double-digit levels. It did a terrific job in handling the near-crisis of 2013. It implemented the Asset Quality Review (AQR) that accelerated the resolution of the TBS problems. More recently, it has been commendably resolute in dealing with the less viable banks under the so-called Prompt Corrective Action Framework, forcing them to reduce their activity. It has also courageously and appropriately facilitated the exit of some leading private-sector bankers. Protecting the RBI must therefore be of paramount importance.

At the same time, the RBI must be held accountable for the scale and severity of the problems in the financial sector. So, going forward, we need a more radical strategy to solving India's banking problems; this is spelt out in Section 2.2.

Both government and RBI need to make major changes, including allowing for privatization of some public-sector banks and serious reconsideration of the RBI's effectiveness as a regulator and supervisor. Without these changes, it will take too long to solve the recent problems, and they are likely to recur. Unfortunately, prospects for such reform remain cloudy; the

Nirav Modi scandal offered a moment of opportunity but, alas, it went unexploited. The more problems that occur in private banks or non-bank companies such as IL&FS, the more difficult it will be to sell privatization to the public.

Even now, I find myself wondering why it took so long to address the TBS challenge, when it was such a serious economic problem. So perhaps it is worth going through the history of action and inaction, not to assign blame but to draw lessons for the future.

The scale of mounting debt was first quantified and highlighted by the outstanding work of Ashish Gupta at Credit Suisse, one of the few heroes in the sordid banking saga, first with his report on Non-performing Assets (NPAs) in the corporate sector in 2010, followed by the 'House of Debt' report in 2011. The RBI had also been aware of the mounting problem in the early 2010s.

Nothing fundamental was done to address the problem between then and 2014, either by the RBI or the previous government, a period of catastrophic neglect. On the contrary, the situation was allowed to deteriorate via what was euphemistically called 'evergreening': banks lending money to over-indebted companies, who turned around and used the funds to repay the interest they owed to the banks. This is a sophisticated form of fraud and to have allowed it to happen was a policy failure.

When the new government came into power in 2014, it took some action by implementing a package (Indradhanush, meaning rainbow) of recapitalizing the banks, and the RBI launched a series of initiatives to facilitate resolution between banks and companies. Not just in retrospect, but even at the time, it was clear that Indradhanush and the RBI's efforts were inadequate financially and also failed to provide any mechanism for debt write-downs, which are at the heart of the TBS challenge.

In January 2015, at the 'Gyan Sangam' in Pune, a sort of bankers' retreat, where the prime minister and finance minister met with all top officials of major banks, the RBI, and officials of the ministry of finance, the government committed to not interfering with decision making in the PSBs. In particular, the meeting focused on PSB governance going forward, rather than the legacy issues that constituted the heart of the TBS problem.

The government's cautious approach owed to a number of reasons. Growth accelerated in the first two years of the government's tenure, creating the impression that the problem would solve itself. It also provoked the question of 'how serious can the problem be if growth is so good?' Moreover, being in fiscal consolidation mode, the government felt it did not have the resources to fill the gap that would have been left in the banks if the problem of the NPAs had been fully recognized and tackled. That made it difficult to go for solutions that are more serious.

Perhaps the deeper caution of the government in grasping the nettle of the TBS could be attributed to the zeitgeist of stigmatized capitalism. The accusation of '*suit–boot ki sarkar*', the perceived differential treatment of indebted fat cats (corporates) versus debt-burdened poor farmers, and the fear that decisions by public-sector bank managers would be the object of investigation by the 4Cs made the writing down or writing off of loans— absolutely vital to any solution—virtually impossible.

But for most of this period, there was a much more basic issue: the system failed to identify the scale of the problem. The government had little view of the scope independent of what the banks themselves were reporting. And the banks were massively under-reporting the problem. To a certain extent, this situation occurred because a series of RBI initiatives allowed a form of 'extend and pretend', postponing repayments to a day of reckoning far in the future. It was only in 2015, two years into Raghuram Rajan's tenure, that the RBI started pushing banks to come clean on the magnitude of the problem, under its AQR.

Once the AQR made the magnitude of the problem public and growth decelerated in late 2016, the government realized the urgency of addressing the TBS challenge. It reacted by passing the new bankruptcy law—a truly major achievement in facilitating exit successfully for the first time in Indian economic history. But this law essentially amounted to handing the problem over to the courts, favouring a 'judicial approach' over an executive-led approach to fixing the TBS problem. 'Long live the Justices!'

It is, of course, nonsensical to blame Raghuram Rajan for the growth slowdown and for banks failing to extend more credit after 2014. If the RBI had not initiated the AQR, there would have been even further delays in tackling the NPA problem; the fraud would have continued, and the cost of cleaning up the mess would have continued to rise.

Even so, some serious questions could and should be asked of the RBI. Why didn't the RBI make the case for stronger action years earlier, as soon as credible estimates suggested there was a serious bad-loan problem? Why did it instead repeatedly downplay the magnitudes in its Financial Stability Reports?

The following chart says it all.

Estimates for Non-Performing Assets in the banks, 2012-2018

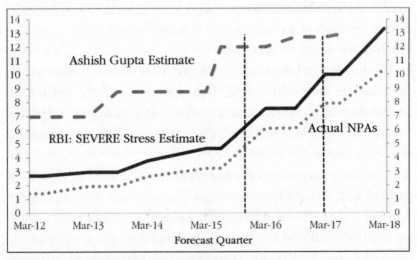

RBI estimate is taken from the Financial Stability Report (FSR) of June every year for March of the coming year. The Ashish Gupta estimate corresponds as closely as possible to the RBI's. Dotted vertical lines mark, respectively, the beginning and end of the Asset Quality Review (AQR) period.

The chart shows that the RBI consistently and massively underestimated the magnitude of the problem. For example, in March 2015, the RBI was forecasting that even under a 'severe stress' scenario—where to put it colourfully, all hell breaks loose, with growth collapsing and interest rates shooting up—NPAs would at most reach about R. 4.5 lakh crores. Meanwhile, Ashish Gupta was forecasting Rs 12 lakh crores, a figure that proved far closer to the actual numbers.

Why was the RBI so clueless about the magnitude of the problem? Given the much larger estimates in the 'market', based on credible research, why did it not start the AQR much earlier than 2015?

Even now, it is difficult to say. Perhaps it truly believed its schemes had a chance of success. More likely, it was waiting for the government to commit sufficient resources, fearing that highlighting the seriousness of the problem without being able to announce a solution would simply unnerve financial markets. This is a classic 'chicken-and-egg' problem, since the government would not mobilize resources until it first understood the true extent of the bad loans. So, for years each side waited for the other, delaying decisive action.

Counterfactual exercises are always risky. But it is interesting to speculate on what might have happened if the RBI had undertaken the AQR much earlier. It's possible that the government might still have balked at providing the necessary resources, especially as the fiscal position in those years was still tight and the government was trying to reduce the deficit. But perhaps not. After all, the problem is fiscally not that expensive. A rough calculation suggests that it requires a maximum of 3-4 per cent of GDP, which is small compared to the government's resources, and the typical emerging market banking crisis of 10-20 per cent of GDP.

Even if the government had balked at the cost, the RBI could have initiated a negotiating dynamic with the government that might have helped move things forward. For example, the RBI could have said, 'We put up some of the resources from our own balance sheet, as other central banks have done in the wake of the global financial crisis. In return, you bite the bullet on creating the conditions for writing down debt or even creating a bad bank.'

The RBI, sadly, missed a Draghi-esque (Mario Draghi, governor of the European Central Bank) 'do whatever it takes' demarche of determination, which could potentially have changed the entire dynamic around the TBS challenge.

~

Navigating the aftermath of demonetization was one of my bigger challenges. One consequence of being a public figure is that the CEA must engender public trust. This requires reconciling the privilege of helping the government and being its spokesman with discharging certain fiduciary responsibilities to the country at large. In other words, the incumbent must support the government without spinning on behalf of it and combine fealty to the government with fidelity to the larger good. Put in Mahabharata terms, a CEA must practise both loyalty and dharma, aspire to be both Karna and Arjuna.

Of course, demonetization was something all of us learnt about afresh. Writing the Economic Survey of 2017 in the midst of demonetization, my team and I had to work through the analytics, the attendant costs and benefits for the formal and informal sectors, and the appropriate policy responses. The analysis had to be honest, credible and comprehensive. The title of the chapter was chosen carefully: 'Demonetization: To Deify or Demonize?'

The broad theme running through these analyses was that demonetization imposed short-term costs that were real and substantial, affecting in particular the informal, cash-intensive sector. There were also potential long-term gains (especially digitalization, formalization and tax compliance) that would have to be monitored on an ongoing basis. Chapter 2 of Volume 1 had a detailed discussion of its costs, benefits and appropriate policy responses. Surprisingly overlooked, but no less important, was Chapter 1 of Volume 2, which contained a detailed analysis of the costs of demonetization for the informal sector, reflected in the increased demand for employment via the Mahatma Gandhi National Rural Employment Guarantee Act (MGNREGA). Finally, Chapter 1 of the Economic Survey of 2018 discussed the adverse effect of demonetization on the growth decoupling/deceleration of the economy, beginning in 2016, and also of its positive impact on increasing income-tax collections. The government, and especially the Minister of Finance, deserve credit for allowing me to discuss both the real costs and potential benefits in the Economic Surveys.

Leaving aside the prurient 'who knew what when' questions and demonetization's rights and wrongs, the questions that puzzled me then, and continue to puzzle me now, relate to the measure's impact.

Puzzle 1: Why did demonetization turn out to be an electoral vote winner in the short term (in the Uttar Pradesh elections of early 2017) if it imposed so much hardship on so many people?

Puzzle 2: Why didn't the draconian 86 per cent reduction in the cash supply have bigger effects on overall economic growth? To put it provocatively, the question was not why demonetization imposed costs—which it clearly did—but why it did not impose much greater costs.

Honesty on the part of demonetization's apologists demands that they confront its significant costs. Equally, honesty on the part of its critics demands that they understand why it turned out to be politically advantageous (first puzzle); and honesty on the part of analytical economists demands that they understand why its economic costs proved much lower than expected (second puzzle).

If my hypothesis for the first puzzle (discussed in detail in Section 2.4) is right—and readers should judge that—it does affect my understanding of the political economy of 'reforms' more broadly. It seems to suggest, counterintuitively, that perhaps in some cases, at least where there are charismatic leaders, policy actions that adversely affect more people are more likely to succeed than actions whose impact is confined to a narrow few. Apparently, they find it difficult to take on, say, public-sector bank unions, entrenched bureaucrats, or rich farmers, but less difficult to take on the entire informal sector.

On the economic costs of demonetization (also discussed in Section 2.4), I remember having breakfast with Paul Krugman, the Nobel Prize winner and *New York Times* columnist, in New Delhi in late 2016 and asking him how he would model the GDP impact of demonetization. Given the magnitude of the monetary shock, he anticipated a severe loss in output, significantly greater than what actually transpired. Any reasonably plausible model would have predicted the same. The measured GDP outcome has been mercifully incommensurate with the policy action. Why that is the case and which of the hypotheses I offer in Section 2.4 is right will surely launch multiple PhD theses.

~

Arguably, the greatest policy achievement of the last four years, and one of the greatest fiscal policy reforms in Indian economic history, was amending the Constitution to implement the Goods and Services Tax (GST). To have been a part of this process, including writing the report that helped forge the political compromise that allowed the Constitution to be amended, and to have been a sort of self-appointed conscience and occasional thorn for the GST Council during its deliberations, was one of the great privileges of being the CEA. On 3 August 2016, I recall hugging my wonderful colleague, Dr Hasmukh Adhia, the revenue secretary, after looking up at the screens that displayed the vote on the Constitutional Amendment bill flashing numbers close to 400–0. That moment ranks as one of the high points of my tenure.

The decline of parliamentary debate and decorum is one of the abiding tropes of our times. But in content, tone and repartee, the parliamentary debate on the Constitutional Amendment bill in August 2016 was a spectacular exception. It pitted two terrific constitutional lawyers, finance ministers and veteran parliamentarians, Arun Jaitley and P. Chidambaram, whose substance-laden sparring made me (and I am sure the million others watching, not to mention India's founding fathers, in spirit) goose-pimply proud of Indian parliamentary democratic procedure. That was Indian democracy at its finest.

Intellectually, the GST was decades in the making, involving many of India's greatest economists, from Raja Chelliah, who first mooted the idea of a value-added tax for India decades ago, to Vijay Kelkar, who boldly recommended a single-rate structure for the GST.

To be sure, there have been glitches in the initial implementation, and the tax as a whole is yet to stabilize fully. Nevertheless, the GST was an astonishingly successful feat of:

- political deal-making, inconceivable without the deft skills of Finance Minister Jaitley;
- administrative implementation, for which enormous credit is due to the revenue secretary, Hasmukh Adhia, the officers of the Central Board of Indirect Taxes and Customs (CBIC)

and their counterparts in all the states, and the department of
revenue;

- technology design, facilitated by the Goods and Services Tax
  Network (GSTN);
- and, above all, remarkable institutional innovation, namely,
  cooperative federalism in the form of the GST Council.

For all its early glitches, we should not forget the magnitude of the
GST achievement: thirty or more regional governments coming
together, giving up their sovereignty for the larger common
good of creating one market in India; improving tax compliance;
creating a robust revenue base for the country; and creating
the fiscal environment for higher investment and growth. This
would be unimaginable in any other federal system, including the
European Union and the United States. In the latter, states would
rather secede than enter into any such collective tax arrangements,
and the rabid upholders of states' rights would probably pick up
pitchforks in revolt.

I have had the privilege of attending most of the initial GST
Council meetings. The quality of debate, the technical support
provided by the Indian tax bureaucracy, the instances of ministers
rising above the narrow interests of their party and state, and
the establishment of a fantastic tradition of decision making
by consensus, all left me with great faith in the possibility of
cooperative federalism. Again, all this would have been impossible
without the skills and unperturbably calm temperament of Arun
Jaitley, and the tactically shrewd 'good-cop, bad-cop' routine
practised by him and Hasmukh Adhia, respectively.

Amongst the many thoughtful participants in the GST
Council were Sushil Modi of Bihar, Dr Thomas Issac from
Kerala, Dr Haseeb Drabu from Jammu and Kashmir, Krishna
Byre-Gowda from Karnataka and Manish Sisodia from Delhi.
One of the more amusing constants of the GST process was to

watch the Uttar Pradesh representatives, after the 2017 elections, obsessing with reducing the GST rates on agarbattis (incense sticks) and pooja samagris (prayer offerings) to the point of raising this in meeting after meeting. Little else seemed to be of pressing concern to the representatives of this relatively poor Indian state of 200 million people.

Perhaps the high point of democratic decision making occurred when Dr Issac (politically opposed to the government on a number of policies, including demonetization) politely asked to walk out of the meeting because he could not go along with the emerging consensus on taxation of gambling. Jaitley went out of his way to cajole him back and accommodate his views, all the while ensuring that the delicate consensus amongst the other twenty-eight ministers was not ruptured.

One under-recognized point. A key reason why the GST was finally passed in 2016, after more than a decade of debate, is that the political constellation changed dramatically once the NDA government came to power. Major producing states, especially Gujarat and Maharashtra—which had opposed the GST for years—were now politically aligned with the party in power at the Centre. With the Centre pushing for the GST, they had to be supportive. The main non-BJP states in 2015—Uttar Pradesh, Bihar, Kerala and West Bengal—had strong economic incentives to support the GST because they were populous states, which stood to reap a fiscal bonanza from the introduction of a consumption-based tax. In the event, the Opposition states seem to have calculated correctly, because in the first year their GST revenues have indeed performed well.

Another important and obvious reason for passage was that the Centre and BJP-ruled states could muster a substantial majority in the GST Council. However, the way that political constellation played out was more subtle. The offer by the Centre to compensate the states for any revenue shortfall for five years became credible because many of the states that feared revenue shortfalls—Gujarat and Maharashtra—were also BJP states. Under the pre-GST UPA-2 regime, the Centre had to compensate states for reductions in the central sales tax (CST) but those obligations were more breached than honoured in timely fashion, in part because the flow of money was to Opposition-led states. The dynamic and credibility of compensation—a critical part of securing buy-in from the states for the GST—changed as BJP governments came to occupy power at the Centre and in the states.

Even so, the passage of the GST was a very close thing. Reading the political signals as late as October 2015, I didn't think that the deals required to pass the GST could be struck. Discussions suddenly moved forward in early December 2015, and the government seized the political opportunity. I was given the important task of writing a report to recommend the revenue neutral rate (RNR) and the structure of GST rates. I vividly remember my boss, Minister Jaitley, for the first and only time in my stint, asking me to advance a deadline so that he would have the technical wherewithal for his critical political discussions with the Opposition.

A committee helped me write the report. I was advised not to publish it because there was dissent within the committee: in fact, senior officials in the revenue department (other than Dr Hasmukh Adhia) distanced themselves from the report. But I had the conviction that public acceptability would depend not on whether there was unanimity but on the quality of the report, including the recommendations and the underlying analysis. I am glad that I did not let the default bureaucratic position of abundant caution and inertia influence me. It also helped that I had the backing of knowledgeable and committed younger officers of the indirect and direct tax departments (Alok Shukla, Amitabh Kumar and Arbind Modi).

This experience reinforced some sagacious advice given to me by one of my illustrious predecessors, Rakesh Mohan: that to be effective, CEAs should work closely not just with their counterparts (the secretaries) but also with joint secretaries (and their equivalents) in the government because the latter are the real seat and source of decision making. I would go further and say that CEAs should work with all officers in the bureaucracy, regardless of rank. If a strong vertical hierarchy is what distinguishes all bureaucracies—and India's is particularly vertical—the CEA as outsider and academic should strive hard to horizontalize that verticality with an ethic of openness and equality.

In retrospect, my report served two critical purposes. It helped the government convince the Opposition and the public that GST rates did not have to be as high as was being feared. My report suggested a revenue neutral rate of about 15.5 per cent, whereas the prevailing view based on work done by one of the think tanks (National Institute of Public Finance and Policy) was around 21–22 per cent. As a result, the report helped forge the political consensus in favour of the GST.

The second purpose of the report was to provide a reference point for the GST rate structure. My report argued for a three-rate structure. The vast bulk of the goods should be taxed at the standard rate, essentials (food items, for example) at a low rate, and products whose consumption society wanted to discourage (like cigarettes and luxury cars) at a higher rate. These recommendations were not adopted in the initial design but were important for the debate and the process as it moved forward.

Why were they not adopted? Essentially, there were two camps. The first, mostly officers within the bureaucracy, anxious about the opposition that could ensue, wanted virtually no increase in the rate on any product (the experience of Malaysia's troubled VAT introduction weighed heavily on their minds). This led to the adoption of the design principle that every GST rate would be close to, and no higher than, the existing excise-cum-VAT rate. This principle ruled out, almost from the start, a simple rate structure.

This camp also feared the revenue losses from a simple and low rate structure. I was adamantly opposed to the 28 per cent rate and confident that there would be enough revenue, since the introduction of the GST would improve tax compliance. Subsequent events have broadly borne out my analysis and optimism. But to be fair to the GST Council, there has been important learning, leading to downward GST rate revisions that are bringing the regime closer to my report's vision.

There is still considerable distance to traverse. The report has become the focal point around which debates on the structure of rates and exclusions and additions to the GST base (petroleum, electricity, land and real estate) have been conducted. As the CEA and author of the report, there is nothing more I could ask for.

On the GST, I have two wistful reflections about the past and one anxiety for the future. I wonder whether if there had been more conviction about, and stronger political commitment to, simplicity (say no more than three rates) and lower taxes, the rate structure could have come closer to the one I had proposed. Especially with the Centre having promised compensation to the states, it might have been possible to prevent the 28 per cent rate. Once the principle of simplicity and few rates was replaced in favour of the principle that no new rate could be greater than the old rate, the compensation commitment led the states to start haggling for lower rates but in a somewhat arbitrary fashion.

I wonder also whether the implementation of GST was handicapped by being the second shock that had to be imposed on the system, especially on small traders in the informal sector. To be sure, implementation could have been significantly better but the GST's public reception was surely contaminated by demonetization having preceded it.

My anxiety for the medium term is this: the GST has been and seen cooperative federalism at its magnificent best. Yet, as with all things political, equilibriums can be fragile. Chafing at the inability to respond to some local concern, states may start 'defecting': granting a GST exemption here, raising a rate there, imposing a cess elsewhere. Especially if the political constellation changes, with the Centre unable to nip these defections in the bud, we could get a proliferation of small defections that cumulate over time and eat into the integrity of the GST as one country, one market, one tax. I fervently pray this will not happen.

~

One of the real learning and humbling experiences of my tenure related to agriculture. Before becoming the CEA, I had delved into India's manufacturing, services and trade sectors. But I had never really done any serious work on Indian agriculture, subconsciously believing that since development is a process of getting out of agriculture—a 'sunset industry'—research and policy ought to focus on where people should be headed, not where they are leaving from. How wrong I was.

Agriculture is critical for India in so many ways, not least in its ability to hold the entire economy back by generating inflation, agrarian distress and political restiveness. In the last four years, agriculture has played a prominent role in shaping both Indian economics and politics. Agriculture has also been critical to my thinking about cooperative federalism in India. Many of the areas that need reforms such as labour, land, agriculture, power, fertilizer, education, health fall under the Concurrent or State list of the Constitution. It is states that will have a key role in shaping these sectors. If the Centre wants to drive reforms, it will have to work with the states as it did in the GST process.

There are two agricultural welfare policies that stick out like carbuncles, not just for their negative consequences but also as an affront to my understanding of Indian political economy. The first is the fertilizer subsidy, the fact that farmers can have access to unlimited supplies of fertilizer at prices well below those prevailing in the market. This is arguably one of the worst policies imaginable. It is costly (nearly Rs 1 lakh crore, or 0.6 per cent of GDP) and regressive (disproportionately helping larger farmers), with devastating consequences for soil quality, water and health. In fact, there is a 'cancer train' running through agricultural Punjab, bringing the disease to an extraordinarily high proportion of the residents because of excessive fertilizer use. Almost nothing redeems this subsidy.

Yet it persists—a telling, chilling monument to lousy economics masquerading as lofty politics, puncturing any pretensions I may have had in understanding or improving the world. Of course, I'm not alone in this. Two finance ministers in the previous NDA government, Yashwant Sinha and Jaswant Singh, had to roll back urea price increases (which reduced the subsidy) in the face of strong push-back; evidently, even their boss, the epitome of old-world tahzeeb (refinement) and poetic persuasiveness, Atal Behari Vajpayee, could not get the backing of the political system for eliminating the fertilizer subsidy.

The second agricultural policy is the minimum support price (MSP), the guarantee that the government will purchase agricultural products from farmers at this price and not allow prices to go below this threshold. Now, much has been written about the large MSP increases announced and implemented in 2018–19. These increases covered many products but the action to raise paddy prices was particularly egregious—violating even the minimal demands of 'do no harm'—because of its unfairness to poorer farmers who cultivate unirrigated crops, its impact on the depleting water table, worsening soil quality, and its potential conflict with our international obligations. Not to mention that we already produce far too much rice and are in the process of accumulating Kumbhakarna-esque rice mountains that will eventually rot for the rats.

My failure in nudging these policies in the right direction was one of the biggest disappointments of my tenure. My continuing inability to understand the political economy and to figure out how to get the exit process started must count as a personal failing.

But agriculture has suddenly also become exciting because it is the locus of new experiments with direct benefit transfers (DBTs), that is, payments in cash to designated beneficiaries. The Rythu Bandhu scheme—essentially giving Rs 5000 per hectare to every farmer in every sowing season—being implemented by the Government of Telangana is at the vanguard of progressive thinking about first-best agricultural and social policy. It has the potential to be a universal or at least quasi-universal basic income (UBI or QUBI). These are topics dear to my heart because of the extensive research we had done in the economic survey (building on excellent academic research by Vijay Joshi and many others) which have raised the profile of UBI in policymaking and discussion. UBI was not something I had even heard of when I took up the job of the CEA. Four years later, I had become one of its main proponents, and the list of converts (including the thoughtful Bihar chief minister, Nitish Kumar) is growing.

UBI, of course, can only become meaningfully implementable if the delivery mechanism is in place. Which leads to one of the other big achievements of the government, namely, to complete the construction of the JAM pipeline, the acronym I coined, to connect Jan Dhan (financial inclusion), Aadhaar (biometric identification), and Mobile (the telecommunications revolution). Clearly, the recent Supreme Court ruling will have an impact on how Aadhaar can be used going forward, but JAM has played a critical role and will probably do so to an even greater extent in the future in underpinning what might be one of the government's terrific initiatives.

If we have seen the return of the old statism to some extent as a consequence of stigmatized capitalism, the government and especially the prime minister should get credit for a new kind of statism to realize a fresh welfarist vision. In this new statism/welfarism, the animating idea is the public provision, especially for the poor, of essential private goods and services such as bank accounts, life insurance, toilets, power, cooking gas connections, housing, and more recently, protection against serious illnesses. (Note that this is about the provision for more private goods, rather than public goods such as health and education; on the latter, less progress has been made.) The new welfarism is about harnessing technology and state capacity at and from the Centre to deliver good social outcomes; At least in principle, this new vision is about moving away from the provision of handouts or subsidies to providing goods and services. If this endeavour succeeds—it is still a work-in-progress and its implementation could benefit from greater doses of cooperative federalism—it could arguably be an alternative model of social welfarism that could endure in the political consciousness for years to come. This could be a major economic legacy of Prime Minister Modi.

~

I said that the theme of the book is how the Indian economy surprised me. That's true in a more personal way. One of the important roles of a CEA is to be someone who engenders public trust, which is achieved in part by speaking truth to power. What I discovered during the course of my tenure was that often, as an insider, I had to be more critical of policies than the outsiders.

In particular, the business, financial and analyst communities tend to be extraordinarily coy when it comes to commenting on

RBI policies or even those of the government. Their relationship with officialdom is not arm's length. Bankers are careful not to get on the wrong side of the government or the RBI, because they worry about losing access since they are the regulatory bodies. Here the famous Upton Sinclair quote comes to mind: 'It is difficult to get a man to understand something when his salary [or perhaps his banking licence or invitation to RBI press conferences] depends upon his not understanding it.' The desire to be on the right side of power affects incentives, even if only subtly. In their eyes, RBI monetary policy actions are always on target, and every Union budget, including its 2018 avatar, is the best budget ever.

The sociology of this phenomenon needs greater examination but one consequence was that I found myself as a sort of lone voice questioning RBI actions (with all the risks that created internally and publicly) and sometimes government policies. My V.K.R.V. Rao lecture (Chapter 7) is an example of my role as a public dissenter vis-à-vis RBI actions; my Darbari Seth memorial lecture (Chapter 4) tries to critically examine how much India should really be in love with renewables; and my National Academy of Agricultural Sciences lecture (Chapter 5) is a critique, albeit circumlocutory, of agricultural policies, especially regarding the livestock sector.

My public disagreements with the RBI in particular need explanation. It is true that in general the Ministry of Finance and the RBI should sort out their disagreements internally without any public airing of them. I think very highly of the RBI and its senior staff and it truly is one of India's illustrious institutions. But the RBI does make mistakes and must be held accountable.

The problem is that for various reasons—compromised incentives à la Upton Sinclair, simple awe of its governors, or inadequate analysis stemming from the difficulty of intelligently analysing international macroeconomics which is a hard subject—

this accountability tends to be weak. Rightly or wrongly, I felt I had to fill in that gap.

I chose to speak up only when I felt that RBI policy was demonstrably questionable: for example, the systematic and large inflation forecasting errors, leading to overly tight monetary policy through much of 2017 or the overly tight liquidity policy in the summer/fall of 2015. In some cases, I had ideas I thought would benefit from greater public discussion such as the consequences, for monetary policy, of large discrepancies between consumer and wholesale price inflation that prevailed during 2015, as well as the issue of whether RBI has too much capital.

In each of these instances, either there was some policy response (for example, on the liquidity issue, where Raghu graciously acknowledged I had a point) or a lively debate was provoked. In retrospect and given the context, I do not regret having spoken up publicly on a few occasions.

The targets of my dissent were not confined to the RBI and the government. My team and I savaged the sovereign ratings agencies ('Poor Standards', reproduced in Chapter 7) for their discriminatory treatment of India and China. Although post hoc is not propter hoc, it gave us great satisfaction that following our analysis, some of the agencies downgraded China and upgraded India in their subsequent assessments, a sort of double victory for us.

I also dissented from the N.K. Singh Committee's recommendations on fiscal targets, believing then that there was little justification for proposing a serpentine fiscal deficit path and arbitrary debt and deficit targets. In some ways, I have moved beyond my own dissent. Despite commendable efforts in reducing the measured deficit, the overall fiscal, especially debt, situation has not improved as much as it should have.

It is also true that governments have a lot of policy and accounting freedom in meeting deficit targets such as through share buybacks by public-sector enterprises (in which the government sells shares to the public enterprise itself) or using the National Social Security Fund (NSSF) to finance expenditure, as was done recently for Air India. I have come to the realization that underlying budgetary processes—typically given insufficient attention—are critical, perhaps even more important than mechanical targets for sound fiscal policy and fiscal integrity. To these ends, I would strongly favour the excellent recommendation of the N.K. Singh Committee to create a credible, independent fiscal council.

~

Having described the book, perhaps I should provide a guide to the reader or rather an explanation of who should read the book and how.

The book has eight chapters, covering the main challenges and reforms of the last four years. Some of these were written in collaboration with members of my fabulous Team CEA. I have not been comprehensive, confining my scope to the issues in which I was intimately involved. Each chapter contains a preface which provides context and history to the topics that follow.

- Igniting Ideas for India
- Money and Cash
- The Great Structural Transformation (GST)
- Climate Change and the Environment
- Agriculture
- The State and the Individual
- Speaking Truth to Power
- What Do They Know of Economics Who Don't Know Globalization and Tennis?

I envisage two types of readers. Those in the first category—the informed and serious reader, curious about economics and policymaking but more generalist than wonk—should probably read all the prefaces to all the sections to get a sense of what happened. Then, he or she should read all the chapters that attract his or her interest.

The second category of reader, comprising those more familiar with my work, should hone in on the prefaces and the new material. Just to whet the appetite, the new pieces cover:

- Yes, demonetization;
- A Grand Bargain for the Twin Balance Sheet challenge, which has new ideas on how to solve it (both the RBI and the government will have to take difficult action);
- Whether the RBI has too much capital (yes, yes, yes, it does and enough to fix the banks), on which I had some interesting exchanges with Raghuram Rajan;
- Climate change, written ahead of the Paris Summit of December 2015, for which I was demonized as a lackey of the West when I thought I was doing just the opposite by calling out the West's 'carbon imperialism';
- The precursor to the Economic Survey chapter on Universal Basic Income (UBI), which gives a sense of my thinking on the issue, and how it evolved and how it was framed in the survey (Sabarmati Ashram was the inspiration);
- Some new thoughts on tax sharing (yes, there is a lot of redistribution within India but not just from the southern states but also from the coastal west and towards Uttar Pradesh, Madhya Pradesh and Bihar).

One more guide to the reader. Drawing inspiration from Paul Krugman, individual chapters that are slightly technical or wonkish are asterisked.

~

It is clear that realizing my ambitions for the job required both having a good and influential boss, and enjoying his trust and confidence. In all these respects, Arun Jaitley was a dream boss and some.

I had not known him before, so it was all the more surprising that we hit it off immediately. I would on a normal day barge into his room at least four or five times, shouting, 'Minister, good news first or bad news?' I would give him the most candid, most technical advice I could. He wouldn't always agree with me, of course, but he would follow up on my counsel often enough for me to feel that this was a job more than worth doing. On the occasions that he didn't agree, he was never dismissive or impatient. And that gave me an opening. I would not let up, returning within a few hours, with each of us knowing why I had come back. I knew when he was just allowing me to vent and when he was really listening. He knew that I knew, and so on. The book's cover captures our relationship.

Right from the start, it was easy for me to understand why he had been such a successful lawyer: he had an exceptional ability to persuade others. In my first year, I was anxious that the gains from bringing inflation under control should not be compromised by populist policies. I wasn't sure that I had convinced him, but then learnt that he took the matter to the very next Cabinet meeting—and actually succeeded in staving off the measure I had worried about. Watching him make the case for the adoption of the controversial and uncomfortable (for the Centre) recommendations of the Fourteenth Finance Commission in the Cabinet or summarizing the outcomes of the sometimes tediously long GST Council meetings to the press was to see excellent persuasion and communication in action.

Looking back over these four years, how do I assess the evolution of the economy and economic policymaking? As with most things in life, the answer must be positive but mixed. Some major good was done: the GST and the bankruptcy code were implemented; macroeconomic instability was reversed; the JAM infrastructure of connectivity was completed; and an alternative vision of welfarism—based on using state capacity and harnessing technology to provide essential private goods and services for the less well-off—was put in place.

Some good remained undone or unfinished: privatization, especially of Air India, was postponed indefinitely; health and education remain the objects of relative inattention, especially by the states; and the pervasive phenomenon of stigmatized capitalism remains entrenched, with progress under the bankruptcy code determining whether we can realistically escape from its thrall.

There were some setbacks: agricultural performance and farmer incomes have languished; selective trade protectionism has been re-embraced, legitimized in part by the global backlash against globalization; and manufacturing export performance has remained lacklustre. Thankfully, some major setbacks were avoided, most notably the descent back into serious macroeconomic instability, although the recent turmoil in emerging markets is testing the government's mettle.

It is impossible to escape the human instinct for speculating about counterfactual history. T.S. Eliot's words from the first of his 'Four Quartets' haunt one's retrospective imagination.

'What might have been is an abstraction.
Remaining a perpetual possibility
Only in a world of speculation.
. . .
Footfalls echo in the memory
Down the passage which we did not take
Towards the door we never opened
Into the rose-garden.'

What might have been? What doors were never opened? What rose-gardens were never sighted? Economic historians of this period will examine many counterfactuals, many what-ifs. Of course, the particular questions they will ask will be shaped by their motivations and prior beliefs and affiliations.

What if the Twin Balance Sheet Challenge had been tackled earlier? What if the GST had been simpler in design and what if its implementation did not have to deal with the prior shock of demonetization? At a time when the Centre-states political constellation was so well-aligned to deploying the 'technology' of cooperative federalism—the brilliant rationale of Niti Aayog and so successful in the GST context—could other sectors such as agriculture, power, and direct benefit transfers have seen more reforms?

A great deal was accomplished in these four years for which the government deserves a lot of credit but questions and wistfulness about the paths not taken will forever provide fodder for future historians.

When I was first approached for the job, if I had been told that four years down the road I would have had the extraordinary privilege and good fortune to undertake such indulgent reflections, I would have dismissed that as fantasy, as dreamlike as the Incan ruins I was beholding in Machu Picchu.

Stepping back from these four years, a longer-term perspective shows that history and India's founding fathers chose a unique path for the country's development, what I call the Precocious Development Model. Marked by many successes, afflicted by some shortcomings, this model is still a work-in-progress, and there's still a lot of hope in it. Perhaps by 2047, a hundred years after being midwifed at midnight, we will know with greater clarity whether this gamble of uniqueness pays off.

But for all that is problematic about India, we must never forget that the standard of living of nearly all Indian citizens is immeasurably better today than fifty or even twenty years ago, and that there is an essential hopefulness that comes from the widely shared belief and the rising, restive expectation that tomorrow will be better than today, that our children's lives will be much better than ours.

As a believer in reincarnation, I hope I have retained enough karma to be able to come back in future births not just as chief economic adviser to the Government of India but as chief economic adviser to all the Indian states to contribute to and participate in pulling off this gamble, in making this Precocious Development Model a success. That way, the best job I ever had, I will get to keep forever. Or, as the Argentinian man of letters, Jorge Luis Borges, might have better put it, that way I will get to keep the best job forever and a day.

Chapter 1

Igniting Ideas for India

1.0

Igniting Ideas for India

George Stigler and Milton Friedman were two brilliant economists at the University of Chicago, both of whom went on to win the Nobel Prize. Apparently, the modest George Stigler used to say, 'Milton down the corridor is trying to change the world, I am just trying to understand it.' Similarly, all chief economic advisers want to contribute to policymaking to change the course of the economy. But they also aspire to thinking more deeply about the economy to perhaps just understand it—the economy, its historical development, its politics—better.

So, this first chapter in the book contains four or five of what I think are big ideas about the Indian economy: that it has been an unusual model of development, which I have called the Precocious Development Model (Section 1.1); that India is in the thrall of stigmatized capitalism (Section 1.2); that exit from economic activity, and perhaps even more than entry into it, is one of India's big policy challenges (Section 1.3); that regional disparities within the country are rising despite rapid growth (Section 1.4); and this disparity is paradoxical because India is becoming more integrated in terms of flows of goods and workers (Section 1.5).

During my time as CEA, I have changed the way I think of Indian development, and the country's prospects for reform going forward. For many years, I had been proud of the unique Indian development trajectory, calling it the Precocious Development Model. I remain proud, and I still believe that India's future is bright. How could it be otherwise for a country that is so dynamic, so full of youthful and entrepreneurial energy? Even so, I have become concerned about the costs of India's development model. And I have become increasingly aware of the many obstacles that stand in the way of reform.

India's development model has two distinctive features. First, there is an atypical sequencing of politics and economics. In the successful model of the now-rich countries of North America and Europe, the franchise was initially limited and was slowly, progressively expanded as the economy developed. In the successful post-World War II model of East Asia, economic development came first, followed by political development so that democratization happened only recently. In contrast, India granted universal franchise immediately after Independence so that economic development has had to be attempted and achieved in the context of full democratization.

The second distinctive feature relates to the relatively low importance and contribution of manufacturing compared with services in the development process.

The advantage of this model is obvious: we are rightly proud of our democracy, and our IT sector. But premature democratization has imposed a 'democracy tax' on development, since the government has had to redistribute resources far before efficient delivery mechanisms had been established. Premature reliance on high-skilled services such as IT has curtailed employment opportunities for low-skilled workers. These are issues I discuss in the first section of this chapter in a conversation with Professor Karthik Muralidharan of the University of California, San Diego.

Aside from the inherent difficulties of the development model, there have also been persistent problems in advancing reform. Again and again, I have been asked: why is it so difficult for India to reform, to adopt policies that have proved successful elsewhere? The answer to this question is complex, obviously so, since if there was just one barrier to reform it could have been removed a long time ago. Instead, there are several, interrelated problems.

To begin with, consider the problem of exit. Governments of all stripes have found it difficult to get out of bad policies (such as subsidies) or unwind inefficient enterprises, especially in the public sector, or resolve the problem of over-indebted corporate-sector balance sheets. It seems that India has gone from 'socialism with limited entry to capitalism without exit', a problem which I termed the 'Chakravyuha challenge', drawing upon the fate of Arjuna's son Abhimanyu in the Mahabharata. This challenge is elaborated upon in Section 1.3.

Reform has also been impeded by what I call 'stigmatized capitalism', meaning, India's ambivalent attitude towards, and its half-hearted embrace of, the private sector and private capital. Section 1.2 traces three stages in the evolution of public attitudes towards capitalism, from the 1970s and 1980s, when the success of private enterprise was linked to its proximity to government; to the early years of the new millennium, when the IT sector boomed, creating a brief era of 'good capitalism'; to the rents raj of the recent years, characterized by major corruption scandals and overlending that has led to today's Twin Balance Sheet Challenge.

A final idea in this chapter relates to regional inequalities in India (Section 1.4) and the puzzle of why they continue to grow despite the overall dynamism of the economy and despite the fact that the equalizing forces of greater integration—greater internal flows of goods, services, people and capital—within the country are becoming more powerful (Section 1.5). Economists call this phenomenon—the persistence of inequalities—'divergence'. The world over and in other large countries such as China we see convergence. But within India, we see Integration Big Time but also Divergence Big Time. Go figure as the American expression goes.

1.1

Precocious Development

In July 2015, nine months after taking over as chief economic adviser to the Government of India, I did an interview with the brilliant young economist Karthik Muralidharan, who has done exceptionally good research on India based on large, randomized control trials. The interview happened at India International Centre on the occasion of the annual event of the International Growth Centre. Karthik and I have always good-naturedly sparred about the relative merits of a micro (him) versus macro (me) approach to development. Looking back, the interview covered a lot of ground on Indian development and Indian economic policy.

Karthik asked me to give the audience an overview of the Indian economy—how we got to where we were, with a focus on the past year, and my forecast for the most important things going ahead. I felt it was important to set the Indian development experience in a broader context before coming to the more recent period, which was what everyone was interested in. I had many things to say about the Indian development model, where we were, and how to understand it. This piece is expanded from the conversation that took place in that interview, in which I tried to address a wide range of fundamental subjects.

The first and the most exciting thing for me as someone who has studied growth across countries from a macro perspective was that there is something truly unique about the Indian development model. I call this the 'precocious development model', since a precocious child does things far ahead of its time—in both the good and bad sense.

Political scientists have often observed that India is a complete outlier in having sustained democracy at very low levels of income, low levels of literacy, with deep social fissures, and with a highly agrarian economy. Almost no country in the world has managed that under these conditions. I think the only continuous democracies have all been small countries (Costa Rica, Barbados, Jamaica, Mauritius and Botswana) with higher levels of literacy and fewer social divisions.

The second part of the precocious model is that it entails not just precocious politics but also precocious economics. There are many ways of explaining this precocious economics model, but I focus on two.

Most countries grow by either specializing in or exploiting their minerals—as in the old model—and in some cases, exploiting their geography. But most of the post-war growth experiences have come about by becoming manufacturing powerhouses, especially starting with low-skill labour and going up the value-added spectrum. Korea, Taiwan and China are classic examples, specializing in textiles and clothing initially and now becoming major exporters of electronics, cars, IT products, etc.

Of course, everyone knows that the Indian development experience, certainly in the last thirty to thirty-five years, has been driven by services, and that's special. We have specialized in IT-related services that are highly skill-intensive, and even Korea and Taiwan today—at much higher levels of income—have not done this. The other way of understanding this precocious model is that in some ways, India is trying to grow and develop not by worshipping or deifying its comparative advantage but by defying it. We have a lot of unskilled labour but we are not using it; we are using much more of our skilled labour.

For me, the most striking manifestation of this precocious development model is that India exports a lot of foreign direct investment (FDI). If you think of the international pattern of development, countries at our stage of development are meant to get capital, labour and technology, and then export labour-intensive goods. But we have been doing something else, so this is actually a fairly unique development model. Our entrepreneurs have bought and are running companies in the US and Europe (think the Birlas, INFOSYS, etc., owning and running companies in the US, and the Tatas running car plants in the UK and steel factories in Europe).

It is a work in progress; we can't say yet if it's a success or not. Provisionally, in the last thirty years, the economy hasn't been doing too badly: 6–6.5 per cent growth rates for thirty-five years, but with lots of problems. So, if India can pull it off in some sense, it would be quite a unique development model, maybe a model for others to follow down the road.

The second thing which strikes me as special is related to India's precocious politics model. There is a combination of what American development economist Lant Pritchett calls a 'flailing state' on one hand, but India is also a perennial democracy, as it were, on the other. I think democracy has created these pressures to redistribute and spend at levels of development, which advanced countries reached much later in their development process. This creates a lot of challenges: Can you spend well? What kind of spending should you do? For example, we have spent a lot on anti-poverty programs. But we have done it in inefficient ways by giving various kinds of subsidies rather than giving money that can directly benefit the poor. Similarly, we have a lot of affirmative action programmes (what we call 'reservations').

Politics and history dictated that these policies were unavoidable in a poor, fractured country like India, but it creates costs. We are seeing the tugs of these conflicts to some extent. One manifestation of that is, in some ways, what went on in the UPA years: increasing food subsides, providing employment guarantees, creating more rights, for example, to education. We have a country or model that is trying redistribution without the state having established its credibility and legitimacy by providing essential services. Professor Indira Rajaraman of IIM Bangalore said that even the Western world redistributed much later in the process because it had established its credibility to spend. And so we are trying to spend and redistribute without, perhaps, the legitimacy or ability of the state to do it well.

The other part of this, which is very important and which gets neglected, is taxation; the fiscal contract between citizens and the government is very important for accountability and institutional development. In India, for example, the number of taxpayers in relation to voters in the economy has been about 4–4.5 per cent for a long time. So, we still don't have that fiscal contract and that creates a lot of challenges in that the glue of accountability between the state and its citizens is weak.

The third thing, which has happened in the last ten years, is what I would call the Latinization of Indian macroeconomics (maybe that is unfair to the Latins because they have moved on). By Latinization I mean that we have become much more vulnerable macroeconomically—high deficits, high inflation, great reliance on foreign capital over time, which has created this volatility. The Turkish economist Dani Rodrik has this important idea that if you are going to integrate, you actually need bigger government because there is more volatility and you have to cushion the shocks. So, we have a situation where we have become more volatile macroeconomically—we have become more exposed—and that has also created a lot of challenges. The 2013 experience that we had—the so-called Taper Tantrum, in which the US Fed signalled that it would be dialling back its unconventionally loose monetary policy that nearly led India to a full-blown macroeconomic crisis—I think was, in some ways, a culmination of the Latinization of Indian macroeconomics. Remember in the late 1990s, when Asian countries had their crises, we were spared because we had not fully integrated—at least financially—into the world economy.

The fourth point in terms of the challenges we face is as follows: one way to understand India—on the model side and the micro side—is that we went from socialism with restricted entry to capitalism without exit. This is now a real problem in India. You take power, fertilizer, banks, public–private partnership (PPP) projects, civil aviation, or even agricultural commodities like rice and sugar—the problem is you can't get out. Inefficient firms or inefficient production can't be easily wound down, and that poses a really big problem for all the things that you think are desirable. It is a fiscal burden; it affects the economy in so many ways.

Summing up, India has a unique development model and there are at least three challenges to it. First, the weak state and what politics has done in terms of redistribution and taxation; second, the Latinization of Indian macroeconomics; and third, we have gone into capitalism without exit (we will talk about crony capitalism later).

I strongly believe that there is going to be a lot of endogenous change in India. One example is that we talk a lot about what the state has or has not done for education. Educational outcomes are very poor. But I think, to some extent, if you look at what has powered the drive to enrolment and people seeking more education, this has been the noteworthy growth pick-up over the last twenty years. By virtue of having a particular pattern of growth, it has increased the demand for education. Outcomes are still a question mark but at least we are not talking now about just supply driving educational outcomes, but also demand doing so. This has had a huge impact and is an example of endogenous change.

The other big agent for change in India is going to be competition among states. That is why I am—subject to some caveats—a big fan of the Fourteenth Finance Commission, which gave much more fiscal autonomy back to the states. States will get more revenues and will have greater freedom to spend. This will allow the states to compete—what we call competitive federalism—which will create a powerful dynamic for change. It has maybe not gone far enough—competitive federalism has to embrace cities as well; that is, cities should also compete with each other and with the states at large.

Lastly—again a work in progress—there are signs that some of this endogenous change can come about because in India, good economics, perhaps slowly, not always, not everywhere, could be on its way to becoming good politics. We have seen that in the last two or three election cycles; we have seen that in 2014. The great sage and philosopher Donald Rumsfeld said, 'You go to battle with the army you have.' So, when people in India talk wistfully about the Chinese model with its top-down development and unencumbered decision making, it's almost a silly wistfulness because you know you're stuck with the system you have.

Are we seeing enough endogenous change from within the system? I think this good economics becoming good politics could be combined with competitive federalism, and could be an endogenous agent of change in India. So, on the whole I would say, yes, there are challenges, but in the long term I'm quite hopeful about endogenous change.

Some big institutional reforms are under way, like the GST and the whole DBT (Direct Benefit Transfers)/JAM (Jan Dhan Yojana, Aadhaar, Mobile Money) vision. These could be game changers if we can get them done right. So, between competitive federalism, good economics being good politics, a few institutional game-changing reforms, I'm certainly bullish enough to want to do this job with hopefully more energy.

Coming back to the last twelve months or so, from 2017–18, of the big enabling changes that are setting the stage for some of the cautious optimism, one has been the stabilization of macroeconomic indicators. Oil prices have helped, but we have also contributed to the decline in inflation; the RBI has also done that. To the extent that price inflation was coming through from agriculture and minimum support prices, the government has contributed by moderating them and keeping them manageable. So the macro side is looking less vulnerable than it did a couple of years ago.

In terms of the two or three big-ticket reforms, that spectrum and coal were auctioned cleanly and transparently sets the model in terms of what the government is seeking to do on governance reform. That gold has been liberalized—which people don't realize—is actually a governance reform. All the deregulation that has taken place on the energy side is another part of it. On the real-sector side, a lot of opening up to FDI has happened.

In terms of institutional reforms, the GST will hopefully be passed soon and get implemented in April 2017.[1] The JAM is being done for salaries and pensions to some extent. We've had this cooking-gas experiment—of providing direct transfers instead of subsidized prices—which has been quite successful. We have seen tremendous gains and are now looking to extend them to other commodities. However, the lessons from cooking gas don't easily transpose to other sectors and the policy design has to be just right.

The whole vision for JAM is really an institutional change, which is important for the following reasons. Firstly, apart from fiscal savings—which is the smallest part of it—if the government can do something well, it legitimizes the state and builds state capacity. It chips away at the cynicism about government and the delegitimization that takes place. If we can do that, we can also allow the price system to function better; there are efficiency gains to be reaped from that. It's amazing that for many goods and services, consumers and producers still don't face market prices. Above all, any democratic government wants to protect the vulnerable and the poor and direct transfers are really the best, most efficient way of doing so.

Another interesting point is that not only have oil prices been deregulated but people have noticed that the government has stuck to its commitment. International prices have gone up to some extent after the low, and pump prices have adjusted accordingly, unlike the earlier era when the whole thing collapsed. So, as long as prices don't soar too high, say, if they go to 100 dollars per barrel, all bets are off all over the world, not just in India—but that said, I think the deregulation commitment can be maintained.

On the short-term macro side, we made a strong pitch that the government needed more public investment because of the state of corporate-sector balance sheets. To some extent, the government has made more allocations by saying that they'll delay the fiscal consolidation targets. So, all these things add up to something we can build on and work towards. Of course, the big challenge is the exit problem. There are lots of contenders related to exit—banks, PPPs, corporate sector. Otherwise, in terms of governance, institutions, the macro and real sector, I see enough having taken place that if we persist at this pace, there could be meaningful change and higher growth in the future.

~

As our discussion wore on, Karthik shared his beliefs that the government deserved credit for its monetary policy framework. I talked about how earlier, there was a political consensus that inflation was politically bad, but in the past ten to fifteen years we seem to have accepted a permanently higher level of inflation, whereas this was something we were all once worried about. So, this is actually a big game changer, because it is committing credibly to restricting the government's ability to inflate away debt. He probed me on how this agreement on the monetary policy framework actually came about, what were the costs and trade-offs I would worry about, and since I had tied my hands to this, he expressed the concern that fiscal space gets limited in terms of running deficits that one may think are warranted for investment reasons.

I explained to Karthik that when Raghuram Rajan took over as the RBI governor, the Urjit Patel Committee Report came out, which recommended inflation targeting. There is some dispute whether it was inflation targeting or flexible inflation targeting—and we need to talk about that to some extent. The experience of high inflation provoked enough people into recognizing that this is a problem going forward and that we need some institutional constraints on it. The RBI and the government have been on the same page on this. In fact, the monetary policy framework was actually announced in the August budget in 2017, and this budget was the first agreement we had with the RBI. Going forward, this is going to be a part of the monetary landscape, because both the government and the RBI have a common commitment to inflation reduction. The strong belief is that when you have high inflation, there is no trade-off between inflation and growth—and that's the theory behind it.

Now, tackling the second concern, the point is whether we are going to have a rigid inflation-targeting framework or something more flexible, which is a discussion the government and the RBI are going to have. I don't think the fear that the government is going to inflate away its debt is a serious concern, certainly not at this stage. Maybe, down the road, that might happen. The irony is that we are in this situation because we did inflate away our debt over the last fifteen to twenty years. Our debt to GDP ratio has come down. Initially that happened because we grew very rapidly, but then we had high growth and high inflation, so debt levels have come down for India. Going forward, prudent fiscal and macro management is a shared commitment of the government and the RBI, and so in that sense, inflation targeting merely codifies that we will stick to it.

Karthik then pointed to a pretty fundamental constraint, which is that India needs major investments in infrastructure. But, for the reasons that I have described, there were commitments to categories of spending. Most of today's developed countries invested in public goods (roads, railways, bridges) before they invested in redistribution (the social safety net). We are kind of in a place where redistribution commitments have been made and therefore, this severely restricts the fiscal space available for such investments which we know we need. What is interesting is that from a basic capital budgeting perspective, as long as the internal rate of return (IRR) of an investment is positive, you should be willing to borrow for it. But then the bond markets won't let you do that beyond 3–4 per cent, or whatever the fiscal targets are. So, what are the conventional options to create fiscal space for these infrastructure investments, and how out of the box can we get?

Even if you look at the latest budget (of 2015), the constraint on public investment in India, today at least, is not on resources but just the ability to spend, spend well and spend quickly. That's why in the short run, I have no fears at all that public investment is going to be constrained by a lack of fiscal resources.

In some ways, I am more anxious that we actually implement what we have budgeted for. Partly, it's because the ability to spend, generally, is not great. There are a few pockets that can spend well like the National Thermal Power Corporation Ltd (NTPC), railways, highways, roads, and so on. But it is not easy to do so especially when the legal institutional environment is such that the CBI and the CVC are watching out for bad spending. There is a natural caution in the bureaucracy, which further limits how much you can spend. So, I don't worry about the resource problem in the short run.

In the medium term, I have a slightly strong view on our model of understanding the macro savings investment picture. In India, I have been surprised by how in thrall we are to what I would call the Ragnar Nurkse–Rosenstein–Rodan Lewis kind of framework, which argues that growth is held back only because of inadequate savings. In the last five years, there has been this notion that this is the investment, we need so much saving, but where will the savings come from? In fact, the East Asian experience tells us that savings actually rise to meet investment, and so savings don't become that much of a constraint on growth.

Even if you look at our own experience in India, our savings shot up enormously during the boom period, and it's not as if we had to run huge current-account deficits. The big current-account deficits happened when we started decelerating for all kinds of different reasons. So, while we need to devote time to getting better intermediation on domestic savings—to then asking if we need more innovative sources of finance—I think my first-order concern in the short run is with implementation capacity and the natural caution that actually deters public investment. In the medium term, I worry less about savings because the East Asian experience, whether it's China, or Korea or Japan earlier, certainly shows that savings endogenously increase as you grow. In a sense there is a certain kind of finance fetish that I don't completely buy into.

'Maybe I was channelling Mr Suresh Prabhu [the railways minister at the time],' began Karthik, perhaps because his ministry has the capacity to spend, but seems to need to look for off-budget resources to fund some of these large capital expenses. 'How do we unblock the banking system and how do we get it to start lending again?' he asked.

I digressed a little into Indian economic history here—planning and import substitution were de rigueur in those days, so in real time, those were not major mistakes or bad choices. If you were to ask me what the two egregious economic sins we committed in our past were, they are the Industrial Policy Resolution, which started the licensing of industry, and bank nationalization in 1969. The reason is that while in all the other cases we tried to protect Indian industry against competition (import substitution, public sector, etc.), in this case we taxed and expropriated domestic investors. So, in that sense, this was a very costly mistake.

In terms of banking reforms going forward, we had a chapter in an Economic Survey which my colleagues Rohit Lamba and others helped write. Allow me a small digression into the 'McKinsey way' of talking about these things: I called this the four 'Ds' of bank reform: deregulation, differentiation, diversification and disinterring.

If you look at the banking system, we actually practise severe financial repression. We've been doing it on the liability side, but we do this on our asset side as well as with our priority-sector lending and the statutory liquidity ratio. I think we need to address those by deregulating, which is the first thing that generally improves intermediation. Second, we need to differentiate—we don't merely have public-sector banks in India; we have public-sector banks and public-sector banks and public-sector banks (that is, PSBs with varying degrees of efficiency).

We do need to differentiate between how we approach this. Any recapitalization strategy should differentiate across banks.

For example, there are clearly some categories of banks which you want to shrink, where maybe even the regulator can shrink, through mergers and so on; some where you aggressively need to recapitalize; and some in which governance reform should be undertaken. So, the whole one-size-fits-all approach does not work in banking.

Third, we must diversify sources of financing—whether by introducing many more banks, many more types of banks, payment banks—and our licensing has to become more permissive. And, of course, we have to gradually begin to develop our bond markets. In some ways it's possible that the way to get out of the problem is to grow the non-banking sector rather than to frontally shrink the public sector. The last is to disinter, since exit is very difficult from this framework. We need to get better bankruptcy laws. We need much more creative quasi-political exit mechanisms. This may even address the overhang problem we are experiencing. Because clearly, the legal mechanism for exit that we have right now is not effective and needs to be reformed. That's the way I see banking reform—in terms of the 4 'Ds'—and we have got to work on all of them.

Karthik acknowledged the chicken-and-egg situation we're in with respect to banks where at one level, the government feels the asset values are so depressed that it's not the right time to exit. About twenty years ago, American economist and public-policy analyst Jeff Sachs famously said, 'State-owned hotels irritate me, state-owned firms annoy me, state-owned banks terrify me,' precisely because it is a misallocation of resources across the whole economy. But then, you're never going to get that valuation as long as you have the political economy of public-sector bank lending.

So, when I talked about differentiation, Karthik asked me: why not bite the bullet on, say, one bank? He wondered if we were to proceed with one bank and say that we would bring equity down below 50 per cent, we will get to see how much the market gives a control premium, or rather a de-control premium. He believed in the 'let us just de-risk the process of taking this on' approach—pick one guy and see what happens.

I told him that was great advice and it certainly should be a part of the menu of options. However, it runs against the exit problem. I alerted him to a sense of the political challenge, without disagreeing with what he was saying. A sector that I have been studying a little bit with my colleagues is fertilizer. In fertilizer, for example, we have this perverse system—you can't make it up—where the more inefficient you are, the more the subsidies you get. The interesting thing is that some of these very inefficient firms are not employment-intensive. But it's not easy to wind them down, and I prefer not to try and second-guess my political masters in terms of why that is so. So, that's where we stand—when you think about the proposed solution for public-sector banks, that kind of problem in fertilizer is magnified n-fold.

Referring to his smart-cards work with Sandip Sukhtankar and Santhosh Mathew, Karthik said that the deeper question is not whether smart cards reduced corruption, but why it was allowed to be implemented when political rents were being shut down. Karthik felt that the basic economic road map of what needs to happen is almost so obvious to many of us that the highest value-add comes from thinking through which are the winnable political battles, and finding ways in which you can get some of these things through. He told me that for what it's worth, it seems that there are two or three ways to cut through the political economy gridlock. One is that reforms happen in sectors where rents are controlled by the Opposition party. Given this diversity in banks and the diversity in where those rents are, that might be something that one could consider putting on the table.

I thought that was a very good notion, and I would like to digress towards a point related to that. Crony capitalism in India is well known; I think it is older than capitalism itself. What is really interesting about India is that the markets for the 'cronier' and the 'cronied' are both contestable. On the crony side, one man is in favour today but the other man can be in favour tomorrow. But equally, the guy who is in the government and doing the crony-ing changes because of politics. This is to say that one constraint on my misbehaviour as a politician today is that tomorrow I'll be out of office and in opposition and therefore, liable to scrutiny and investigation. That is an aspect of crony capitalism that I think is quite interesting.

But more seriously, there are some political constraints that we have to keep pushing and pushing as unacceptable. We may not win that battle, but there are other constraints where we have to see how we overcome the opposition. One way is what Karthik said. The other way is reform by stealth. The third way is to act where you find the minimum resistance. The fourth is sharing the gains that materialize from eliminating the rents. For example, if we want to reduce the kerosene and food subsidy sold through the public distribution system (PDS), we may have to incentivize the states by giving them a share of the gains; we may have to give the PDS shops a share of the gains as well. There are various ways and I think that's what makes the economist's job so interesting and challenging, because as Karthik said, the big items that need to be done are well known.

Karthik then added one more possible approach. As economists, we think that certain status-quo situations are inefficient. This means that rent-seeking is probably captured by relatively few people in the classic American economist and social scientist Mancur Olson's 'concentrated costs, diffused benefits' kind of world. The former chief economist of the World Bank Kaushik Basu said that in many, many settings the problem is just ossified bad ideas. One approach that might be promising in various sectors is to do an incidence analysis of some of our most distortionary subsidies, whether it's fertilizer or free electricity, and to plot out how regressive that is. The basic political economy in this case is that if you have a highly regressive subsidy, the median or average amount of that is going to be something that is covered by the 80th percentile. So you could take stock of your subsidy and repackage this by saying, 'a certain number of free units for everybody'. You use less than that, you sell at the market price; you spend beyond that, you pay the market price. But the key thing is, if you were to put that proposal to vote, you suddenly have an 80 per cent majority in favour of your reform. Besides looking at ideas and pushing things through, it feels like there might be creative ways of designing approaches to reform that allow us to uncover consumer preference.

I do think—and this is what I discovered from my job as the chief economic adviser—that there is a lot of value in just presenting simple facts clearly. For instance, the numbers that Karthik produced on teacher absenteeism were phenomenally useful in changing the discourse around public education. In fact, we were doing some work on the power sector in India, and we were looking at how regressive or progressive the tariff structures are, state by state. If we could potentially bring to light how much it departs from some fairly egalitarian social-welfare function, that itself would be valuable. This can be done in a number of areas; you don't even have to put it to vote (how you would do that is a difficult question). I certainly think that we underestimate how little the facts are understood, and there is a lot of scope for presenting these facts through simple analyses; you don't have to do complicated, randomized, controlled trials.

Picking on these simple facts, Karthik went back to something I had said earlier about the structure of Indian fertilizer subsidies, which I suspect not very many people know. To put it simply, say, there are thirty fertilizer (urea) firms in India. Say, the internationally competitive price is about USD

300/ton. Say fifteen of them actually produce at USD 300 or below. But then, there are fifteen firms that are producing either at USD 400/450/600 and sometimes even more—so that is two to three times. If you are producing at USD 650/ton, the amount of subsidy that you get in terms of rupees will be much more. In a sense, the aim is to equalize the returns to all fertilizer firms. So, the more inefficient you are, the more you need to get to equalize returns. These are firm-specific subsidies and they are perverse in this manner.

Karthik then turned to privatization, on which I elaborated that if you look at the more successful cases of introducing competition and efficiency into markets in India, whether it was airlines or telecom or even to some extent banking, it has been not by shrinking the public sector but by allowing entry for the private sector, and thus reducing the market share. In the case of banking, one of the things that strikes me is that if you look at the period of rapid growth in India (2003–11), it was the most private-sector–led growth and yet, the share of the private banking system barely rose.

It's a bit odd. Of course, ex post, it seems like they were very wise and prudent. But there is something about why private-sector banking hasn't picked up more. And I still think the privatization, the shrinking, the holding company, all have to be part of the mix, but there also has to be more and more entry. That is privatization by stealth, as it were; that's why more generous licensing of conventional banks and payment banks is going to be very important.

And that, Karthik pointed out, is where bankruptcy legislation is potentially a big thing, just by allowing the sort of exit that I have been talking about.

One of the big challenges which we haven't studied enough is that when you move towards a more regulatory state but are stuck with weak regulatory capacity, what does it mean for the design of regulatory policy in the first instance? You can design a bankruptcy law, but then it's not as if we don't have them at the moment. We have debt recovery tribunals, for example—understaffed, lack of talent, governance issues, etc. So, I think the bankruptcy legislation is no guarantee that you will get a smoother exit. We need to think about how we can improve capacity, or take into account weak capacity in designing it in the first place, or how we can try and take insights from behavioural economics to improve capacity at the margin. These are ideas we need to explore because these are the ways in which change will happen, more than by frontally attacking the exit problem.

Karthik highlighted how, in a way, conceptually, it appears that fiscal space is the constraint to getting the investments. 'But what I'm hearing time and time again is that it is the implementation capacity, it's state capacity, it's the ability to write decent contracts, the ability to follow through on regulation—and all of this capacity simply doesn't exist in the state,' he said. He brought up two points regarding self-financing in some ways for the wave of infrastructure that we need.

The first was property taxes—unless you have a robust property-taxing mechanism at the urban level that's reflecting the appreciation of these property values, you will not have the resources to fund urbanization. The second idea was again one of the core principles of public finance—taxing 'bads' and reducing the taxes of 'goods'. In this case, it would be something like a graduated carbon tax that would be put into an escrow account, explicitly for infrastructure. There are two things—one is that the environmental position is stuck behind this somewhat sanctimonious international negotiating position of saying that we need our turn to pollute. But even without the global and domestic health externalities, in terms of the environment this is a win–win–win if it's done in a gradual and transparent way. A creative political communicator can get the message across that the majority of the incidence is perhaps on the high end of the income distribution.

I responded that, in fact, the graduated carbon tax-plus what we had called earmarking is in some ways exactly what we had done in 2017. Petroleum taxes were raised, and in the Economic Survey we calculated what the implicit de facto carbon tax was as a result of the increases in excises on diesel and petroleum. For example, in the case of diesel, we went from carbon subsidization to taxation, with a tax of about USD 62/ton of carbon dioxide. The international norm—Nordhaus, Weitzman, Stern—is about USD 25/ton. In the case of petroleum, it is about USD 120/ton of carbon dioxide. Some of these were levied as cesses, which have been earmarked for the public-sector infrastructure programme. So, the government has been doing exactly what Dr Karthik ordered. I think there is more scope for that, but we will come back to climate change later in the book. Even the coal cess was increased from Rs 50/ton to 100 and then to Rs 200/ton in the last budget (2015) and again earmarked for a 'Green Fund', which is meant for investment in green projects.

Regarding land, for instance, in the last fifteen years or so, if you take into account how much land prices have gone up and how little has been captured in taxes, it is a travesty. It really comes down to how we are going to address this third tier of governance, and the experience hasn't been great. Even the Fourteenth Finance Commission, perhaps, didn't go far enough in terms of giving these third-tier fiscal entities the power to generate taxes. Here again, we run into this question of, 'But why hasn't it (raising property taxes) happened?' And clearly, the urban local bodies (ULBs) don't have an interest in doing this because it's unpopular.

Again a digression here, which I think is very interesting. If you look at the fiscal history of the United States after the civil war, they had restricted franchise. Restricted franchise meant the property owners were the voters as well. They had an incentive because infrastructure was financed mostly by property taxes but it was a self-sustaining equilibrium because the taxes led to increases in land values. One lesson we could draw is that we should go back to restricted franchise, which, of course, is a decision no one in this day and age would make.

Karthik found this quite surprising because he thought it would be the opposite. The landless should be happy to vote for more property taxes. So, this seems to be the sort of tax that universal franchise would actually push in favour of. It's the opposite if you restrict it to just having landowners as voters; then they are the ones who are not going to want to have property taxes. What are we missing here?

I would think in our setting, the political economy is rather in the opposite place, in the sense that you raise the greasy pole of power up to the state but then the money is controlled in the cities, which means you don't want to let go. When Karthik asked if that's what has been happening in India rather than an inability to tax per se, I explained that if urban bodies will have to tax, the losers will be the propertied class to some extent and that's where all the opposition is going to come from. It is a case of concentrated losers, diffused beneficiaries (as I mentioned previously in the Mancur Olson framework)—so you get a difficult equilibrium.

'Then the argument has to rely more on the nature of the public goods that are financed, which has to be more benefitting for those who hold land,' Karthik said.

One question we could ask here is: given that property taxes are what they are, what can the Centre do to incentivize some of these things? There is a bit of a struggle here. On the one hand, recognizing the bad political economy equilibrium at the local level, you want the Centre to use either carrots or sticks to make this happen. But then, T.V. Somanathan—someone who comes from the states—said that some of these decisions are actually

made by the state finance commissions and so it's kind of an
intrusion into democratic legitimacy for the Centre to do so. So,
you struggle with these competing things, and frankly, there is no
clear answer in this case.

This set the stage for Karthik's next pivot—one broad view
of this government in the past year (2015) has been that there
is a fair bit of movement in the domains that are directly in the
control of the central government, whether it's foreign policy,
railways or defence. Then when we look at something like 'Ease
of Doing Business' or 'Make in India', the vast majority of the
web of regulation and the last mile rent-seeking that plagues
businessmen is still at the state level. He asked about the levers
the Centre has to meaningfully push on this in a way that delivers
on the promise of this government.

I told him that with the Fourteenth Finance Commission,
there are fewer and fewer levers because more untied resources are
going to the states, but it's not that it's beyond the Centre. This
is why competitive federalism is so important; you need to have
change from above but also change driven by competition among
states. In terms of what the Centre can do, here are a couple of
possibilities. One is that expenditure management systems can
be improved considerably; reducing the float/idle balances in the
system is something you can use to incentivize states to follow up.

The second possibility is that, at this juncture, we have all
this work by people at the World Bank saying that the greater
the alignment between the states and the Centre, the likelier it is
that resources will flow and change will follow. Similarly, insofar
as there are states aligned with the Centre, there could be more
political direction to make this happen as well. It's not for me
to say how it should be done. I think that is the opportunity of
this current mandate. The constitutional levers are receding but
there are still some left and now we also possibly have political
alignments working in a way that we can push some of these

things around. To some extent, these things are happening—
Rajasthan reformed the labour laws; Gujarat and Madhya Pradesh
are following. The public distribution systems are good in some
states such as Andhra Pradesh and Chhattisgarh.

In the context of expenditure reforms, what ends up happening
in practice is that every department has a request for a certain
amount of money for its dream set of projects. Finance doesn't
really have the wherewithal to go into assessing the quality of
spending because this is the department's ask and the department's
domain. It is incentive-compatible for every department to ask for
as much money as possible; it was then my job to say you can't get
it all. But then that becomes an alibi for this low-level equilibrium,
saying we didn't get the money; the same thing happens with the
states. So, it seems like there is a structural weakness, whereby
departments are penalized for being cost effective at delivering
what they need to.

As we thought more deeply about architecting expenditure
management and improving the quality of spending, Karthik
asked if there was something that the ministry of finance could
do. Take the example of teacher absenteeism, where the fiscal
cost is Rs 9000 crore a year. Karthik documented this problem
in 2003. He then went back to the schools seven years later and
while there was massive improvement in every input, the absence
number hadn't gone down very much. And this is just one line
item of one sector. But that's just not on the radar.

He then asked how I would reward departments for delivering
better quality of expenditure. I believe there are two problems
here. One is the monitoring of outcomes. When you say quality
of delivery, start with whether we really focus on outcomes.
Pratham and the Annual Status of Education Report (ASER)
Centre have been focusing on the lack of learning outcomes. But
I think here we have an opportunity because the prime minister,
as chief minister of the state of Gujarat, was really obsessed with

outcomes, and even now he wants to focus on outcomes at the central level.

In fact, during a meeting, he suggested this idea: 'Why don't we have one to two universities or think tanks in every state that will undertake assessments of the quality of expenditure in that state?' Maybe we should have twenty-nine joint poverty action labs (J-PALs) in the country and not one. I think we have to start with that because if you can show value for money or lack of value for money, that can be an important input into the first-level decision of what gets financed and what does not. So far, it's fair to say that we have not focused enough on outcomes. So, in terms of any ideas that people may have for improving the translation of expenditure to outcomes, I think this is an opportunity.

Going back to the Fourteenth Finance Commission, Karthik agreed that it was a game changer, but still thought that globally there is one concern, which is that if you look at the evidence on public-service delivery after decentralization, the general sense is that the average improves a little bit. The average improves because the better units pull away and the weaker units fall behind and that exacerbates inequality. Maybe at the state level we can't get away from this phenomenon—you need those leaders at the state level to demonstrate what they do, before the laggards catch up. I guess there is a genuine concern that with great power comes great responsibility, and the states have not always shown the ability to spend wisely. The state electricity boards are kind of exhibit A in the perilous condition of public finances at the state level.

I had three responses to that. One is that if you plot fiscal transfers (finance commissions) per capita against state GDP per capita, and do the same for expenditure per capita handed out by the (erstwhile) Planning Commission, you find that fiscal transfers are more progressive than plan transfers have been. Why? It's simple—because the formula of the Fourteenth Finance

Commission is more progressive; it has all these redistribution-intensive indicators. Also, plan transfers are discretionary and they moved away from formula-based transfers. So, I certainly do not accept prima facie, based on the limited evidence I've seen, that moving from Planning Commission transfers to finance commission transfers is regressive (that is, it discriminates against the poorer states).

Secondly, in terms of the fear that the states will fritter it away, if you look at the aggregate numbers on fiscal discipline and fiscal profligacy, the Centre, on an average, has been more profligate than the states. Clearly, there is some variation amongst the states, and we need to think about that, but it is not that all states are irresponsible.

Now this brings me to my third point. Dilip Mookherjee of Boston University, who has done a lot of work on decentralization, was present. Certainly, there are those who want the Centre to spend more, because they think that the Centre will spend on more important things such as health and education, and spend it better. But I struggle with that because in some ways, even if that were true, that is in tension with the other principle we believe in, which is that it should be done closer to the people, that is, there should be greater decentralization. So, I don't know how to reconcile that. One way of doing this in a cooperative federalism framework would be to have more accountability mechanisms or loose forms of conditionalities, say, via NITI Aayog (the successor to the Planning Commission) for this kind of mutual surveillance—something like what the European Union was conceived to do.

Stepping back from the big picture, on a more personal note, Karthik asked me to reflect on my role as the chief economic adviser. 'What does a day in the life of a CEA look like? How does this beast work? How do you feed inputs into the complex policy process?'

I didn't want it to sound either cute or glib or self-laudatory, but I was honest. I wake up every morning and think about how I came to get this job, because it really is the most exciting job in the world. At any point in time, there are so many issues to work on, so much to do. I have this fantastic team of government officials and youngsters from the outside, which enables us to work on so much. For example, before the last budget (2015), we made the case for public investment. There is a generic case for public investment, which we all know about, but this was a circumstantial case for public investment because of weak balance sheets, and the interaction between the public and private sectors. We did a lot of work on that and, to some extent, it did translate into a budgetary decision. We are working on fertilizer, power, DBT, water, savings, and so on. The fact is there are just so many issues where intelligent analytics, good careful data collection, and data exposure can be useful. I praise this government for being so open to listening to not just me, but to what several people have been doing. As to whether they finally act on it, one can't second-guess the political constraints. But at least feeling that they want new ideas and they want to listen has been an absolute joy and delight.

'We've got states that have more people than most countries in the world, now with large amounts of money. How is it that we don't have the equivalent of an office of CEA in every state, because as CEA, you are also the head of the Indian Economic Service? So, to the extent that we are talking about building state capacity, you can't control the overall state, but this is still something that's more directly within your purview. It seems like it could be a great institutional legacy if you could create the space for a CEA in every state because just as you talk about the issues in the country, I'm sure each state needs exactly that level of depth and analysis,' Karthik pointed out.

This year (2015) after the Economic Survey, we actually went to twelve to thirteen different cities to disseminate the survey. The reactions were remarkably encouraging. In fact, three states—Jammu and Kashmir, Bihar and Kerala (and I'm sure this could've been true of the other states as well)—said that they wanted help from us to do economic surveys, like we do for the country, for each of the states. There is a real interest in this—many states actually do economic surveys already—and this is something I was very serious about following up. Of course, this is something that state governments have to agree to. Gradually, this can morph into something ambitious like having a CEA office in every state. The Indian Economic Service has fantastic people, and certainly, we could have people from there or from outside.

Thinking back to my conversation with Dr Karthik, in sum, I am reminded of how India is a very unusual development model. It is still a work in progress. But if it works, it would be the object of envy and imitation by other countries. A lot remains to be done and the government has certainly embarked on the task—with the GST, JAM, etc. Ten or fifteen years from now, I imagine Karthik and I will have a similar conversation, perhaps with the roles reversed, with me as the éminence grise and him as the CEA, to see how this unique model has fared.

1.2

From Crony Socialism to Stigmatized Capitalism—and Its Consequences Today

The phrase 'stigmatized capitalism' occurred to me at a talk I gave at the University of Pennsylvania in October 2017. I prefer it to the more popular 'crony capitalism' because it is more nuanced and actually richer in its implications for the reform process in India.

It has now been more than a quarter century since Prime Minister Narasimha Rao and Dr Manmohan Singh put India's economy on a new growth path. Their reforms were carried forward by Prime Minister Atal Bihari Vajpayee in the early years of the new millennium, and every other leader since. And their efforts have reaped a tremendous reward: a dramatic improvement in living standards for the nation. Yet, despite this success and recent reform efforts, the government is still struggling to deliver the country from the legacy of its socialist past.

The 2017 Economic Survey of India noted that capitalism—and specifically the private sector—evokes feelings of deep ambivalence. Some of these feelings arise from the circumstances of its birth. India's private sector still bears the stigma of having been midwifed under the pre-1990s 'Licence Raj'—an era remembered for the Kafka-esque system of extensive controls, red tape and corruption. To this day, some of India's most successful entrepreneurs are believed to have built their empires by mastering the minutiae of India's tariff and tax codes, and then manipulating them brazenly to their advantage.

The private sector's stigma was lessened by the boom in information and communications technology that started in the 1990s. The information and communication technology (ICT) sector developed itself by virtue of its distance from, rather than proximity to, the government. Indian ICT firms adopted exemplary governance standards, were listed on international stock exchanges, and thrived in the global marketplace. And, by extension, they improved the standing of Indian capital within India and globally.

But after that era of good capitalism, the stigma returned. During the infrastructure boom between 2005 and 2010, public resources were captured under a 'Rent Raj', which put up for grabs every possible type of rent (rent here denotes massive, undeserved returns): terrestrial rents (land and environmental permits), sub-terrestrial rents (coal) and even ethereal rents (spectrum). Unsurprisingly, the defining moments of that era were consequently the 2G and coal scams.

The boom era gave rise to other problems as well. Some of the infrastructure investments were funded by reckless and imprudent lending by public-sector banks, which funnelled resources to high-risk, politically connected borrowers—a good example being a booze baron-turned-wannabe airline tycoon who fled India after he ran his business into the ground. James Crabtree, in his recent book, *The Billionaire Raj*, takes us through the world and lives of India's stigmatized capitalists, whose reach extends from petrochemicals and telecommunications to renewable power, finance, steel, iron ore and, of course, even cricket.

As a result, the Indian public concluded that the promoters of these enterprises actually had little financial stake in the success of their firms, especially because 'limited liability' seemed to mean no liability at all. And now that rapid technological change is threatening the ICT sector's business model—providing low-cost programming services to foreign clients—even India's 'cleanest' capitalist industry is confronting governance challenges.

More broadly, one could say that India has moved from 'crony socialism' to 'stigmatized capitalism'. Crony socialism refers to the selective favouring that happened under the Licence Raj, and stigmatized capitalism is the resulting legacy. It is important to understand that the stigma attaches not just to the private sector but also to the state/government that is seen to be deeply complicit in the process.

Seen against this background, it is easier to understand why it has taken so long to address India's Twin Balance Sheet challenge, the twin problems of overly indebted private-sector firms and under-capitalized public-sector banks. During the East Asia crisis of the 1990s, these countries managed to put a resolution framework in place within a year, and solve the bulk of the problem within two years. But in India, it has taken nearly a decade simply to introduce a (potentially) viable framework, the new insolvency and bankruptcy code.

'Stigma' captures the essence of the problem: the suspicion of the private sector, the complicity of the government, and the difficult relations between them. For example, because there was fear of a political backlash, it was difficult to create the bad bank that I had been advocating since 2015. Because of stigmatized capitalism, it is always easier to pass the decision-making buck to the judiciary which is perceived to have more legitimacy. Because of stigmatized capitalism, it was necessary to ensure that promoters could not regain access to their assets even if they weren't at fault for their firms' bankruptcies. All of this has led to delay and driven up fiscal costs, ironically, further burdening the beleaguered taxpayers.

The good news is that the new bankruptcy law, for the first time in Indian history, has created a legal framework for resolving creditor–debtor relations and for being able to write down debts in a way that the public seems to find reasonable and legitimate. There have been some early successes under this law. But the system remains far from a cure, and further reforms are needed.

The more sobering news is this. The pall of stigmatized capitalism is likely to make a morality play of all efforts at economic reform, favouring a more punitive, heavy-handed approach. For example, because of stigmatized capitalism, government agencies have recently been arresting promoters and bankers, in some cases without even registering cases or following the due process. Apart from raising issues of personal rights, all this could instil fear in the private sector and chill the climate for investment, thereby depressing growth for some time to come.

Perhaps even more sobering is this: even if the bankruptcy process works and stigmatized capitalism is checked, it will reinforce imbalances in the governance system. The process involving the Insolvency and Bankruptcy Code (IBC) has been and will be an explicitly legal one, and key decisions have been taken and/or sanctioned by the courts, especially the Supreme Court. In that case, the broader institutional disequilibrium in India, with declining authority and legitimacy for the executive and the legislature, and conversely greater authority and legitimacy for the judiciary, will be aggravated. In a democracy, there are and should be limits to the power of unelected bodies, including the courts. But if other institutions are unable or unwilling to deliver reasonable governance that power will only increase.

Nothing less than the future of Indian democracy and institutions depends on India's coming to grips with stigmatized capitalism.

From Socialism with Limited Entry to Capitalism without Exit

The Chakravyuha Challenge[1]

The idea that exit, not just entry, was a key problem afflicting the Indian economy occurred to me on the day I was preparing for my conversation with Karthik Muralidharan (Section 1.1). It was a minor eureka moment because it put into an analytical framework several of the issues—the Twin Balance Sheet problem, fertilizer subsidy, agricultural reforms, etc.—my team and I were working on at that time. I remember excitedly asking one of my bright (and demanding) colleagues Siddharth George to come to my room to run the idea by him, to see if it seemed plausible, to which he gave a cautious green light.

A market economy requires the unrestricted entry of new firms, new ideas and new technologies so that the forces of competition can guide capital and labour resources *towards* their most productive and dynamic uses. But it also requires 'exit' so that resources are forced or enticed *away* from inefficient and unsustainable uses. It is no surprise that the great Austrian economist Joseph Schumpeter spoke about capitalism as a gale of 'creative destruction'. In terms of the Hindu pantheon, it is worth recalling that Siva the destroyer is as important a creative force as Brahma or Vishnu.

Structural impediments to India's economic progress have often been identified in relation to entry, reflected in that wonderfully evocative phrase of India's original economic liberal, C. Rajagopalachari: 'licence, quota, permit raj'. That is, socialism made it difficult to start new enterprises, expand existing operations, bring in foreign goods, allow foreign investment or technology. Since the 1980s, remarkable progress has been made in facilitating entry: dismantling industrial licences; liberalizing inflows of foreign trade, capital and technology; allowing firms to come into new sectors such as airlines, telecommunications and banking.

However, the inability to facilitate or engineer exit either out of inefficient policies or situations that are clearly unproductive has now emerged to be a first-order constraint on economic progress. The Chakravyuha metaphor from the Mahabharata—Abhimanyu's ability to enter and break through a complicated war formation of the Kauravas but his inability to get out, resulting in tragic consequences—is an apt one for today's situation. Hence, my somewhat glib characterization of India's economic development as having moved from socialism with limited entry to capitalism without exit.

Where is this exit problem most acute in India? Unfortunately, it is present almost everywhere. The problem of exit is all-pervasive, applying to industry and agriculture, private and public sectors, at the central and state government levels, inputs and outputs, small- and large-scale enterprises. With the notable exception of the newer sectors such as IT, there is no part of the economy that is not afflicted by the problem of exit.

We see it in the airline industry because Air India has really no business to be in business, having bled the state and the taxpayer for decades. We see it in the fertilizer industry where at least half the firms producing urea do so well above internationally efficient levels. They should have been out of business long ago, instead they are mollycoddled and in perverse ways, because the more inefficient they are, the greater the subsidy they receive.

We see it in spades with public-sector banks where many are under the 'intensive care' of the RBI, disallowed from expanding, and even others are saddled with high levels of non-performing loans. We see it in other public-sector enterprises whose accumulated losses (as of 2013–14) was over Rs 1 lakh crores: many have been certified as 'sick' for decades. We have seen it with the electricity distribution companies (the DISCOMs) which have been bleeding until recent measures taken by the government under the UDAY (Ujwal DISCOM Assurance Yojana) scheme have stopped the haemorrhaging to some extent.

Exit extends also to the private sector and to government policies. We see overproduction in the cereals sector, especially rice because of a plethora of policies in the form of high minimum support prices and extensive subsidies for fertilizer, water, power and credit. Especially egregious is the overproduction of sugar, a water-guzzling crop, in water-scarce Maharashtra.

Finally, exit also applies to government schemes. Analysis of centrally sponsored schemes in the economic survey of 2015–16 showed that about 50 per cent of them were twenty-five years old. And out of the 104 schemes, ninety-two have been ongoing for fifteen years or more. There is even a scheme that is ninety-six years old called 'Livestock Health & Disease Control' under the department of animal husbandry, dairying and fisheries. In the Union Budget 2015–16, it was allocated Rs 251 crore. If a similar analysis were conducted for schemes operated by the states, it is almost certain that we will find new schemes being added with virtually no 'deaths' of existing ones.

The costs of exit are captured when comparing the average age and size of firms in the US with those in India. In the US, the average forty-year-old plant is eight times larger than a new one, whereas that number is 1.5 for India. What this shows is that firms that survive in India don't grow large enough, and second, too many unproductive firms survive. In principle, productive and innovative firms should expand and grow, forcing out the unproductive ones.

The costs of impeded exit cannot be overstated. In a capital-scarce country such as India, misallocation of resources has long-term economic costs. Think of two groups: one with an economic idea that maintains status quo economic productivity; and the other that can double it. Repeatedly providing the former with greater resources results in a large misallocation gap which shrinks the economic surplus. The exit problem contributes to this by not incentivizing the first group to quit the fray. The fiscal costs are substantial too. The Economic Survey of India has documented the total bill of inefficient subsidies pursued by the state at around 0.8–0.9 per cent of the GDP.

So the question arises: what can be done to tackle the problem of exit?

First, the emphasis on free entry in industry should be continued; but it is a battle only half won. Greater entry through a level playing field is the easiest way of ensuring the exit of the inefficient—natural competition will support the survival of the fittest.

Second, we must look into reviving or shutting down infrastructure projects, and here, radical progress has been made thanks to IBC. The most striking recent successes are in the steel sector, where several loss-making firms have been bought by more efficient firms: Bhushan Steel by Tata Steel, Electrosteel by Vedanta, and Monnet-Ispat by JSW Steel-AION. But a lot remains to be done.

Third, greater transparency must be pursued aggressively by reaching out to the populace. For example, the economic and environmental costs of encouraging the production of cereals must be widely known so that farmers can make an informed decision about their harvests, and pressure the government to incentivize pulses and other less water-intensive crops.

Fourth, both central and state governments themselves must commit to two rules: for every new administrative scheme that they want to start, they must commit to phasing out two old ones; and every new scheme has to come with an automatic sunset clause, expiring no later than, say, five years after its inception.

Finally, facilitating exit can be seen as an opportunity. In many cases where public-sector firms need to be privatized, the problems of exit arise because of opposition from existing managers or employees' interests. But in some instances, such action can be converted into opportunities. For example, resources earned from privatization could be earmarked for employee compensation and retraining. Most public-sector firms occupy relatively large tracts of land in desirable locations. Parts of this land can be converted into land banks and made into vehicles for promoting the 'Make in India' and 'Smart City' campaigns. If the land is in dense urban areas, it could be used to develop ecosystems to nurture start-ups, and if located in smaller towns and cities, it could be used to develop sites for industrial clusters.

One concern with privatization is the fear that social policies—of reservation, for example—will become casualties when the underlying assets move from public-sector to private-sector control. Credibly ensuring that the spirit of such policies will be maintained is necessary to secure wider social acceptability for exit.

Abhimanyu died a valiant warrior because he could not get out of the Chakravyuha. Unless, we see wholesale exit, the Indian economy could face similar tragic consequences.

1.4*

The Big Puzzle of India

Diverging Regional Economic Development despite Equalizing Forces[1]

Persistent regional inequalities could pose serious challenges to Indian democracy and even to Indian unity, as the recent debates over sharing of tax revenues suggest. Therefore, if India is to do well, the Indian states must also do well; the large differences in economic development among them—for example, a nearly five-fold difference in per capita income between Maharashtra and Bihar and a 12 percentage point difference in life expectancy between Kerala and Madhya Pradesh—must narrow over time. Economists call this narrowing—the reduction in disparities on important indicators of performance, including standards of living, and health and educational outcomes—'convergence'.

The 2017 economic survey showed, however, that convergence is not occurring. It showed that while standards of living (measured in terms of Gross State Domestic Product [GSDP] per capita) have increased significantly in all the states, the poorer states have made no progress over the past three decades in catching up with the rich ones. To the contrary, the disparities between rich and poor states have increased.

Even more disconcerting, the survey showed that these disparities relate not just to per capita GDP but also per capita consumption. This distinction is important because there is a view that in terms of consumption, states such as Bihar may not be doing too badly, because Biharis migrate and send back remittances. The data, however, do not support this comforting view.

In other words, there has been 'divergence' across the states. This is puzzling, because both theory and evidence suggest that economic performance should converge. In theory, if a state or country is poor, it will be short of capital. But if capital is scarce, it is valuable, and there should be high returns available to anyone willing to provide more of it. In that case, investment should pour in, increasing productivity and enabling catch-up with richer states or countries. A good example of this process at work is the clothing sector in Bangladesh, where inflows of trade and foreign investment have dramatically raised wages and living standards.

Bangladesh is far from an exceptional case. In fact, all around the world, convergence is occurring. That is, poorer countries are on an average closing the gap with richer countries (measured by their per capita GDP).

India as a whole is also converging towards rich country standards. But the same process is not working within India. Consider the data. The figure below shows the good news—the general improvement in living standards across states. It plots the level of real per capita GSDP over time between 1983 and 2014. There has been an across-the-board improvement, reflected in the whole per capita GSDP distribution shifting right. For example, between 1984 and 2014, the least developed state (Tripura) increased its per capita GSDP 5.6 fold, from a per capita GSDP of Rs 11,537 to Rs 64,712, measured in constant prices.

Figure 1. Income Levels over the Years in India, All Indian States

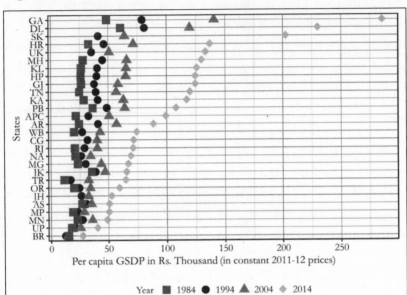

But now consider the convergence data. Convergence occurs when a state that starts off with a lower level of per capita GDP sees faster growth of per capita GDP so that it catches up with the better-performing states. If we plot the initial level of per capita GDP on the x-axis and per capita GDP growth on the y-axis, convergence would show up in the form of states being distributed around a downward sloping line. (Conversely, divergence would be reflected in an upward sloping line.)

This is represented in the figure below, which plots convergence trends for the period 2004–14 for three groups: the Indian states (upward sloping), Chinese provinces (dotted line) and other countries in the world (dashed line). As expected, the line for the Chinese provinces and other countries are sloping downward,

meaning that the poorer provinces/countries are catching up with
the richer ones. But the Indian line slopes upwards, showing that
state performance is diverging.

**Figure 2. Income Convergence: India, China and the World,
2004–14**

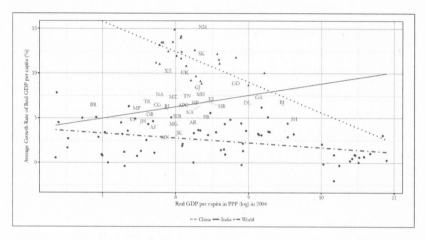

India's performance poses a conundrum on many levels. First,
spatial. Within India, where inter-state borders are porous (there
are no restrictions to the flow of people and capital), convergence
has failed whereas across countries where borders are much
thicker (because of restrictions on trade, capital and labour), the
convergence dynamic has occurred. That is not easy to explain.
This is the cross-country puzzle.

Second, there is an intertemporal puzzle. In the 1990s,
India's growth pattern was similar to China's—neither country
was showing strong convergence at the state/provincial level. But
in the new millennium, convergence started to occur in China.
The driving force behind this convergence dynamic has been the
migration of people from farms in the interior to factories on the
coast, raising productivity and wages in the poorer regions faster
than in richer ones.

Contrary to public perception, India has also benefitted from a similar dynamic. Section 1.5 documents that trade within India is quite high and the mobility of people has surged dramatically— almost doubled in the last couple of decades. Yet disparities have been widening.

Although further research is required to understand the underlying reasons, one possible hypothesis is that convergence fails to occur in India due to governance or institutional traps. If that is the case, capital will not flow to regions of capital scarcity. For example, in the 1980s and 1990s, Bihar despite its cheap labour was unable to attract investment because of the perception that the general climate of lawlessness would make the private sector vulnerable to theft, extortion and expropriation. Adjusted for this risk, the returns to capital were thus extremely low.

A second hypothesis relates to India's pattern of development. India, unlike most growth successes in Asia, has relied on the growth of skill-intensive sectors rather than low-skill ones. (One can see this not just in the dominance of services over manufacturing but also in the patterns of specialization within manufacturing.) If the binding constraint on growth is really the availability of skills, there is no reason why investment would necessarily be high in capital-scarce states. Put another way, convergence will not occur until the less-developed regions are able to generate skills, in addition to providing good governance.

Both these hypotheses, in turn, raise questions of political economy. Given the dynamic of competition between states, where successful states serve both as models (for policy emulation) and magnets (attracting capital, talent and people), why isn't there pressure on the less-developed states to reform their governance in ways that would be competitively attractive? In other words, persistent divergence amongst the states runs up against the dynamic of competitive federalism which impels, or at least should impel, convergence. When Gujarat was able to lure the

Tata Nano project away from West Bengal, that was a successful example of competitive federalism. But why did it not spread more broadly? When Tamil Nadu offers a model of good social service delivery, why isn't Uttar Pradesh able to learn from it?

It is true that over the past two decades, less-developed states such as Bihar, Madhya Pradesh, Odisha and Chhattisgarh have responded to these competitive forces, undertaking reforms to encourage development. But the data suggests that the reforms were neither strong nor durable enough to change the underlying picture of divergence or growing inequality. Why were they so weak?

The move towards economic divergence across India in the face of the equalizing forces of trade and migration is a deep puzzle waiting to be unravelled. When the Hindi hinterland becomes as prosperous and rich in human capital as peninsular India, when the acronym BIMARU loses its second metaphorical meaning (of sickness), we will know that that puzzle has disappeared.

1.5*

India Is More Integrated
Than Anyone Thinks

I had always been obsessed with wanting to quantify the flows of goods and work-related people within India. The former did not exist and I had a strong feeling that the available estimates of internal migration seriously underestimated people flows within India. Leading up to the Economic Survey of 2017–18, my team and I came up with two new ideas for measuring inter-state movement of goods and of people based on two new data sets that had never previously been available and, hence, never exploited. In the pre-GST system, some transactions between states carried an inter-state tax, which the newly created GSTN network was beginning to capture. We used the tax data to track every sale of goods across states. For inter-state migration, we had an even bolder idea of tracking the railway passenger flows between nearly all the major stations for the last ten years. Specifically, we identified those travelling unreserved as potential work-seeking migrants. This was a truly novel data set and idea. The railway minister Suresh Prabhu was kind enough to share what eventually turned out to be nearly 100 million data points, with his young officer on special duty, Hanish Yadav, providing able assistance.

The results were striking and changed at least my understanding of the Indian economy and how integrated it is. The whole effort also showed that the government could create, use and exploit 'big data' for policy purposes.

When Raj Kapoor famously sang '*Phir bhi dil hai Hindustani*' ('Still, my heart is Indian') several decades ago, he was expressing what in hindsight appears to be a deep insight into comparative national development. To the Bismarckian sequence, and paraphrasing the Italian statesman Massimo d'Azeglio, 'We have created Europe. Now we must create Europeans,' the Raj Kapoor counter seems to be that India's founding fathers favoured creating Indians in spirit and political consciousness first. The current difficulties of European integration reflected in the Brexit vote and in the acrimonious debates on the design of the Euro seem to suggest that perhaps the Indian sequencing was not only appropriate but prescient.

The open question is whether the founders of the nation created one economic India, one marketplace for the free, unimpeded movement of goods, services, capital and people. A cautious reading of the Constitution and the Constitutional Assembly debates intimates uncertainty; a less-cautious reading indicates that the needs of creating one economic India were actually subordinated to the imperatives of preserving sovereignty of the states.

For nearly seventy years, the citizens and elites have continually affirmed and reaffirmed the political idea of India. But is India de facto and de jure one economic India? At a time when international integration is under siege and when India is on the cusp of implementing transformational reforms to create 'One India, One Market, One Tax', via the GST, it seems appropriate to ask how much internal integration India has achieved.

Contrary to perception and to some current estimates, the Economic Survey of 2017–18 illustrated that India is highly integrated internally in relation to the flow of people and goods.

India and Indians are on the move. A new methodology that analyses cohorts of Indians across censuses suggests an annual migrant flow of about 5–6 million in the period 2001–11. The first-ever estimates of internal work-related migration using railways' data for the period 2011–16 indicate an annual average flow of close to 9 million people, significantly greater than the number of about 4 million suggested by successive censuses (see Figure 1). If these trends continue, India may not be far off from reaching the magnitude of migrant flows within China.

Figure 1: Estimates of Annual Migrant Flows Based on Railway Traffic Data (Millions)

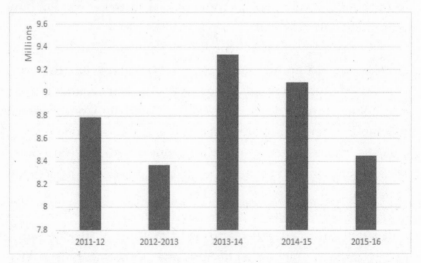

Interstate trade is relatively high. The first-ever estimates for interstate trade flows indicate a trade to GDP ratio of about 54 per cent, a number that is comparable to other large jurisdictions and that contradicts the caricature of India as a barrier-riddled economy (see Figure 2); the ratio of India's internal and international trade also compares favourably with others. De facto, at least, India seems well-integrated internally. A more technical analysis confirms this: trade costs reduce trade by roughly the same extent in India as in other countries. So, both India's international trade to GDP ratio (now greater than China's) and India's internal trade ratio appear quite robust.

Figure 2: India's Internal Trade Compared to Other Large Countries (As Per Cent of GDP)

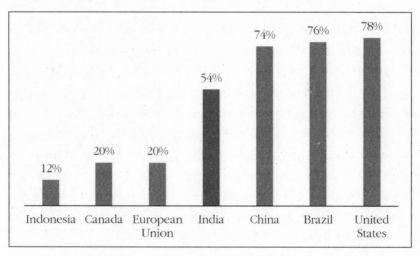

Language may not be a barrier to the flow of goods and people. A potentially exciting finding for which we have tentative, not conclusive, evidence is that while political borders impede the flow of people, language does not seem to be a demonstrable barrier to either the flow of goods or people across state lines. For example, political borders depress the flows of people, which is reflected in the fact that migrant flows *within* states are 300 per cent greater than migrant flows *across* states. However, not sharing Hindi as a common language appears not to create comparable frictions to the movement of goods and people across states. If true, the founders of India may have been vindicated in allowing the organic evolution of a lingua franca rather than dictating it. This prescient permissiveness—not to mention Bollywood— appears to have succeeded in making language less salient an axis of cleavage across India, a remarkable achievement given the early anxieties about language documented in Ramachandra Guha's *India After Gandhi*.

Sensible and surprising patterns. The patterns of flows of goods and people are broadly consistent with those earlier but also throw up some surprises:

- On migration, poorer states such as Uttar Pradesh, Bihar and Madhya Pradesh witness the greatest outmigration while richer states such as Delhi, Tamil Nadu, Maharashtra and Goa are the largest recipients of migrants.
- Smaller states like Uttarakhand, Himachal Pradesh and Goa trade more; the net exporters are the manufacturing powerhouses of Tamil Nadu, Gujarat and Maharashtra.
- Otherwise agricultural, Haryana and Uttar Pradesh are also trading powerhouses because Gurugram and Noida, respectively, have become part of the greater Delhi urban agglomeration.
- The costs of moving are about twice as great for people as they are for goods.
- There is a surprisingly large ratio (68 per cent) of intra-firm trade across states to inter-firm trade (or arm-length sales); intra-firm trade also faces more trading frictions than inter-firm trade.

Just as the world is turning against integration across borders, it seems that at least within India we are making borders more and more porous to allow more goods and more Indians to flow through them. Long live internal integration.

Chapter 2

Money and Cash

2.0

The Tale of Shrinking Three Balance Sheets

Companies, Banks and the RBI

Two months into my tenure as chief economic adviser, our team diagnosed a serious problem facing the Indian economy. A large number of major corporates were heavily overextended and were unable to repay their bank loans. We called this problem the 'Twin Balance Sheet' (TBS) challenge, because the corporate and bank problems were inextricably entwined, and would need to be addressed at the same time. We made this point the key message of my first public document as CEA, the Mid-Year Economic Analysis of December 2014.

I must give a lot of credit to my counsellor Josh Felman who, presciently, kept hammering on the seriousness of the problem and the urgency of addressing it, even in 2015 and early 2016 when the problem appeared to recede amidst a generalized bullishness about the economy. I must also thank Ashish Gupta at Credit Suisse, who would periodically brief me on the magnitude of the problem, based on his thorough research.

Those who had followed India since the boom years between 2005 and 2010 had a gut grasp of the excesses in lending that were taking place then. Hence, they were more alert to the consequences of TBS, which a decade later were exerting a big drag on India's growth. This boom-and-bust conformed to the classic financial cycle, one that is as old as history. As Byron's Don Juan said, 'Let us have wine and women, mirth and laughter / Sermons and soda-water the day after.' We are today—and have been for some extended period—in sermons and soda-water times, for which economists have a more boring term called 'deleveraging'.

In our second Economic Survey in 2016, we set out four key steps for dealing with the TBS problem. I called them the 4 Rs (recognition, resolution, recapitalization and reform), a term that became part of the lexicon when discussing banking-sector issues. I have since added a fifth R, regulation, to that list.

~

This chapter spells out the evolution in my thinking on the TBS challenge, starting with my idea for a 'bad bank' (Section 2.1) and ending with my current proposal for a 'grand bargain', involving a multi-pronged approach to the problem (Section 2.3).

Early on, I was a strong advocate for creating a 'bad bank'. Mind you, I was told that I should not actually use that term because it had some bad connotations in political circles. Therefore, we resorted to the more roundabout Public Sector Asset Rehabilitation Agency (PARA). Still, the underlying idea was the same, namely, that the bad loans of large stressed debtors would be transferred to a government-run agency, which would convert the debt to equity and then auction off the firms. To me, this approach seemed to offer the only timely, reliable way of resolving stressed companies, in the absence of a workable bankruptcy system. Section 2.1 spells out the rationale and mechanics.

We had foreseen some political difficulties in the original proposal, and we knew that a bad bank would run counter to the long-term trend of allowing companies and individuals to take their case to the judiciary. In the end, the real obstacle proved much simpler. There was just no appetite amongst the government or any government agency for taking responsibility for the inevitable debt write-offs that would have to be made in favour of large companies.

Accordingly, a different strategy was chosen. The bankruptcy system was overhauled and in June 2017, the first set of large stressed companies was sent to the courts for resolution. Such a 'legal strategy' for resolving bad debts had been tried several times in the past, and each time it had failed, most famously under the Sick Industries Company Act (SICA) of the 1980s. But times had changed, the new IBC was well designed, and so it seemed worthwhile to give this strategy a try.

In the event, the IBC has had some success in resolving a few high-profile cases. At the same time, many of my initial fears have been realized. In most of the key cases, there have been prolonged delays, the result of repeated appeals by firms seeking to use the courts to block sales of bankrupt companies to their competitors. As a result, backlogs in the system have been growing, resolutions have been receding into the distance, and all the while costs have been climbing.

I now believe that a more radical solution will be necessary to solve the TBS problem. In this case, the government will have to take bold actions such as changing the Bank Nationalization Act—one of the holy cows of India's socialist past—to allow privatization of public-sector banks. So too must the RBI.

The RBI has done an excellent job of maintaining macroeconomic and financial stability, often in difficult circumstances, thanks to its illustrious governors and the strong team behind them. For example, in 2015, the RBI initiated the Asset Quality Review, which had an important impact on advancing the TBS challenge. More recently, it has been enforcing some discipline on some of the most troubled public-sector banks via the Prompt Corrective Action (PCA) framework. In recent months, it has taken impressive actions by calling the heads of some private commercial banks (ICICI, Axis, Yes Bank) to account, and ensuring their exit.

As a result of the RBI's strong track record, it has become one of India's key public institutions, like the Election Commission, the Finance Commission and the Supreme Court, mainstays of the nation that research has repeatedly found to be critical for long-run economic development.

That it has a good reputation, however, does not mean it is always right. For years, the RBI was unable to grasp the seriousness of the loan repayment problems or identify the prolonged frauds of Nirav Modi. Now, with the recent shenanigans involving IL&FS being revealed, this failure seems to have encompassed not just commercial banks but also non-bank financial companies. For these failures, the RBI needs to be held accountable.

The RBI's contributions must be in two key areas. It must credibly step up its supervisory abilities, or even be willing to hand this over to a new agency explicitly created for this purpose. A second area is recapitalizing public-sector banks in decisive fashion, putting them back on their feet so they can lend again. Of course, this will require finding the resources, at a time when India's government finances are once again looking tight. Resources can, however, be obtained from the RBI, which has excess capital that can be profitably deployed for this purpose. How, why and under what strict conditions are discussed in Section 2.2.

I realize that in making this suggestion, I am up against all the eminent current and former RBI officials, who argue that the RBI actually needs all the capital it has. These officials command the respect of the public, and for good reasons. I think they are wrong. As Margaret Thatcher used to say, 'One man and the Truth is a majority.'

The last section in this chapter is on demonetization. As I said in the introduction, there are two big puzzles here: why it was politically successful and why its adverse, short-term impact was not substantially more adverse. These are explored in Section 2.4.

In a sense, this chapter is about shrinking three balance sheets. In the case of companies, their debt has to be written down; in the case of the banks, their assets have to be written down. The third balance sheet is that of the RBI. The RBI has two important liabilities—equity from the government and currency. Section 2.2 is about my recommendation to reduce the equity and transfer it to public-sector banks. Demonetization involved a massive shrinking of the RBI's balance sheet by reducing currency in circulation. Of the four shrinkings, the only one that was actually implemented was demonetization. The challenge lies in moving forward with the other three.

2.1

The Festering Twin
Balance Sheet Problem

Why We Need a Public-Sector
Restructuring Agency

Ever since the global financial crisis of 2008, India has been trying to come to grips with the TBS problem. Perhaps it is time to consider a different approach—a centralized Public Sector Asset Rehabilitation Agency (PARA), a euphemism for what is popularly called a 'bad bank', that can take charge of the largest, most difficult cases, and make politically tough decisions to reduce debt.

For some years in between it seemed possible to regard the TBS as a minor problem, which would largely be resolved as the course of economic recovery took hold. However, the problem has only continued to worsen. Earnings of the stressed companies have kept deteriorating, forcing them to borrow more and more to sustain their operations. Since 2007–08, the debt of the top ten stressed corporate groups (Essar, Adani Power, GMR, Lanco, Jindal Steel, etc.) has multiplied five times, to more than Rs 7.5

lakh crore. Even with such large infusion of funds, corporates have still had problems servicing their debts, so much so that by September 2016, no less than 12 per cent of the gross advances of public-sector banks had turned non-performing. According to some private-sector estimates, these numbers are considerably greater.

This situation of overleveraging is beginning to take a toll on the economy. With balance sheets under such severe strain, the private, corporate sector has been forced to curb its investments, while banks have been reducing lines of credit in real terms. To sustain economic growth, these trends will need to be rectified and reversed. The only way to do so is by fixing the underlying balance sheet problems.

The fundamental question, as always, is how to do this. So far, the strategy has been to solve the TBS through a decentralized approach, under which banks have been put in charge of the restructuring decisions. The RBI has put in place a number of such schemes. As we have been discussing in most cases, this is indeed the best strategy. In the current circumstances, however, effectiveness has proved elusive, as banks have been overwhelmed by the scope of the problem confronting them.

Here I highlight eight steps that lead to the conclusion that the time may have arrived to try a centralized approach, or a Public Sector Asset Rehabilitation Agency (PARA). A detailed case is set out in the Economic Survey of 2016–17 (Chapter 4).

1. **It's not just about banks, it's about companies.** So far, public discussion of the bad loan problem has focused on bank capital, as if the main obstacle to resolving the TBS issue was finding the funds needed by public-sector banks. Securing funding is actually the easiest part, as the cost is small relative to the resources the government commands (no more than 2–3 per cent of the GDP in a worst-case scenario). It is far

more problematic to find a way to resolve bad debts in the
first place.

2. **It is an economic problem, not a morality play.** Without
   doubt, the stench of crony capitalism permeates discussions
   of the Twin Balance Sheet problem. It is also true that there
   have been cases where diversion of funds have caused debt
   repayment problems. However, unexpected changes in the
   economic environment—timetables, exchange rates and
   growth rate assumptions that have gone seriously wrong—
   have exacerbated the problem. A persistent narrative of crony
   capitalism risks leading to punitive rather than incentive-
   compatible solutions.

3. **The stressed debt is heavily concentrated in large companies.**
   Concentration creates an opportunity, because it is possible
   to overcome the TBS problem by solving a relatively small
   number of cases. But it presents an even bigger challenge,
   because large cases are inherently difficult to resolve.

4. **Many of these companies are unviable at current levels of
   debt, requiring debt write-downs in many cases.** Unviability
   varies across sectors and companies. A rough estimate would
   be that debt reductions of about 50 per cent will often be
   needed to restore viability.

5. **Banks are finding it difficult to resolve these cases, despite a
   proliferation of schemes to help them.** Among other issues,
   banks face severe coordination problems, since large debtors
   have many creditors, with different stakeholder interests. If
   public-sector banks grant large debt reductions, this could
   attract the attention of the investigative agencies. Moreover,
   converting debt to equity by taking over the companies and
   then selling them at a loss—even in transparent auctions—
   will be politically difficult, as well.

6. **Other mechanisms haven't worked—and won't work.** Private
   asset reconstruction companies (ARCs) haven't proved any

more successful than banks in resolving bad debts of companies, and in any case are too small to handle larger cases. Moreover, it is possible to distort the incentives facing the ARC–bank relationship. For example, ARCs earn management fees for handling bad debts, even if they don't actually work them out. The new bankruptcy system is not yet fully in place. Even when it is, it will take considerable time before it is ready to handle larger cases.

7. **Delay is costly.** Since banks cannot resolve the big cases, they have simply refinanced the debtors, effectively 'kicking the problems down the road'. This is costly for the government, because it means that bad debts keep rising, increasing the ultimate recapitalization bill for the government and the associated political difficulties. In the same vein, any further delay will be very costly for the economy.

8. **Progress may require a PARA.** Developing a centralized PARA could eliminate most of the obstacles currently plaguing loan resolution. It could solve the coordination problem, since debts would be centralized in one agency; it could be set up with proper incentives by giving it an explicit mandate to maximize recoveries within a defined time period, and it would separate the loan resolution process from concerns about bank capital. For all these reasons, many countries facing the TBS problems, notably the East Asian crisis cases, have adopted asset rehabilitation agencies.

To this point, we must consider how the PARA would actually work. There are many possible variants, but the broad outlines are clear. The PARA would purchase specified loans (for example, those belonging to large, over-indebted infrastructure and steel firms) from banks and then work them out, depending on professional assessments of the value-maximizing strategy.

Once the loans are off the books of public-sector banks, the government will recapitalize them, thereby restoring them to financial health and allowing them to shift their resources—both financial and human—back towards the critical task of creating new loans. Similarly, once the financial viability of the over-indebted enterprises is restored, they will be able to focus on their operations rather than on their finances, and they will finally be able to consider new investments.

Of course, all of this will come at a price, namely, accepting and paying for the losses. This is inevitable. Loans have already been made, losses incurred, and because state banks are the major creditors, the bulk of the burden will necessarily fall on the government (though the shareholders in the stressed enterprises will need to lose their equity as well). In other words, the issue for any resolution strategy—the PARA or decentralization—is not whether the government should assume any new liability. Rather, it is how to minimize a liability that has already been incurred by resolving the bad-loan problem as quickly and effectively as possible, and this is precisely what the PARA would aim to do.

That said, the capital requirements for such rehabilitation would be large. Part of the funding would need to come from government issues of securities. Part could come from the capital markets, if stakes in the public-sector banks were sold off or the PARA were structured in a way that would encourage the private sector to take up an equity share. A third source of capital could be the RBI. The Reserve Bank would, in effect, transfer some of the government securities it currently holds to public-sector banks and the PARA. As a result, the RBI's capital would decrease, while that of the banks and the PARA would increase. There would be no implications for monetary policy, since no new money will be created in the process.

Creating the PARA is not without its own difficulties and risks given that the country's history is not favourable to public-sector endeavours. Yet, one has to ask how long India should continue with the current decentralized approach, which has still not produced the desired results eight years after the global financial crisis, even as East Asian countries were able to resolve their much larger TBS problems within two years. One reason, of course, was that the East Asian countries were under much more pressure: they were in crisis mode, whereas India has continued to grow rapidly. However, in their case an important reason for the relatively quicker turnaround was that they deployed a centralized strategy, which enabled them to work out their debt problems using the vehicle of public asset rehabilitation companies.

2.2*

Government's Capital in RBI

Prudence or Paranoia?[1]

An important area where the RBI needs to be held accountable is in the swelling size of its capital base. Here, two simple questions arise: is the RBI over-capitalized, in the sense that it has too much government equity? If so, where else should that equity be deployed and under what conditions?

I first became interested in this issue when a senior colleague in the Ministry of Finance alerted me to a note written by one of my predecessors, in which he had argued that the RBI had too much capital. I never found the note, but nonetheless decided to investigate the matter further.

It turns out that there is no clear answer to the question of how much capital a central bank should hold, either in theory or in practice. In theory, economists hold a spectrum of views. At one end is the view that central bank capital holdings do not matter, for three reasons. First, central banks can always deliver on their obligations regardless of their net worth because they can always issue liabilities ('print currency'). Second, central banks are part of the government, and it is the broader government balance sheet that matters, not that of any of its constituents. Third, as long as overall conditions are reasonable, the stream of profits will eventually make up for any capital shortfalls because central banks have a unique ability to generate income or 'seigniorage'. Seigniorage refers to the fact that central banks earn interest on their assets (foreign exchange reserves and government securities) but pay zero interest on a large portion of their liabilities (the currency they print), a situation generating large profits, which should continue until the world becomes cashless or crypto-currencies take over. As a result, central banks will always remain solvent, even if at the moment they have negative equity.

There is some evidence that these theoretical points are borne out in practice. Indeed, a number of highly respected central banks such as those of Israel (including under the legendary economist, Stan Fischer), Chile, the Czech Republic and Mexico have continued to operate quite successfully for long periods with negative capital.

Against this, some economists have argued that if central banks run short of capital, they may be tempted to print money to protect their balance sheets, which could result in higher inflation. In a variant of this argument, financially weak central banks, on average, tend to have lower interest rates than might otherwise be warranted, in order to protect their capital positions.

Yet another view is that central banks need capital not so much for economic reasons but for political ones. For example, if central banks are short of capital and need to turn to governments for resources, their independence might be compromised. A twist to this argument is that if central banks are unable to make profits and unable to contribute to the government's finances, they could come under public scrutiny and even attack.

Finally, Raghuram Rajan has argued that if government finances are themselves fragile, central banks cannot rely on the government to recapitalize them in difficult circumstances and that they should protect themselves by building up their capital.

In practice, the range of the central banks' actual capital position reflects this ambiguity. Figure 1 depicts the ratio of shareholder equity to assets for various central banks.[2] This ratio varies from over 40 per cent in the case of Norway to negative capital in the case of Israel, Chile and Thailand, with a median central bank holding of 8.4 per cent (in a sample of fifty-four major developed and emerging market economies for 2016–17).

Figure 1 also reveals that the RBI is an outlier among major central banks. It holds about 28 per cent in capital, which is the fifth largest amongst all major central banks. Two of the four above India in this ranking are oil exporters, which are special cases because these countries are highly vulnerable to the swings in the price of petroleum.

Figure 1: Capital As a Per Cent of Total Assets

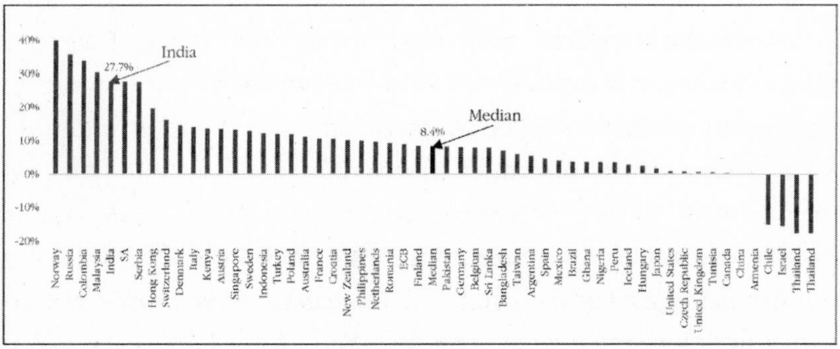

Source: Annual reports of respective central banks. Shareholder equity includes capital plus reserves (built through undistributed earnings) plus revaluation and contingency accounts.

Prima facie, then, it seems that the RBI is holding too much capital. For example, compared to the typical central bank (8.4 per cent ratio), it has excess capital of about Rs 7 lakh crore. That, however, might be too crude a way of calculating excess capital. Central banks across the world are now using an analytical framework (ECF, for Economic Capital Framework) to arrive at the optimal level of capital. This framework essentially involves conducting a Value-at-Risk (VAR) analysis for the various sources of potential risk for a central bank.

These risks are:

1. *Market risk*, which captures the risk arising out of change in the value of their assets, such as foreign reserves, gold and government securities;
2. *Credit risk* in the form of losses arising due to default by counterparties;
3. *Operational risk*, which arises from losses incurred from inadequate or failed internal processes, people and systems; or from external events (including legal risk); and
4. *Contingent risk*, which arises from:

   a. Emergency Liquidity Assistance operations and their impact on the balance sheet size and structure (for example, losses on collateral obtained when injecting emergency liquidity into troubled banks)
   b. Inflation management operations
   c. Currency stabilization operations

Of these four risks, market risk is quantitatively the most important. Once the risks have been measured, the next step is to determine the central bank's risk tolerance. Should it have enough capital to absorb events that happen 5 per cent of the time, or 2 per cent or 1 per cent or .001 per cent? The more conservative the central bank, the more capital it will want to hold.

We looked at the practices of all the major central banks and the Bank for International Settlements (BIS; the organization of central banks). In a technical paper soon to be published, we found that nearly all the other central banks chose a risk tolerance level of 1 per cent of the time. When we applied this tolerance level to the risks facing the RBI, the formula showed India's central bank had an excess capital amounting to Rs 4.5 lakh crore.

Our estimate is that the RBI is holding excess capital between Rs 4.5–7 lakh crore. In the Economic Survey of 2016–17 and later, I suggested that, since the public sector needs to manage its resources efficiently, this excess capital should be redeployed, shifted from where it is not needed and put instead where it is needed urgently, namely, in public-sector banks. I further noted that this redeployment should be subject to stringent conditions being imposed on the government and the banks for using the RBI's balance sheet in this manner.

This proposal has evoked a fierce push-back from various RBI governors and deputy governors, past and present. Since these are eminent people, it seems important to respond to their objections.

First, there are several technical objections.

Objection 1: The RBI's own calculations for excess capital based on this same framework suggest there is no excess; indeed, there might even be a shortfall. The explanation for this discrepancy between our calculations and the RBI's is simple. To begin with, the RBI calculates risk based on a sample that almost no other central bank does. It confines the estimation of risk to periods of unusual volatility whereas other central banks calculate risk over longer periods.

Then there is the matter of risk tolerance. There is one important thing that all readers should understand. The risks that the RBI is worried about do not include the most common type of crisis: a sharp currency depreciation. The RBI holds large foreign exchange reserves so that when the rupee depreciates rapidly, the RBI actually makes a profit.

In contrast, the events that would result in large losses for the RBI are very unlikely. Indeed, the RBI has set for itself a risk tolerance that is ultra, ultra conservative, almost bordering on paranoia: whereas other central banks want to cushion against events with 1 per cent probability of occurring, the RBI wants to cushion against events that can occur with .001 per cent probability.

In any case, if there is an extreme event, the government can commit to filling in any shortfall that the RBI might face.

Objection 2: Redeploying excess capital to the government would increase inflation. There's no reason why inflation should increase, since no money would be printed, no credit extended, and no aggregate demand created. Instead, capital would merely be shifted from one public institution (the RBI) to another (the PSBs). This could be done as follows: the central bank would declare a special dividend and give some of its government securities (g-secs) to the government, which could then give them to public-sector banks as capital.

Objection 3: Redeploying excess capital would reduce the future flow of profits of the RBI. This is true, but largely irrelevant. Obviously, if the RBI gave some of its g-secs back to the government, its future earnings would be smaller. Equally obviously, as long as public-sector banks lack sufficient capital, they will not be able to extend much credit and economic growth will suffer. So it makes sense for the government to forsake some future dividends from the RBI for the wider benefit of improving the economy.

We can actually measure the benefits of redeployment by calculating the average return on the central bank's assets and comparing them to the average debt servicing cost for the general government, which is a very conservative measure of the costs of deploying the funds where they are most needed.[3] If the interest cost of issuing government securities is far higher than the rate of return on the central bank's capital, prudent financial management suggests that the excess capital should be returned to the government and used to repay debt.

The figure below shows that there would be large gains to such a strategy, because rates on government bonds are far higher than the RBI's return on assets. An illustrative calculation suggests that using excess capital to retire debt could save the government Rs 33,000 crore to Rs 45,000 crore per year, based on the current returns, g-sec rates and estimates of excess capital.

Figure 2: Return on Assets for RBI vs Debt Servicing Costs for General Government

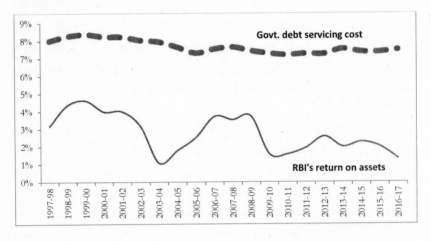

Beyond these technical objections, there are some more serious political economy concerns.

Objection 4: Redeploying excess capital amounts to the government raiding the RBI. There is an important principle involved here. Any redeployment of RBI capital must be seen not as a government demand but as a voluntary commitment of the RBI for the greater good. It should be done only after extensive consultation, with the plan fully agreed by the government and the RBI.

This may sound quixotic, but there is in fact a very recent precedent. The Malegam Committee, in its report submitted in 2014, observed that the total capital to cover various risks faced by a central bank like the RBI was in excess of what was required. It recommended the transfer of the surplus to the government over a period of three years, starting from 2014. That recommendation was implemented and no complaints of raiding arose then.

In fact, what I am suggesting is far more prudent than this precedent. In that case, the money was transferred to be used for general government deficit financing. In contrast, my current proposal is that the government's excess capital in the RBI be redeployed as additional government capital in the public-sector banks (but only after instituting all the necessary reforms I have proposed in the Grand Bargain in Section 2.3). This capital should not be used for routine financing of the government's fiscal deficit.

Moreover, if a transfer of excess capital does take place it would be important to address any lingering concerns on risks to the RBI's balance sheet. A clear rule, enshrined in law and agreed upon by the central bank and government, could stipulate that the government will never allow the central bank capital to fall below a jointly agreed threshold. That way, the benefits of excess capital can be reaped without compromising the integrity of the central bank's balance sheet and without undermining its policy effectiveness.

Objection 5: Redeploying excess capital would let the government off the hook and encourage it to be profligate. In public perception, the government is bad and the RBI is good; the government is profligate, the RBI is prudent. In that light, this objection carries weight. But if there is a real need—for example, to find the resources to fix the financial system—it is in the joint interest of the RBI and the government to find the resources. If there is one strong balance sheet and one weak, there is no good reason the former should not come to the rescue of the latter. We build up strength in balance sheets not for strength's sake but to use that strength. Savings are meant for rainy days and when rainy days come, savings should be run down. This is what distinguished the actions of the major central banks, especially the US Fed and the European Central Bank (ECB).

Objection 6: Redeploying excess capital would be radical. Especially in India, any suggestion of using the RBI's balance sheet encounters resistance because it smacks of financial engineering (which is bad enough) and that too involving a highly respected institution. It also goes against some innate sense of financial conservatism. But, during and after the global financial crisis, major central banks across the world (including the Fed and the ECB) have lent the heft of their balance sheets to pull economies out of dire economic circumstances, and generally pushed the frontiers of central banking. Indeed, more recently, there are even proposals to use central bank capital as 'helicopter money'. Against this evolving view of central banking, the suggestion that the RBI's excess capital should be deployed elsewhere is actually tame and perhaps even conservative.

Moreover, the lesson of the past decade is that when serious problems occur, the legitimacy of central banks is actually enhanced when they take actions to address them. Strong balance sheets are there to be used in times of stress, the proverbial savings to be used on rainy days and not squirrelled away forever. When reputations and strong balance sheets are put on the frontline in service of the economy, these assets, far from getting depleted, are actually replenished.

~

I have a dream. Perhaps it is a nightmare. There is a public event and on one side of the stage are lined up Messrs Bimal Jalan, C. Rangarajan, Y.V. Reddy, D. Subbarao, Rakesh Mohan, Raghuram Rajan, Urjit Patel and Viral Acharya. I am alone on the other side.

I am being lectured on the RBI's balance sheet by this eminent group of current and former RBI officials, and the hordes—especially the fawning elites in journalism, TV, financial community, etc.—are cheering them on. One of the group lectures me that I don't understand monetary economics because transferring excess capital would increase inflation, forgetting that he too made my case when he was in my job. Another asks how I dare raise such a proposal to raid the RBI and destroy a great public institution. Yet another harangues that I am just another Ministry of Finance lackey. I respond with my arguments. The eminences are dismissive.

Suddenly Ben Bernanke and Mario Draghi appear. They had been bold in deploying their balance sheets during their respective financial crises, taking risks that eventually paid off. I appeal to them. They examine the case and pronounce their verdict. 'This is such a no-brainer,' they say. 'Obviously, you should *do whatever it takes*.'

2.3

The Twin Balance Sheet Challenge

Taking Stock and the Grand Bargain?

I. Taking Stock

Vijay Mallya, Nirav Modi, Chanda Kochhar, Rana Kapoor, Ravi Parthasarathy. Hearing this roll call of names is to be reminded of India's 'stigmatized capitalism'. It also suggests, to paraphrase from Shakespeare, that 'something is rotten in this state of Indian banking' for having allowed stigmatized capitalists to survive and thrive for so long.

Where do we stand on the Twin Balance Sheet challenge in late 2018? What is the way forward? To answer these questions, we need to go back to the 5 Rs—recognition, resolution, recapitalization, reform and regulation—that constitute the necessary actions that must be taken:

- banks must value their assets as close as possible to their true value (*recognition*);
- once they do so, their capital position must be safeguarded via infusions of equity (*recapitalization*);

- the underlying stressed firms must be sold and/or rehabilitated (*resolution*);
- future incentives for the private sector and corporates must be set right (*reform*) to avoid a repetition of the problem; and
- finally, check-ins and oversight of the banking system must be in place to ensure that the shenanigans we have seen over the last several years from Vijay Mallya to Nirav Modi to ICICI Bank to IL&FS are minimized; they can never be fully avoided (*regulation*).

Consider the current status of these 5 Rs.

Recognition: After years of denial by the RBI and government (as we showed in the chart in the Introduction), despite credibly grave warnings starting as far back as 2011, we have finally come a long way in publicly admitting the magnitude of the problem. The RBI's Asset Quality Review, initiated in late 2015, played an important role in this regard. Today, total stressed assets are about Rs 13 lakh crore or about 15 per cent of total lending; of this about Rs 11 lakh crore are in the PSBs, amounting to nearly 20 per cent of their loans.

But there is what I self-referentially call the Subramanian Iron Law of Non-Recognition: despite the progress, we know in our bones that the amount of stressed assets is always and everywhere at least 20–25 per cent more than what people believe and what the RBI claims. I say this not because I am a doom-monger or know something that others don't. Rather, the law is based on knowing that banks are always trying to hide bad loans to paint a rosy picture of their finances. For example, until IL&FS began to default, its problems weren't even on anyone's radar, and their bad loans certainly weren't included in the estimates of stressed assets. So, it would only be prudent to assume that we still have not identified all the stressed loans, especially amongst non-bank financial companies which would also feed back into the banking system; we should plan for matters being worse than they currently are.

Resolution: Here, too, after serious delays, the government undertook a truly major—potentially transformational—reform. In the budget of 2016–17, the government passed a new bankruptcy bill, the IBC, which provides a legal framework for the timely resolution of companies unable to pay their debts. For reasons I have discussed earlier—essentially, the inability and unwillingness of the government to take tough decisions on write-offs—the Bad Bank approach to resolution had had to give way to a more judicial approach, which is what the IBC offers.

The RBI followed up decisively by identifying, on 13 June 2017, twelve loan accounts to be taken up under India's new bankruptcy law with its tight deadlines and well-specified resolution process. These loans account for about 25 per cent of the current NPAs (not the overall stressed assets) in the banking system. Another thirty to forty cases have since been added to the list, and if settlement does not take place, they may also enter the bankruptcy process.

In the summer of 2018, India's economic history reached a milestone. For the first time, a major industrial firm, Bhushan Steel, was declared bankrupt and was sold in auction to a new owner, Tata Steel. As of end-October 2018, another four companies have been successfully sold under the bankruptcy process. These transactions have demonstrated that 'exit' is possible, that it can be done through the legal system, and that banks can recover substantial sums in the process. In other words, the sale showed that the new insolvency and bankruptcy code is working.

At the same time, these cases demonstrated the limits of the IBC. They revealed that the process is going to take far longer than originally envisaged: for example, at the current rate of disposal of cases by the National Company Law Tribunal (NCLT), it could take another five to six years for the most important cases to be settled. They suggested that the corporate insolvency resolution process (CIRP) may not be suitable for some assets. Moreover, there is now a serious risk that the process is getting overloaded, with too many cases being thrown into the bankruptcy process.

Recapitalization: The government has injected a considerable amount of money since 2015—first under the 'Indradhanush' programme and then in late 2017 and again in the budget of 2018—into public-sector banks, amounting to nearly Rs 2 lakh crore. The aim is to ensure that all banks are in compliance with the capital adequacy standards laid out by the Basel Committee (the minimum amount of equity a bank must have relative to the size and riskiness of its assets).

The longer it takes to resolve the stressed assets issue, the lower their value will be when they are finally sold. Consequently, the larger will be loss to the PSBs, and the greater the amount the government will need to spend to recapitalize them. Meanwhile, the resources available for this task have shrunk, since PSBs will not be able to raise the planned amounts (about Rs 60,000 crore), owing to their recent poor performance and the consequent sharp drop in their share prices. So, it is almost certainly the case that more money will be needed to make banks healthy and, for the good ones, healthy enough to be able to provide enough credit when the economy starts picking up again. It is possible that the government will need to provide anywhere between Rs 3–5 lakh crore—in addition to the amounts already spent—to restore the fundamentally viable PSBs to health.

Reforms: As if the foregoing problems are not enough, another has become apparent. Recent scandals have underscored that there are fundamental governance problems in the PSBs which need to be addressed. There is currently no strategy in place to do this. Nor is there a clear path forward for the smaller, less viable banks. About eleven PSBs have been placed by the RBI under the Prompt Corrective Action (PCA) framework (some more might follow), which will have the salutary consequence that their growth will be capped until they reform, forcing them to cede market share to better-run banks. The RBI deserves credit for maintaining the integrity of this PCA process, amidst pressures from the government to dilute it, for example, by having unsound banks resume their expansion immediately.

In addition, two sets of bank consolidation exercises have happened, one involving SBI in 2016 and another now involving Bank of Baroda. We must be very clear. Merging bad banks with tolerably good banks does not improve the health of the overall banking system in any way. Consolidation is at best a Band-Aid for the system, and at worst a distraction for management from their key priority of dealing with their bad assets.

Meanwhile, there is still no serious consideration of privatizing some of the major public-sector banks.

Regulation and Supervision: Perhaps the most problematic area has been bank (and non-bank) supervision. Over the past few years, egregious problems have been revealed in the banking system, ranging from exceptionally poor lending practices, to deceptive accounting practices that hid the loans that had gone bad, to a spate of scandals that involved a breakdown in control procedures (as in the Nirav Modi affair at Punjab National Bank [PNB]). None of these problems were prevented by the regulator, nor were they detected by bank supervision in real time. Instead, they were discovered long after it was too late to prevent substantial losses. Clearly, the record of the RBI as supervisor—along with that of the government as owner of public-sector banks—has not been pretty.

The RBI has reacted to these failures by taking a much tougher approach to banks. It has questioned bank accounting practices more closely, sanctioned banks that were found 'cooking the books', and removed executives at private-sector banks who had allowed such practices to take place. All the same, the central bank has not fundamentally overhauled its supervisory organization, or its procedures, in part because it hasn't been held accountable for its failures. Meanwhile, on the government side, the Banks Board Bureau (BBB) was introduced to improve governance at public-sector banks, but it has so far had very little impact.

~

These problems are all serious ones. As Economic Surveys from 2015 onwards have emphasized, the longer it takes to solve the Twin Balance Sheet challenge, the longer corporate investment will remain low, and the longer it will take for the economy to return to vigorous growth. As more banks are placed under the PCA, there are fewer banks in operation to lend and support growth. Fragile banks also find it difficult to assume the risks of investing in long-term government securities, since any increases in interest rates on these bonds (i.e., lower prices) would result in capital losses for them, further eroding their capital base. Therefore, they are reluctant to bid at government securities auctions, leading to high real interest rates, which further constraints growth and leads to more NPAs. A sort of mini-doom-loop from weak bank profitability to higher g-sec interest rates back to weaker bank profitability has come into play.

Consequently, it is vital that the resolution, recapitalization and reform strategies be strengthened. Less clear, however, is what the potential modifications should be. How can the resolution process be accelerated? What should be done with the power-sector assets? Where can the government find the resources to meet the banks' recapitalization needs? What can be done to improve PSB governance? I attempt to set out some possible answers to these questions.

I have argued that a 'grand bargain' should be struck between the government and the RBI, under which:

- *Recognition* is further advanced by sanctioning financial institutions that are not classifying their loans properly, most notably power-sector loans at banks and other loans at NBFCs.
- Asset *resolution* is accelerated by sending smaller assets to specialized distressed asset recovery firms, while the power-sector assets would be shifted to a new government-run holding company.
- *Regulatory/supervisory* reform is further achieved by granting the RBI greater supervisory powers over public-sector banks. The government should also allow the RBI to implement the Prompt Corrective Action (PCA) framework for less strong banks.
- Fundamental *reform* of the PSBs is facilitated by allowing majority private-sector participation in the PSBs.
- In return, the RBI would deploy its surplus capital to augment the resources for *recapitalizing* PSBs and capitalizing any new holding companies.

The specific measures are summarized in the following table.

Table 1: Grand Bargain to Resolve the Twin Balance Sheet Challenge

Action	Government	RBI
Recognition		Sanction financial institutions that are not classifying their loans properly, most notably power sector loans at banks and other loans at NBFCs
Resolution	Create a Holding Company for some sectors such as power	Modify February 2018 circular to allow special treatment for power. Allow for sale of small loans to specialized distressed asset firms
Recapitalization	Provide say 10-15% of additional requirement	Provide say 85-90 % of additional requirement for recapitalizing PSBs from its balance sheet but conditional on government taking other actions in the Grand Bargain
Reform	1.Change Bank Nationalization Act (BNA) to allow majority private sector ownership of public sector banks 2.Allow RBI to implement Prompt Corrective Action (PCA) framework. 3. Change BNA to give the RBI greater power to more effectively regulate PSBs	
Regulation/Supervision	Government and RBI together must find better ways to strengthen supervision of banks and non-bank financial companies by RBI	

II. The Way Forward

Resolution

The two major challenges facing the National Company Law Tribunal (NCLT) process are clogged pipelines and the unsuitability of the method for some classes of stressed assets, especially power and small and medium enterprises. At current clearance rates, resolving the whole NPA problem could take another six years or so.

What, then, is the way forward? The government needs to diversify its resolution strategy away from the current policy of putting all its eggs in the one basket of the IBC.

The first step would be to make a triage, similar to the degrees of wounds attributed to a casualty or illness. Stressed assets should be divided into three groups:

- assets that should go through the CIRP;
- large assets that need an alternative resolution mechanism; and
- smaller assets that could potentially clog the CIRP.

The precise criteria for classifying assets need to be considered carefully. As a rough guide, the first group should be considered the 'default' option, defined as all the assets that do not qualify for the second and third groups. The second group would comprise the power-sector assets, together perhaps with a few other cases where bidders are unlikely but where the assets are of such national importance that they cannot go through liquidation. The third group could comprise all companies with loans below, say, Rs 100 crore.

1. *Power-Sector Assets: Public-Sector Holding Company:* Stressed power-sector assets pose a major quandary. They are very large, with debts exceeding Rs 2.5 lakh crore, and they are almost impossible to resolve, since power plants can neither be sold easily nor can they be liquidated. That suggests they should be retained in the public sector. The existing public-sector power producers are, however, reluctant to take them, since they are incurring heavy losses.

What, then, can be done? The first step would clearly be to take these assets off the books of the banks, for that would free up balance sheets and management attention, allowing banks to focus again on their core business of supporting economic growth.

Of course, once removed, the assets will need to go somewhere, which is the more difficult issue. A few of the plants could probably be sold off, once their debts are reduced to manageable levels. The bulk of the plants should then be 'warehoused' until they can be returned to the private sector. The government could create a holding company, which would purchase the assets and manage them.

Essentially, the holding company would operate like a public-sector asset rehabilitation agency (or a bad bank) and would be capitalized by the government or the RBI. The prices of power companies would be based on the recommendations of independent parties, such as investment banks, which will be hired to value the plants. This procedure would allow the transaction to be seen as fair by all stakeholders—the holding company, the banks, and perhaps most importantly, the public. In addition, fair prices would give the holding company some chance to make a profit in the long run, as power demand increases. Finally, the prospect of profits might induce private investors to provide some of the capital needed, thereby alleviating the upfront cost to the government.

One may then ask what the holding company would do with the assets. The ultimate objective would be to sell the plants back to the private sector. In fact, this objective should be built into the charter of the company; it should state that the purpose of the company is to sell off the assets within five years, after which it would be dissolved. To realize this objective, the holding company should endeavour to reduce uncertainty, especially by securing strong coal linkages and developing purchasing agreements with state electricity boards. Once this is done, and as demand for electricity grows to the point where the plants can operate at somewhere close to full capacity (at present their plant load factors are abysmally low), the appetite for these assets will gradually revive.

2. *Smaller Assets:* As for the smaller assets (companies with debts less than Rs 100 crore), banks should be encouraged to sell these off, rather than drag them through the IBC process. This is a standard approach, employed all over the world—in the US and Europe after the global financial crisis, and in East Asia after the crisis of the 1990s. In all these cases, private firms, normally operating outside the formal bankruptcy system, did much of the resolution work.

Under this more informal procedure, banks auction off not the firms but rather the loans themselves. The loans are sold to private distressed asset firms, which then negotiate with the existing owners in the hope of recovering more than what they had paid to the banks. This difference is their profit.

Why has this strategy been employed so widely when it means that the banks' proceeds are lower than the ultimate recoveries? For one, because the ultimate recoveries often cannot be achieved by the banks. Asset-resolution firms have specialized skills and experience in dealing with distressed cases that banks often lack. Moreover, these firms have much more flexibility than banks, especially public-sector banks, which are restricted by both formal and informal guidelines, and fear of vigilance agencies.

The question arises, then, why banks in India have not employed this route enough, when, after all, they are already free to sell off assets whenever they wish. There are several explanations. One is RBI accounting: if banks sell off bad assets, they must recognize the loss immediately, whereas if they keep them on as NPAs, they can spread out the losses over several years. In addition, banks typically overestimate the recovery rate that they are likely to obtain. Finally, even if their projection is accurate, they do not take into account the externality involved in taking a case to the NCLT. That is, they ignore the congestion that this causes, which leads to delays, and lower recoveries in the other pending cases.

Only a collective agency such as the RBI can take this externality into account. For this reason, it will be important for the RBI to clarify that the smaller stressed assets, which banks have not been able to resolve even 180 days after their default date, should be sold off to distressed asset firms.

I would like to make two further points, both of them important. First, the distressed asset firms should be allowed to take cases to the NCLT. Most likely, they will not do so, for reasons already mentioned: bidding interest is likely to be low. But the distressed firms must have this option available in order to convince the defaulting promoters to pay. Otherwise, recovery rates will fall, bank losses will rise, and the government will need to fill in the difference. Second, the RBI needs to allow a much wider range of distressed asset firms, beyond the current asset reconstruction companies. Individuals, private equity funds or any other structure should be allowed to participate in the process. After all, the wider the pool of potential bidders, the higher will be the amounts realized in the auctions. Additional regulation will not be needed, since such firms pose no risks to banks, consumers or the financial system.

To allow such special treatment by way of the aforementioned two clauses, the RBI would have to modify its 6 February 2018 circular. The advantage of providing for such treatment would be that the burden on the NCLT process will automatically be lessened.

Recapitalization

If an additional Rs 4–5 lakh crore will be needed to recapitalize the banks, there is only one public-sector entity that has a strong enough balance sheet to deploy this magnitude of resources, namely, the RBI. Conservative estimates (as well as cross-country comparisons) based on our internal analysis suggest that if the RBI were to adopt the practices of most major central banks around the world in deciding how much capital is necessary, it would find that it has about Rs 3–4 lakh crore of excess government capital, some of which it could deploy for the clean-up.

This idea and the objections to it are discussed in detail in Section 2.3. Essentially the RBI would transfer some of its excess capital (in the form of retained earnings) to the government as a special dividend, and the government would then transfer the equivalent government-sector tenders to the PSBs, thereby augmenting their capital. This operation should be seen as the government transferring its excess ownership in the RBI to the PSBs or any new holding companies that are created.

That said, deploying capital is a decision for the RBI to take, and it must be taken voluntarily and proactively without even the whiff of interference from outside.

Reform

Recent developments have revealed manifold governance problems in the operation of banks: weak internal controls, weak boards, and an accounting industry seemingly unable to identify even major frauds.

A critical dimension to improving PSB governance is to allow more majority private-sector participation, which is a euphemism for 'privatization'. For years, this step has been ruled off the agenda: the government has refused to cede control over these banks, claiming that it could improve PSB governance simply by reforming internal procedures. But after five decades of 'reforms', which were meant to reduce political interference and politically directed lending, it is time to accept that this strategy has not worked and a new one is necessary. The government has recently acted boldly to end the monopoly of Coal India. The banking sector calls for similar boldness. The Bank Nationalization Act will have to be amended.

For some people, the case can be closed right here. For many others, privatization is a very contentious issue. So, let me spell out the arguments.

To begin with, it must be acknowledged that private ownership is not a panacea. In particular, private banks also engage in imprudent lending and improper behaviour, as we have been reminded of in recent months. As a result, effective regulation and supervision will always be needed. Indeed, some have argued that privatization should not take place until supervision has been perfected.

This is just not feasible because perfection is impossible in this world. In fact, it will be difficult even to *improve* supervision as long as the government owns public-sector banks because the regulator has little incentive to monitor the financial dealings of PSBs closely. After all, if something goes wrong, the RBI can count on the government to pay up. So, realistically, supervisory reform cannot precede privatization, and insisting on this sequencing will simply ensure that neither reform nor privatization actually happen.

So, what is the case for privatization? Perhaps the most obvious argument is that privatization will release the PSBs from the constraints imposed by the investigative institutions (the so-called 4 Cs—the courts, the CBI, the CVC and the CAG), giving them the freedom to recruit and retain high-quality personnel, and empowering them to take decisions based on commercial criteria. It is striking how much caution, inertia, and yes, even fear, public-sector bank managers' experience thinking that they could be the targets of one or more of these institutions. Going forward, this must be addressed.

A related efficiency argument for privatization is the following. Public ownership creates complicated three-way lines of control, ownership and regulation between the government, the regulator and the banks themselves. One might—to be a bit risqué—almost call this situation a ménage à trois with all the attendant complications. With private-sector participation, some of that three-way complication gets attenuated because banks are under direct lines of authority, accountable to the regulator, namely, the RBI.

Perhaps the most important argument concerns the political economy. It has become clear that in India exit is an intractable challenge. Across the range of sectors, whether in agriculture, fertilizer or civil aviation, it is difficult to get out of inefficient and unproductive production. The exit problem is particularly perverse for public-sector banks, because they typically lend to private-sector companies. Consequently, if these loans turn bad, any move to resolve them could be seen as favouring already stigmatized private promoters, inviting the scrutiny of the 4 Cs, the political establishment and the public.

Put simply, experience has shown that private bank-to-private company lending and private bank-to-public company lending are broadly politically acceptable. It is public-to-private lending model that has proved toxic. We should want to be careful before we repeat that experiment again.

So, privatization is a necessary condition for progress. To be clear, what is being suggested is a policy change that would permit *some* banks to be privatized and not require *all* banks to be privatized. Indeed, what's needed is simply a rebalancing. In the ideal banking world of tomorrow, India needs to have a few strong PSBs (much fewer than currently) and more large private-sector–owned banks, competing domestically and internationally.

Regulation/Supervision

That the TBS problem has persisted for so long, that so many new scandals have erupted, and that problems have spread to non-bank financial companies should now make obvious that regulation of the financial system by the RBI—and to some extent the government—has been ineffective.

What needs to be done? In broad terms, the answer is clear: the RBI needs to intensify its vigilance over the banks. In many cases, the central bank merely needs to step up its supervision to ensure that existing regulations (such as registering international transactions in banks' books, as failed to occur in the Nirav Modi case) are implemented. Wherever gaps are uncovered, banks need to be sanctioned and forced to bring rules and practices into line.

In other cases, however, such as when dealing with errant public-sector banks, the RBI needs additional powers so that it can meaningfully sanction the banks. For example, the RBI should be able to remove board members, convene a meeting of the board, or supersede the board of public-sector banks, just as it can with private-sector banks.

For RBI supervision to be truly effective, and for the playing field to be level between private- and public-sector banks, the RBI needs to be able to treat all banks equally. Giving such powers to the RBI, however, will require amending the Bank Nationalization Act (BNA).

Even these measures may not be enough. It is not sufficient to give the RBI more powers to supervise banks; the RBI must be willing to use these powers. This willingness is not obvious. For example, even though the bad loan problem first became obvious long ago, in the aftermath of the global financial crisis (GFC), it was not until 2015 that the RBI began to force banks to reveal the extent of their bad loan problem.

It's not obvious how to correct incentive problems. There's no standard international practice; different countries employ different models, and it's not clear which one would best suit India's conditions. In the circumstances, I would suggest appointing an independent committee to study the recent failures, to see what went wrong and recommend measures to ensure it doesn't happen again. In particular, the committee should consider whether there is a case for setting up an independent financial regulator as in Australia, whose financial system sailed through the GFC unscathed (although the UK experience was less successful). The sole objective of such a regulator would be to ensure that the financial system remains sound at all times, an objective that would be enshrined into law, together with explicit mechanisms for holding the regulatory accountable for any failures to meet this standard. Whatever the approach, it is simply untenable—in the light of consistent and serious regulatory failure—for the RBI to say, 'Leave it to us, we will find the solution.'

The Grand Bargain

Summing up, there is an opening for a 'grand bargain' between the government and the RBI, which I have outlined in this chapter. On the government's side, it would need to amend the BNA to allow more majority private-sector ownership of the PSBs and also provide the regulator with additional supervisory and regulatory powers needed to prevent a recurrence of past problems at the level of state banks. Meanwhile, the RBI would need to provide the government with additional resources to recapitalize state banks and capitalize the (power sector) holding company.

The grand bargain would include a number of other elements. In particular, the RBI would have to modify the February 2018 circular to allow for departures from the IBC process in the case of power-sector assets and smaller loans.

We have made good progress in identifying and addressing the TBS challenge. There are still 'miles to go before we sleep'. The resolution process is proving much slower than expected, the recapitalization costs are larger, and the fundamental reforms of PSBs and regulation have not yet been embarked upon.

These problems need to be addressed, and quickly. Only through prompt action can the costs of the TBS be minimized, economic recovery hastened, and necessary public support for the measures secured. For, make no mistake, the passage of time will erode the country's resolve and slowly, and quite imperceptibly, the status quo will once again seem acceptable. If that happens, the country will remain mired in the TBS morass for years to come.

Having said that, how realistic is the possibility of some of these bold actions such as privatization or RBI transferring excess capital? In situations such as these, with deeply entrenched beliefs and vested interests, only major crises can galvanize reforms. In the famous words of Rahm Emmanuel, the hard-edged chief of staff of President Obama, 'Never waste a crisis.' There was such a moment in early 2018 when the Nirav Modi scandal erupted, creating a palpable sense of outrage amongst the public that could have spurred policy action. Alas, that opportunity passed. The question is whether things may have to once again turn really bad before they can be made better.

2.4

The Two Puzzles of Demonetization

Political and Economic

On 8 November, in a dramatic nationally televised speech that I watched in my room in North Block, the prime minister announced that the top two high-denomination currency notes of Rs 500 and Rs 1000 would cease to be legal tender; that is, they would no longer be accepted as a government-certified means of payment. It was an unprecedented move that no country in recent history had made in *normal* times. The typical pattern had either been gradual demonetizations in normal times (such as the European Central Bank phasing out the 500-euro note in 2016) or sudden demonetizations in extreme circumstances of war, hyper-inflation, currency crises or political turmoil (Venezuela in 2016). The Indian initiative was, to put it mildly, unique. It presupposed an extraordinary amount of resilience in the economy, especially amongst the vulnerable, because it was going to be the first of two major shocks—along with the GST—to affect those in the cash-intensive, informal sectors of the economy.

Two years on, demonetization still consumes the attention of the commentariat, in part because of the mysteries surrounding its origins. I have little to add to the economics of the D-decision beyond what was said in three economic surveys that I oversaw. I do have some new thoughts, or rather hypotheses, on two demonetization puzzles, political and economic.

Puzzle 1: Why was demonetization so popular politically if it imposed economic costs? Specifically, why did demonetization turn out to be an electoral vote winner in the short-term (in the Uttar Pradesh elections of early 2017) if it imposed so much hardship on so many people?

Today, the political perception of demonetization is confounded by a slew of economic and political developments that have occurred since November 2016. Clearly, many factors influence voters' perceptions and hence affect outcomes, rendering any attempt to tease out cause and effect as unreliable. It is important, however, not to forget history as it happened. At the time (early 2017), the election in Uttar Pradesh—India's most populous state and the world's eighth-largest 'country-that-isn't'—was widely seen as a verdict on demonetization, arguably the salient policy action of the government, personally and forcefully articulated by the prime minister.

The demonetization experiment speaks to the more pervasive and fascinating global phenomenon of *What's the Matter with Kansas?*, the title of a famous book by American historian Thomas Frank. This book explores the apparent paradox of citizens voting against their economic self-interest. For example, why do poor white males vote for the Republican Party and President Trump when the policy agenda either has no benefits to them (tax cuts for the rich) or is positively harmful (undermining Obamacare and welfare benefits more broadly)? That same question seemed relevant after the resounding victory of the NDA government in the UP election. This particular piece is an attempt to understand that result as a disinterested observer armed only with publicly known facts. It is not an explanation of the motives of demonetization, simply a post facto analysis of one apparently fascinating political outcome associated with it.

How could demonetization that is supposed to have adversely affected so many Indians—the scores of millions dependent on the cash economy—be so resoundingly supported by the policy's very (and numerous) victims? I offer the controversial hypothesis that imposing large costs on a wide cross-section of people (and the fact that the Rs 500 and not just the Rs 1000 note was demonetized increased the scope and scale of demonetization's impact), unexpected and unintentional though it may have been, could actually have been indispensable to achieve political success.

The canonical political economy model of trade explains the persistence of protectionism in terms of an imbalance between the gainers and losers. Protection—which raises domestic prices—helps a few domestic producers a lot while diffusing the harm among many consumers, each of whom loses only a little. Producers, therefore, have both an incentive and ability to lobby for protection, while individual consumers have little incentive to lobby against it. The demonetization case has been very different: hardship was imposed on many and possibly to a great extent, and yet they appear to have been its greatest cheerleaders.

One answer to the demonetization puzzle has been that the poor were willing to overlook their own hardship, knowing that the rich and their ill-begotten wealth were experiencing even greater hardship: 'I lost a goat but they lost their cows.' In this view, the costs to the poor were unavoidable collateral damage that had to be incurred for attaining a larger goal.

This is not entirely convincing. After all, the collateral damage was in fact avoidable. Anti-elite populism, or 'rich bashing', as the *Economist* put it, could have taken the form of other punitive actions—taxation, appropriation, raids—targeted *just* at the corrupt rich. Why entangle the innocent masses and impoverish them in the bargain? As I wrote in the Economic Survey of 2016–17, if subsidies are a highly inefficient way of transferring resources *to* the poor, demonetization seemed a highly inefficient way of taking resources *away from* the rich.

Understanding the political economy of demonetization may require us, therefore, to confront one overlooked possibility—that adversely impacting the many, far from being a bug, could perhaps have been a feature of the policy action. Not necessarily by design or in real time, but in retrospect it appears that impacting the many adversely may have been intrinsic to the success of the policy. Consider why.

First, the breadth of impact could have been a credibility signalling device. The American economist Thomas Schelling famously argued that to convince the public or opponents of the credibility of one's actions, costs must be incurred. It cannot be done cheaply. Hernan Cortes, the first conquistador, is said to have destroyed all his ships after landing in Mexico to motivate his fellow soldiers to fight boldly because there was no possibility of return. By imposing near-universal costs, demonetization could similarly have been a device to signal regime change against black money in particular, and the corrupt rich, more broadly. If a regime could incur such enormous costs, it could surely follow up through similar actions against corruption. Indeed, to demonstrate that the measure was bold and hence more likely to be effective, the felt costs may have had to be high.

Second, the breadth and depth of impact could have served as another signalling purpose. In order to be credible, the masses must somehow be led to believe that the corrupt had been hurt. With demonetization, this may not have been easy to do, at least in the short-run. How better to convince the masses that the corrupt rich were being hit hard than to hit hard the masses themselves? 'If it hurts me so much, it must hurt the rich immeasurably more' could have been the thought process of the typical victim.

Third, the near universality of impact created a sense of solidarity. Sparing some groups would have undermined this spirit and raised questions about the good faith and legitimacy of the policymakers, who could have been seen as favouring some while hurting others. If only a few had been adversely affected in the demonetization process, they would have mobilized and from trade theory we know that their incentives to do so would have been great.

Moreover, if only a few had been affected, suspicion would have arisen about those who were spared: did they have connections? Were they possibly even 'in' on the decision? Did they contribute as quid pro quo for being spared? By impacting the many, these difficult decisions were avoided. In the light of the zeitgeist of stigmatized capitalism, such questions would invariably have been raised and would have been politically awkward.

Fourth, and a related point, is cultural. One legacy of Mahatma Gandhi was to inculcate a spirit of sacrifice as a necessary condition for achieving a larger, loftier objective. Especially if there is a shared recognition that eliminating black money is not an easy task because it has been around for seventy years, the need for sacrifice—and shared sacrifice—could only be enhanced.

None of the points I've raised here is a normative assessment of the economics and politics of demonetization. But honesty requires admitting that the political response to demonetization was puzzling, and confounded most economists and political scientists. So we must be open to the hypothesis that politically speaking, in the case of demonetization, vice may have been virtue.

Puzzle 2: Why didn't the draconian 86 per cent reduction in the cash supply have bigger effects on overall economic growth? To put this more provocatively, the question was not whether demonetization imposed costs—it clearly did—but why did it not impose much greater costs?

Demonetization was a massive, draconian, monetary shock: in one fell swoop 86 per cent of the currency in circulation was withdrawn. Figure 1 shows that real GDP growth was clearly affected by demonetization. Growth had been slowing even before, but after demonetization the slide accelerated. In the six quarters before demonetization growth averaged 8 per cent and in the seven quarters after, it averaged about 6.8 per cent (with a four-quarter window, the relevant numbers are 8.1 per cent before and 6.2 per cent after).

Figure 1: Real GDP Growth, 2015–16 Q1 to 2018–19 Q1

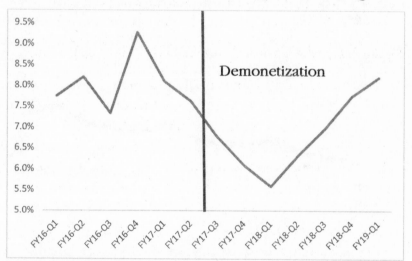

I don't think anyone disputes that demonetization slowed growth. Rather, the debate has been about the size of the effect, whether it was 2 percentage points, or much less. After all, many other factors affected growth in this period, especially higher real interest rates, GST implementation and rising oil prices.

I do not have a strongly backed empirical view apart from the fact that the welfare costs especially on the informal sector were substantial.

As a monetary economist, though, what is striking is how small the effect was compared to the magnitude of the shock. There are many ways of seeing this. Figure 2 compares what happened to cash with what happened to nominal GDP. It is a stunning picture. Prior to demonetization, cash and GDP move closely together. Then, currency collapses and recovers (the dotted line), but through all of this, the economy seems to have been chugging along almost unmindful of the currency in circulation. You have to squint to see any downward movement of the solid black line (for nominal GDP) after demonetization: in fact, there isn't, and all the downward blips reflect seasonality, which leads to a lower level of activity in the first (April–June) quarter every year.

Figure 2: Level of Cash and Nominal GDP (June 2015=100)

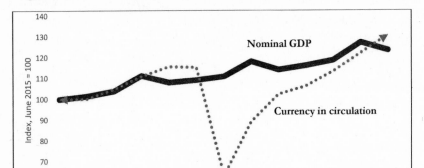

What could possibly explain this apparent resilience? A number of hypotheses need to be considered. First and foremost, it could simply be an artefact of the way that GDP numbers are created. In India, there are no timely measures of informal sector activity, so it is proxied by formal sector indicators. Normally, this is not a problem, since the two move in tandem. But when a shock like demonetization occurs that primarily affects the informal sector, relying on formal indicators to measure overall activity will overstate GDP.

This hypothesis goes only a small way towards explaining the puzzle, since any squeeze in informal sector incomes would depress demand in the formal sector, and this effect should have been sizable.

As a result, we need to search for other explanations. One possibility is that people found ways around the note ban, for example by continuing to use the Rs 500 note even after its use had been formally banned, so the currency shock wasn't actually as big as conventionally measured. Another possibility is that production was sustained by extending informal credit: people simply agreed to pay their bills as soon as currency became available. Finally, to a certain extent, people may have shifted from using cash to paying by electronic means, such as debit cards and electronic wallets.

Or, there may be other, completely different explanations that have eluded my understanding of demonetization, one of the unlikeliest economic experiments in modern Indian history.

Chapter 3

The Great Structural
Transformation (GST)

3.0

The GST: From Good to Better, but No Gold Standard

One evening late in 2017, my wife and I visited the Ramakrishna Math in Belur outside Kolkata, on the insistence of my Bengali colleague, Rangeet Ghosh. As we were heading towards the evening aarti ceremony, I suddenly received an important phone call from the Delhi finance minister, Manish Sisodia. I had always been impressed by Sisodia, because he had put such political capital (not to mention personal commitment) into improving public primary schools in Delhi. Not often in India have we seen politicians make primary education a salient political and electoral issue.

But Sisodia wasn't calling me to discuss education. He was calling because he wanted to improve the goods and services tax. Previously, Dr Hasmukh Adhia, supported by Minister Jaitley, had made a terrific pitch to the GST Council, urging them to include land and real estate in the GST system. And that day I had written an op-ed in the *Indian Express* (Section 3.3) expounding on this theme. As a result of these efforts, Sisodia said he was now inspired to write to his finance minister colleagues in the council to urge them to act on it with urgency.

That experience epitomized the thrills and troughs of my involvement in the GST. My enjoyment of the aarti, especially the final, beautiful composition in Raga Behag ('*Sarva Mangala Mangalye*'), was magnified by that phone call, which conjured up the tantalizing thought that if land and real estate could be brought into the GST, a key channel of black money creation could be tracked and eventually blocked.

My soaring hopes were quickly dashed.

Manish Sisodia did write to all the state ministers of finance. But the reform effort was soon buried by vehement opposition, including from some of the large, BJP-led states such as Gujarat and Maharashtra. Land and real estate remain outside the GST, and will perhaps be for some time. So, for now, I will have to accept failure on this score, my only hope being that one day, others will take up the good fight.

This chapter contains my writings on the GST. The first piece (3.1) was written with Dr Hasmukh Adhia in the aftermath of the Constitutional Amendment Bill in August 2016. We hadn't secured everything we wanted, but then no one ever does. The amendment was still one of the government's and the country's phenomenal achievements. So, the passage was a moment to savour, and we wrote a celebratory op-ed, highlighting the benefits of the GST.

The second piece (3.2) was written when I could sense that the GST rate structure was deviating far from my recommendations in the Revenue Neutral Rate Report. The structure was becoming complex and some very high rates were being considered. I was anxious, even alarmed, and wanted to make one last effort at limiting the damage. So I wrote an op-ed. But then I went one step further. I wrote to the editors of the major newspapers, asking all of them to publish the piece. The request was highly unusual, perhaps even unprecedented, and one of the editors remarked that I was being cheeky in making this request. But they all accepted, and the piece was printed in about ten national dailies. I was really grateful for and impressed by their sense of public interest in not asking for exclusivity, and for not refusing to publish the piece despite not getting exclusivity.

The next two pieces are on extending the GST to land and real estate (the op-ed that prompted Sisodia's phone call) and electricity (3.4). While writing these pieces, I learnt immensely from Alok Shukla and Amitabh Kumar, two terrific joint secretaries in the Central Board of Excise and Customs. This was not an exceptional experience. Indeed, during my years as the CEA, I received extraordinary education from government officers, especially and including many of the junior ones, who shared with me not only their considerable expertise but often also their views on where policies were going wrong, and what could be done to improve things. I was happy to be their vehicle to advance reforms.

The last piece (3.5), written with my colleague Kapil Patidar, makes the case that the GST revenues in the first year did much better than most people believed. One of the challenges for policymakers in India is communication. In the specific case of the GST revenue performance, I was surprised by the constant misunderstandings (even within the GST Council) every time the revenue numbers were released. It did not help, of course, that the 2017–18 budget presentation of the GST numbers was difficult to comprehend. The piece tries to clear up these misunderstandings by suggesting that revenue performance should be measured by the total GST collections rather than any sub-component, such as the central GST (CGST), state GST (SGST), or GST collected on imports, and interstate trade (IGST). These sub-components were either affected by particular transitory factors, or by central government policies, for example, in the case of the IGST.

There was another reason for writing this last piece. In the Revenue Neutral Rate Report, I had argued that low rates would be sufficient because the GST would prove a revenue spinner. At the time, these revenue predictions were considered too optimistic, which is one reason why we ended up with such high rates. We still have to see how the GST does in the long run, but if the current performance continues, there's a good chance that the final GST outcome will come close to what I had recommended in the RNR: low and simple rates, and a broad base that includes land and real estate, electricity and gold.

Gold and the GST make strange bedfellows. In my report, I made the case that gold should be taxed at a below-standard rate between 6 and 12 per cent. This recommendation did not go down well, as gold was traditionally taxed (by nearly all states) at much lower rates, just 1 per cent, and the Centre did not tax it at all. When I say the recommendation did not go down well, I am being euphemistic. A government minister actually shouted at me, the only time this happened during my tenure.

Even so, the Centre's budget of 2016–17 (after my GST report but well before the passing of the Constitutional Amendment Bill) took the bold step of levying an excise tax—also a mere 1 per cent—on gold. When the budget proposal was announced, there was an upsurge of protest from the jewellery trading community. In the post-budget debate, all the usual arguments were made opposing the tax: it would encourage smuggling and evasion, gold was a store of wealth for the poorest, the gold bangle and mangalsutra were items of religious significance for the masses.

The finance minister was able to address some of these arguments by citing numbers that we had calculated in my GST report: more than 80–90 per cent of the gold was consumed by the richest decile of the population, with the poor accounting for a minuscule portion. And gold expenditure was a much higher fraction of the total expenditure for the richest than for the poorest, 3.5 per cent compared to .03 per cent. Keeping taxes on gold low was a boondoggle for the rich, cloaked in socialist rhetoric: the real giveaway was that the communist party in Kerala levied the highest tax on gold in India. In response to an urgent request from the finance minister during the budget session of Parliament, I had to text these numbers directly to him from the United States, where I was travelling. Evidence mattered.

Of course, vastly more important was the resolve of the prime minister, who stood firm against the opposition. As a result of the budget, the important principle that the Centre would tax gold was established.

Since the principle had been established, I thought it would be a simple matter to establish a more reasonable tax of 6 or even 10 per cent when the GST discussions took place a year later in 2017. I soon realized my economic analysis had run ahead of my understanding of Indian gold politics. The GST rate on gold ended up at . . . 3 per cent. Since 3 per cent is greater than 2 per cent, I guess this represented progress. But it was hardly the gold standard!

We live in an imperfect world. But dreams never die. Even today, whenever I hear Raga Behag, I think back to that heady Tagore-esque moment of dusk in Belur when spiritual, musical and professional satisfaction all came together.

At Belur Math, after the aarti, we had an audience with some of the inspiring monks. We covered a lot of issues, including the Math, its spiritual practices and Ramakrishna Paramahamsa. But the monks were also keen to discuss the GST . . . levied on religious institutions!

3.1

The Goods and Services Tax

One India, One Market[1]

Hype and hyperbole are temptations to which government officials, in particular, must not succumb. Yet, it is difficult not to view the GST as a game-changing reform for the country; and, when it happens, it would be curmudgeonly not to acknowledge its passage as a major, historic achievement for the government but also the country.

Consider some questions in turn. Why is GST important? What can be said about its design? How does it compare with similar tax reforms in other countries?

Three major benefits will flow from the GST. First, it will increase the resources available for poverty alleviation and development. This will happen indirectly as the tax base becomes more buoyant and as the overall resources of the central and state governments increase. But it will also happen directly because the resources of the poorest states—for example, Uttar Pradesh, Bihar and Madhya Pradesh—who happen to be large consumers, will increase substantially.

Second, the GST will facilitate 'Make in India' by essentially establishing 'one India'. The current tax structure unmakes India by fragmenting the markets along state lines. These distortions are caused by three features of the current system: the central sales tax (CST) on interstate sales of goods; numerous interstate taxes; and the extensive nature of countervailing duty (CVD) exemptions that favour imports over domestic production. In one fell swoop, the GST will rectify all these distortions: the CST will be eliminated; most of the other taxes will be subsumed into the GST, and because the GST will be applied on imports, the negative protection favouring imports and disfavouring domestic manufacturing will be eliminated.

Third, the GST will improve, even substantially, tax governance in two ways. The first relates to the self-policing incentive inherent in a valued-added tax. To claim input tax credit, each dealer has an incentive to request documentation from the dealer behind him in the value-added tax chain. Provided the chain is not broken through wide-ranging exemptions, especially on intermediate goods, this self-policing feature can work very powerfully in the GST system.

The second improvement in tax governance relates to the dual monitoring structure of the GST—one by the states and one by the Centre. Critics and taxpayers have viewed the dual structure with some anxiety, fearing two sources of interface with the tax department and, hence, two potential sources of harassment. But dual monitoring should also be viewed as creating desirable tax competition and cooperation between state and central authorities. Even if one set of tax authorities overlooks and/or fails to detect evasion, there is the possibility that the other overseeing authority may not.

Other benefits such as the boost to investment have been documented in the Report on the Revenue Neutral Rate that I submitted in December 2015. Of course, these benefits will only flow through a well-designed GST system. The GST should aim at tax rates that protect revenue, simplify administration, encourage compliance, avoid adding to inflationary pressures and keep India in the range of countries with reasonable levels of indirect taxes. To this end, the report recommended a revenue neutral rate between 15 and 15.5 per cent and a standard rate of about 18 per cent. The report also urged that the GST be comprehensive in its coverage, that exemptions from the GST be limited to a few commodities that catered to clear social benefits, and that most commodities be taxed at the standard rate. There is no free lunch here. There is no escaping the fact that more the exemptions or exclusions, the higher will be the standard rate which could affect poorer consumers.

Some have levelled the charge that the inherent design of the GST system is flawed. Clearly, the current design is not ideal and could be improved. But the 'flawed GST' charge fails to appreciate how reforms actually occur. In no country is the GST—even today after many years of implementation—perfect, and was therefore quite flawed at inception. In complex systems, change is introduced and then learning from implementation takes place, leading to further and better change. That is what happened with the implementation of the VAT by the states and that is what will happen with the GST. It is far better to start and allow the process of endogenous change to unfold over time than to wait, Godot-like, for the best time and the best design before it is actually introduced.

That said, we must also be realistic about the timeframe for assessing the success of the GST. The GST is fiendishly and mind-bogglingly complex to administer. Such complexity and lags in GST implementation require that any evaluation of the GST, and any consequential decisions, should not be undertaken over short horizons, say, months, but over longer periods, say one to two years. For example, if six months into the implementation, overall GST revenues are seen to be falling a little short, there should not be a hasty decision to raise rates until such time as it becomes clear that the shortfall is not due to implementation issues. Facilitating easy implementation and taxpayer compliance at an early stage—via low rates and without adding to inflationary pressures—will be critical. In the early stages, if that requires countenancing a slightly higher fiscal deficit, that would be worth considering as an investment which would deliver substantial long-run benefits.

In understanding GST systems around the world, we have been struck by how ambitious and how under-flawed the Indian GST is in comparison. GST-type taxes in large federal systems are either overly centralized, depriving the sub-federal levels of fiscal autonomy (as in the case of Australia, Germany and Austria); or where there is a dual structure, they are either administered independently creating too many differences in tax bases and rates that weaken compliance and make interstate transactions difficult to tax (as in the case of Brazil, Russia and Argentina); or administered with a modicum of coordination which minimizes these disadvantages (as in the case of Canada and India today) but does not do away with them.

The Indian GST will be a leap forward in creating a much cleaner dual VAT, which would minimize the disadvantages of completely independent and completely centralized systems. A common base and common rates (across goods and services) and across states and the Centre will facilitate administration and improve compliance while also rendering manageable the collection of taxes on interstate sales. At the same time, the exceptions—in the form of permissible additional excise taxes on sin goods (petroleum and tobacco for the Centre, petroleum and alcohol for the states)—will provide the requisite fiscal autonomy to the states. Indeed, even if they are brought within the scope of the GST, the states will retain autonomy in being able to levy top-up taxes on these 'sin/demerit' goods.

To have achieved this, in a large and complex federal system of multi-party democracy, with a Centre, twenty-nine states and two Union Territories of widely divergent interests via a constitutional amendment requiring broad political consensus, affecting potentially 2–2.5 million tax entities, and marshalling the latest technology to use and improve tax implementation capability, is perhaps breathtakingly unprecedented in modern global tax history.

Sometimes we are insufficiently appreciative of how much the country has achieved in coming to this point with the GST. Credit should go to all political parties at the Centre and the states for having worked towards, even if all of them have also occasionally worked against, the GST. The time is ripe to collectively seize this historic opportunity; not just because the GST will decisively alter the Indian economy for the better but also because the GST symbolizes Indian politics and democracy at its cooperative, consensual best.

3.2

The GST's Last and Critical Lap[1]

After the Constitutional Amendment Bill that midwifed it, and with the passage of the four laws that have given it elaborate flesh and substance, the Goods and Services Tax has entered its last and critical phase: the determination of the GST's rate structure.

Late in 2016, there was agreement on five broad GST slabs: 0 (the exempted category), 5, 12, 18 and 28 per cent; there was also agreement that cesses—to finance possible compensation to the states—would be levied on certain demerit goods (tobacco and related products, aerated beverages, luxury cars, etc.). Now is the moment of truth when items will be assigned to the different GST slabs and the exact amounts of the cesses decided. The actual rate structure has already become overly complicated, departing from the simple three rate structure I had recommended. Now, it is time for damage limitation.

A few general points must be highlighted at the outset. This is a constitutional moment for the GST, a moment ripe for ambition and visionary decision making which must be seized because it comes but rarely in history. Inevitably, in the future, inertia, 'dead habits' and the unavoidable diversity of interests will reassert themselves, strongly perpetuating the status quo. So, the rate structure decided today is likely to persist for a considerable time.

In that light, the guiding principle cannot be to minimize departures from the status quo. If that were the case—and hence if GST rates were set close to today's rates—the question might legitimately be asked: why bother with a GST at all?

Instead, the guiding principle must be: what will make for a good GST, a GST that will facilitate compliance, minimize inflationary pressures, be a buoyant source of revenue, and command support from the public at large?

It is essential not to saddle the GST with multiple objectives; down that path lies complexity and arbitrariness that will be fatal for the GST. The GST is a consumption tax, so any differentiation of rates—which in any case should be minimal—should be linked to protecting the consumption basket of the poor while imposing a greater burden when there are externalities associated with consumption or where consumption is disproportionately by the rich. The GST cannot be burdened with the task of meeting other objectives such as employment, industrial policy and social engineering.

Another general point and one that will pose a communication challenge is that today's headline tax rate is not the actual tax burden felt by the consumer. What you see is *not* what consumers get. So, if the government imposes a GST rate that seems greater than today's rate (excise plus VAT combined), it does not necessarily follow that the tax burden has gone up. The reason is that today there are a lot of embedded taxes (the so-called cascading).

A numerical example will help understand embedded taxes and cascading. What is cascading? Consider the case of a car, which costs Rs 5 lakh to manufacture. Under the old system, excises would add Rs 50,000 to the cost, bringing it to Rs 5.5 lakh. Then the VAT would add Rs 55,000. So, total tax (excise plus VAT would be Rs 1,05,000 [50,000 plus 55,000]). But under the new GST, the tax would just be Rs 1 lakh, that is 20 per cent of Rs 5 lakh. This difference of Rs 5000 is called 'cascading' duties, which have accrued because the VAT was imposed on the price including excises. This 'tax upon a tax' is eliminated under the GST system.

Under the GST, on the other hand, what you see will be close to what consumers get. So, if a product goes from being exempted pre-GST and attracts a GST rate of 5 per cent, it could well be (as in the case of many agricultural products) that there has been no increase in the consumer's actual tax burden.

I discuss below some key issues with recommendations on the desirable course of action, even corrective action:

1. **Tax Structure:** Under the proposed rate structure, India will be seen, rightly, as a very high GST country because the top rate has been set at 28 per cent, well in excess of that in most emerging market countries. There is still time to consider eliminating the 28 per cent rate and the 18 per cent rate, combining them into a 20 per cent slab, which would then become the standard rate.

   However, if this is not feasible and the 18 and 28 per cent slabs are here to stay, a second-best option must be considered. In order to credibly signal an 18 per cent GST rather than a 28 per cent GST, the number of goods that are placed in the 28 per cent slab must be kept at an absolute minimum.

   In my view, the 28 per cent slab should include only demerit goods (no services) on which additional cesses will be levied and a few real luxury items such as air conditioners and cars. The bulk of consumer goods (refrigerators, electrical appliances, basic cosmetics, furniture) that are currently envisaged to be in the 28 per cent category should be moved to the 18 per cent category. Otherwise, India will be a high GST country and there will be no escaping that stigma and all the consequences for tax administration and compliance that will follow from it.

As a rough rule of thumb, if the 28 per cent slab contains items that comprise more than, say, 5–7 per cent of the value of all GST taxable products, India will be seen as a high tax country.

If there is a risk of too many goods being put in the 28 per cent category, there is now subtle pressure from the states (which have been guaranteed a minimum growth of 14 per cent in revenues associated with GST-taxable goods) for placing many goods and services in the lower rate slabs of 5 per cent and 12 per cent. This too must be resisted because the more number of goods in the lower rate slab, the greater will be the pressure to overload the 28 per cent slab in order to maintain adequate revenues.

The result will be a populist GST where several goods and services are placed in the low-rate categories; then revenue considerations and populism will force lots of goods also being placed in the 28 per cent category. One bargaining chip that the Centre could consider is to lower the compensation threshold (from, say, 14 per cent to 12 per cent) if states insist on placing goods in the lower-rate slabs.

2. 'GoodsandServices', not 'Goods and Services' and Certainly Not 'Many Goods, Many Services': One of the big virtues of a simple GST system with one or at most two rates was that it would have completely abolished the distinction between goods and services (it would have been a lexicographer's dream and a GST bequest if a new word, 'goodsandservices', could have been created). Technology and the modern economy are blurring the distinction between the two; our tax policy and system must reflect that. Tax authorities should not be burdened with distinguishing a good from a service. (A single rate will also avoid misclassification between services.)

Given the multiple rate structure that has been adopted that is going to be difficult to achieve. But damage limitation will require that an overwhelming majority of the goods be taxed at the standard rate of 18 per cent, and nearly all services (with the exception of road transport) also be taxed at 18 per cent. If services are also allocated between the different rates, the result will be a messy system with multiple categories for both goods and services.

Consider the following example. Suppose a dealer sells an air conditioner and also provides installation and other post-sales services. Under the proposed GST structure, a rate of 28 per cent will apply to the former and 18 per cent to the latter. This immediately creates an incentive for the dealer to allocate the costs of the air conditioner towards the services that he is providing. Examples like this abound in real life (downloading of software = service; sale of that same software in a physical medium = goods, possibly). In fact, it could get worse: if the dealer is deemed to be providing a composite supply, even the services he provides could be taxed at 28 per cent.

3. **Textiles and Clothing:** The current system of indirect taxation is a mess of exemptions and complications. If India is to become a serious clothing exporter—especially in the dynamic man-made fibre segment—the GST must provide for a simple structure. Ideally, all textiles and clothing products should be subject to the standard 18 per cent tax with no favouritism displayed towards cotton-based products (consumed mostly by the rich) over those based on synthetic fibres. As a second-best option, it may be necessary to move to a 12 per cent rate but that should be applied uniformly across the entire value chain from raw materials to intermediates to the final goods. Any differentiation within the sector would be very damaging.

The same applies to leather and footwear. Since these are items of general high-end consumption, there is no reason to tax all these products at anything other than the standard rate of 18 per cent.

4. **Gold:** In the 2016 budget, a 1 per cent excise was levied on gold and jewellery products, which elicited strong reactions from the gold-trading lobby. The government, to its credit, resisted demands to roll back the levy. Having bitten that bullet, it is time to take the next step to treat gold like any other item of luxury consumption.

    Ideally, of course, the tax on gold and jewellery should be the normal 18 per cent, especially since the rich and very rich consume it disproportionately. But the argument that high tax can lead to evasion has some merit in the case of a high-value product such as gold.

    Today, even though the total headline tax on jewellery is 2 per cent (1 per cent by the Centre and 1 per cent by the states), the effective burden faced by consumers is about 10–12 per cent because of cascading and non-availability of input tax credits. So, there would be no increase in burden if the GST rate is set at 12 per cent (with free flow on input tax credits). It would be an absolute travesty if gold and gold products were taxed at anything below a GST rate of 12 per cent.

5. **Tobacco Products:** Today, most tobacco products are taxed at very high rates reflecting their potential to cause cancer and other diseases; they are classic demerit goods. Bidis, on the other hand, attract very low taxes in some states on the grounds that bidis are made in the small-scale sector and create livelihoods for millions. This is a classic case of multiple objectives leading to distortionary taxation. In terms of consumption, bidis are no less harmful than cigarettes. So, the GST as a consumption tax should treat the two similarly. The objective of helping bidi workers should be addressed

through other fiscal tools such as subsidies (and in any case, small bidi establishments will fall below the GST threshold).

In the new regime, therefore, the cess on all tobacco products should be broadly similar. In fact, bidi taxation is going to be a test for the GST Council because there are some states such as Karnataka and Rajasthan that tax bidis heavily. Since taxes have to be uniform across states, it will be interesting to see if the GST lurches towards undesirably low levels as in West Bengal or moves to desirably higher levels as in Karnataka and Rajasthan.

6. **Countervailing Duty (CVD) and Special Additional Duty (SAD) Exemptions:** CVD and SAD levied on imports are not import duties because they are the counterpart of the excise tax and VAT, respectively, levied on domestically produced goods. Thus, CVD and SAD serve to prevent discrimination against domestic goods. Currently, numerous exemptions are granted on the CVD and SAD levied on imports, which lead to favouring imports over domestic production. Under the GST, both will be combined and a uniform IGST will be applied on imports. If any import IGST exemptions are allowed under the GST (to mimic the current CVD and SAD exemptions), it would make a mockery of the prime minister's 'Make in India' initiative.

In conclusion, it must be accepted that the GST suffers from weaknesses largely related to the exemption of so many items from its scope: alcohol, petroleum, electricity, land and real estate, health and education. But warts and all, the GST has been a great achievement and worth pursuing, not least because of being a daring experiment in the implementation of cooperative federalism. But in order to minimize the damage from these warts, at least the structure of rates on those products that are not excluded from the GST should be low, simple and efficient.

It is asserted in politics, and rightly so, that the best should not become the enemy of the good. At the same time, political practices must yield outcomes that are passably good. Otherwise, they are not worth having. Can the GST Council, at this constitutional moment, deliver such an outcome?

The country will be watching, oscillating between hope and anxiety.

Black Money's Next Frontier

Bringing Land and Real Estate into a Transformational GST

After the steps taken to reduce black cash and streamline election finance, the next step will entail cleaning up one of the biggest sources of black money—land and real estate. And the natural way to do that is to bring the supply of land and real estate (hereafter referred to as LARE) into the GST. At the moment, the GST law does not include LARE but there is still a window to fix that in the GST Council meetings in the months ahead.[1]

Before we spell out the details, a few clarifications are in order to clear up the misconceptions and misinformation, some of which appear to be perpetrated deliberately by vested interests with a stake in preserving the murky status quo.

Misconception 1: Stamp duties will be brought into the GST. Many states have refused to entertain bringing LARE into the GST, fearing that their right to levy stamp duties on the sale of land—a big source of state revenues—will be taken away from them. This fear is unfounded. There is no such intention and stamp duties will remain untouched.

Misconception 2: Agricultural land will be taxed. There is similarly no intention to bring transactions relating to land for agriculture into the GST. The fear that there is a slippery slope that will lead to taxes on agricultural land and income is also unfounded.

Misconception 3: Low-cost housing will be taxed and made unaffordable. There is also no intention to bring transactions relating to low-cost housing into the GST. The fear that the price of housing for poorer sections will go up because of new taxes is also unfounded. Housing below a certain cost (or below a carpet area of 60 square metres) will not be subject to the GST.

Misconception 4: The tax burden will increase and hence the prices of LARE will go up. There is no intention to increase the current taxation on LARE. As elaborated below, bringing LARE into the GST will keep current effective rates of taxation broadly unaffected; what will happen is an increase in taxes at the final stage but because refunds on taxes paid on inputs at previous stages of production will be available, the real burden of taxation will not increase.

So, what will come into the GST? Answering that requires understanding the current system.

Currently, an annual property tax is levied on land as a source of wealth by urban local bodies. When land or property is sold, there is a stamp duty levied by state governments to register the sale. Neither of these will be brought into the GST.

In principle, the GST can be levied as a service tax on the supply of land and real estate. In which case, one may ask what exactly is the service? The service in question relates to the service provided by those who develop and construct commercial and residential property (the LARE service provider). This service can be provided either as a 'works' contract, when the buyer gets the LARE to build and develop the property, or the service can be provided as the supply of an already constructed property by, say, developers (this might be called ready-made property).

Today, the law makes an arbitrary distinction between works contracts and ready-made property. There is a service tax on works contracts both for commercial and residential properties. This tax is about 4.5 per cent, levied on the total value of the property but no credits are available for taxes paid on inputs such as iron and steel, cement and fittings and fixtures (many of which are transacted informally) that go into the construction of a property. The lack of input tax credits means that the effective rate of tax is not the headline 4.5 per cent, rather the rate plus the cascaded sum of all the input taxes. A rough estimate is that the effective tax rate even today is actually over 12 per cent.

In contrast, there is no tax levied on ready-made property, be it commercial or residential. Because there is no tax, there is also no provision for input tax credits. This means that here too the effective rate of taxation is not the headline 0 per cent but the sum of all the cascaded taxes on inputs. One technical reason that ready-made properties are not currently taxed is because some economists argue that immovable property is excluded in the Constitution from the definition of a 'good'. But going forward, ready-made properties—or rather, the service provided in building them—can easily be taxed as a 'service' because the definition of what can be taxed under the GST is quite broad: the supply of goods or services or both (excluding alcoholic liquor for human consumption).

So, today, the playing field is not level; the service underlying works contracts is taxed more heavily than the same service embodied in ready-made property. The way forward is to recognize that this distinction between works contract and ready-made property is artificial and to uniformly tax the service that went into the development and construction of both, and hence address the arbitrariness of the distinction between the two.

The main purpose behind proposing such uniformity in the inclusion of LARE in the GST would be to tax both works contracts and ready-made property at a standard rate and allow full input tax credits. It is the flow of credit that will strike at black money because the self-policing nature of the GST will kick in. All input transactions, notably the sale of cement, iron and steel, and fixtures and fittings that go into the construction of property will have to be accounted for. So, even as the tax on the consumer can be kept the same as today, the sales and purchases of inputs can be brought into the tax net. This would be a real transformational step in the fight against black money in real estate.

Despite the implementation of these very important changes, another key problem still stands to be addressed: the exclusion of transactions relating to the sale of land per se from the GST net. For that to happen, the sale of land (for non-agricultural purposes) must itself be taxable as the supply of a good or service. Only if the sale of land is taxed can an input tax credit be levied for it further down the chain. Moreover, only if there is input tax credit will the self-policing GST mechanism for disclosing the sale of land transactions kick in when, later, the same land is further developed. It is this disclosure that will strike at black money in land-sale transactions. Another advantage of imposing the GST on the first sale of land is that it will deter hoarding and encourage land development because when the latter happens, the GST can be claimed as a refund. In contrast, the hoarder of land will have to bear the full burden of the GST.

There are several international precedents for taxing the sale of land under the GST, including in the VAT systems of Australia,

Singapore, Malaysia, Indonesia and South Africa. However, Indian constitutional provisions are less clear as mentioned, for one because of the exclusion of land and immovable property from the definition of 'goods'. But it is also quite defensible and intuitive to consider the sale of land or the sale of the *right to land* as a service, which will then be covered by the definition under the GST. (Singapore, for example, considers the sale of the right to land as a good.)

In the GST Council, the Centre and some of the pro-governance states have expressed their support for bringing LARE into the GST. But many of the largest states have expressed opposition; those who are for the murky status quo are hiding behind the four misconceptions stated earlier. At a time when there is a drive to root out black money creation, it is imperative to attack the source of the problem—the flow problem—and not just the symptom (which is the stock problem).

Bringing LARE into the GST is thus a litmus test for whether state governments are serious in their efforts to address the scourge of black money, and hence supportive of the prime minister's drive in relation to reducing black money circulation in the country. But we must be clear. If you are against bringing LARE into the GST, you are for the continuous generation of black money. If so, please stand up and be identified. It is as simple as that.

3.4

Why, How and When Electricity Must Come into the GST[1]

As the GST overcomes the transitional implementation challenges, discussed in previous sections, it is time to look ahead at further improving it. The impact of the highest rates has been reduced by substantially paring down commodities in the 28 per cent bracket. Simplification of procedures for small enterprises, especially those that sell to large enterprises, is under way. Bringing land and real estate into the GST is also on the agenda for discussion. High priority must now also be accorded to the inclusion of electricity in the GST. Pertaining to electricity, the next questions arise: why, how and when?

Currently, there is a bewildering multiplicity of electricity taxes that vary by state and across user categories, which are low for consumers and high for industrial users. Taxes levied by the states thus vary from 0 per cent to 25 per cent. Taxing electricity consumption is an important source of revenue for state governments, amounting to about Rs 31,000 crore for all the states combined. On an average, electricity taxes account for about 3 per cent of state tax revenues, even going up to 9 per cent in some states. Most states are therefore reluctant to give up the right to levy these taxes, but the status quo imposes large costs that seriously undermine the government's 'Make in India' initiative.

Costs to industrial users of electricity are high because they include the taxes on inputs that have gone into the supply of electricity, such as raw materials (coal, renewables) and other equipment (solar panels and batteries). When electricity is not part of the GST, it means that no tax refund on input taxes can be claimed, which results in embedding of the tax in the final price. For the textile industry, for example, these embedded taxes amount to about 2 per cent of the price. This embedding of taxes hurts manufacturers selling both to the domestic market and to exporters. Normally, exporters would not be affected but in India no relief is provided for the taxes levied by the states (such as the electricity tax) that get passed to exports.

Moreover, there is a subtler way in which these embedded taxes hurt industrial buyers of electricity, creating a double whammy for them. Electricity is finally purchased by consumers and industrial users. Politics, and especially populist politics, have ensured that consumers (and other users in agriculture) pay either nothing for electricity or very little. As a result, and in order to make up for the resulting losses, distribution companies (DISCOMs) cross-subsidize, that is, they charge higher prices to industrial users to make up for undercharging others.

The embedding of taxes adds an extra layer of cross-subsidization. Industrial users are also charged higher rates to make up for the embedded taxes that cannot be recouped from the consumers. Totalling up all of these effects could lead to increased costs and lower margins of between 1–3 per cent for several industries such as clothing. These margins are significant, especially for exporters who face ferocious international competition where even a 1 per cent extra cost could be fatal to their business.

Another argument calls for its inclusion in the GST. Currently, there is a large bias in favour of renewables in the GST policy. In terms of numbers, inputs in renewables' generation attract a GST rate of 5 per cent while inputs in thermal generation attract higher rates of 18 per cent. Supporting renewables might be conscious policy (and also good policy), but we are in a situation where subsidization is proliferating across policy instruments, making it difficult to quantify the overall support. As we have discovered, complexity in the GST rate structure arises because it is burdened with having to meet multiple objectives. Likewise, support for renewables should be direct, conscious and transparent—the GST should not become an instrument for adding (non-transparently) to that support.

If electricity were to be included in GST, there would be no discrimination between renewables and thermal energy because all inputs going into both forms of electricity generation would receive tax credits. The GST would then essentially become neutral between different forms of electricity generation, as any good tax policy should be.

Thus, the case for including electricity in the GST is compelling. The question is: how? Recall that including electricity in the GST would reduce or eliminate embedded taxes in electricity-using products. This means that both the central and state governments would lose revenues that would accrue as input tax credits to the private sector. In addition, state governments would lose taxes from the use of electricity itself. So, there would be two sources of losses. What should be the response?

Several options can be considered. One would be for the Centre and the states to bear the losses of the embedded taxes, since the benefits would also be shared between them. The Centre would then compensate the states for only the direct loss of revenues. Another option is a halfway solution, which would be to impose a 5 per cent tax on electricity in the GST—allowing inputs tax credits to flow through the GST pipeline—but then allow the state governments to impose a small non-GST-able cess on top of the GST rate.

In the case of the latter, however, the greater the cess, the more it would resemble the status quo with all its problems as described above. So, this halfway solution comes with some limits on state governments' freedom to levy further taxes on electricity. But in both proposals the central government would lose revenues from the loss in embedded taxes and from having to compensate the states.

The final question of bringing power into the GST loop relates to timing. The likelihood of fiscal losses suggests that implementation should perhaps wait till the GST revenues have stabilized, say, by the end of the fiscal year 2018.

To sum up, there are four clear benefits from bringing electricity into the GST, which are: reducing the costs for manufacturing; improving the competitiveness of exporters; reducing the cross-subsidization of electricity tariffs that further undermines the competitiveness of manufacturers and exporters; and eliminating the large biases, and hence restoring neutrality of incentives in electricity generation.

Against these large benefits, there would be costs in terms of forgone revenues, but these costs can be shared between the Centre and the states. After all, that is what cooperative federalism is about.

3.5

A Buoyant Force

Understanding GST Revenue Performance[1]

One fiscal year into the implementation of the GST, it is worth asking how it has performed in terms of revenue generation both for the country and for individual states. And here the news, based on analysing nine full months of data, is encouraging. Three important and new points stand out.

1. **Aggregate Revenues Are Highly Buoyant:** In the Economic Survey of 2018–19, we had argued that confusion reigns in understanding GST performance because of focusing on one or more of the bewildering sub-categories of the GST (CGST, SGST, IGST, cess, etc.). To assess how the new system is doing, we need to understand overall GST performance, from both actual collections and collections, stripping out some of the clearly transitional factors (call it 'steady state' or likely long-run performance).

   Based on the first nine months of data (and including April 2018 collections in those of March 2018 as they should be), revenue collections for nine months were Rs 8.2 lakh

crore (11 lakh crore annualized), yielding a revenue growth of
11.9 per cent, compared with the relevant pre-GST numbers.
The implied tax buoyancy (which indicates the responsiveness
of tax growth to nominal GDP growth) is 1.2, which is high
by the historical standards of indirect taxes.

But another measure (more indicative of the medium-
run) of revenue performance is to strip the actual collections
of transitional factors. Some of these will boost future
performance (for example, a large overhang of CGST credit
has kept last year's revenues down), and some may depress
them (uncleared export and other pending refunds have
inflated last year's revenues).

It is difficult to precisely quantify these factors but rough
estimates yield an annual (steady-state) aggregate GST
revenue growth that is likely to be greater than the actual
collections' growth of 11.9 per cent.

A moment of reflection indicates that these revenue
growth and buoyancy estimates are, in fact, quite surprising
considering three significant headwinds that the GST faced:
implementation challenges in the first year of a massively
disruptive tax change; decelerating growth in the economy
(both nominal and real) which tends to dampen revenue
growth; and finally, the large GST rate reductions that were
effected throughout the first nine months, but especially after
November 2017, which should have also lowered revenue
collections.

2. 'True' Compensation Requirements Are Minimal: Recall that
   in the period leading up to the Constitutional Amendment
   bill in 2016, the need for compensating the losing states
   animated the discussions and created deep anxieties. How has
   the GST fared on this score?

   The government itself produces estimates, undertaking
   such a notional analysis by making a few assumptions, which

show that compensation, although financeable from within the GST, has been substantial. But compensation from a legal perspective is quite different from compensation from an economic perspective. The true measure of compensation is one that arises after all the revenues (from the unsettled IGST and the cess) are first allocated to the individual states. The fact that the unsettled IGST and compensation cess are in a centralized kitty does not mean that they do not accrue to the Centre and individual states.

Once all the GST taxes are allocated to individual states, we find that very few states should require compensation and that the sum of all these compensation amounts is between Rs 5000 and 10,000 crore. Again, this low compensation requirement is surprising given the early anxieties, but it was something that was predicted in the Report on the Revenue Neutral Rate that one of us from the ministry of finance had written for the government in December 2015. What it shows is that even in the first year, nearly all the states have seen their revenues grow by at least 14 per cent (this against a background of decelerating growth and reductions in rates).

Another implication of this new finding is that on current trends, and given likely improvements in compliance with the introduction of e-way bills and invoice matching, nearly all the states will register revenue growth in excess of the 14 per cent guarantee in the years ahead. The Centre's commitment to compensate the states for five years might be rendered largely moot and that too quite soon. If so, scope will be created for revisiting the structure of GST rates and cesses.

3. **The GST Is Boosting Revenues of Consuming States:** One of the factors contributing to the political acceptability of the GST was that many of the then-Opposition (i.e., prior to the GST being accepted) states (for example, Uttar Pradesh, West Bengal and Kerala) were net consuming states that

stood to gain from the GST, or so they thought. Has that expectation been met? Evidence from the first nine months suggests that it has, with a few exceptions. How do we know this? Once we correctly attribute all the GST revenues to the states, we can compare the share of the different states in the GST revenues compared with their share in taxes in the pre-GST regime.

This analysis highlights a few patterns. There are very few states where there is a significant decline in the post-GST share compared to the pre-GST share, which is consistent with the finding that 'true' compensation requirements are small. Many of the net consuming states such as nearly all the north-eastern states as well as Uttar Pradesh, Rajasthan, Madhya Pradesh, Delhi, Kerala and West Bengal have indeed increased their post-GST shares. States that have seen a small decline in their shares are those that had special tax regimes in terms of incentives or in agriculture. Therefore, the GST appears to be, desirably, a force for fiscal convergence.

After the first nine months of implementation, there is, of course, a full agenda for future reform: further simplifying the rate structure, widening the base to include currently exempted sectors, and streamlining procedures for filing and refunds.

But on the revenue front, performance has been very encouraging. Aggregate GST revenues have performed optimistically (despite three headwinds); there has been a desirable and equitable shift in revenues towards the consuming states; and this has happened without threatening the revenues of the producing states reflected in the small compensation requirement.

On this (revenue) score, at least, the GST has surprised on the upside.

Chapter 4

Climate Change and the Environment

4.0

Carbon Imperialism, Climate Change, Power

'Chief Economic Adviser (CEA) Arvind Subramanian has suggested Prime Minister Narendra Modi and Finance Minister Arun Jaitley to radically alter India's climate-change policy and negotiation strategy before the new global climate-change agreement, to be finalized in Paris by December this year. In a note to the two ministers— which has been reviewed by Business Standard*—Subramanian has recommended that India should stop insisting that the developed countries provide financing for poor countries to fight climate change, as they are required to under the UN climate convention.'*

That was the news story and picture that screamed out of the front page of the *Business Standard* one day in December 2015, just as we were gearing up for the climate change negotiations

(COP-21) in Paris. The story claimed to summarize a long policy note I had written and sent to the key interlocutors within the government (Section 4.1). The note was radical in its analysis and prescription, proposing a robust new way of protecting Indian interests. But somehow the *Business Standard* reporter had spun it as an anti-national piece, combining it cleverly with a picture of me looking furtive in dark sunglasses, all of which evoked a James-Bond–like character who was 'mentally un-Indian'. The article infuriated me. Back then, I hadn't developed the thick skin that is essential to survival as a public figure.

I had coined the term 'carbon imperialism' to castigate advanced countries that, having used their coal resources to become rich, now wanted to discourage coal-rich developing countries from doing the same. These hypocrisies were the subject of an op-ed that I wrote in the *Financial Times* the day before the key Paris negotiations (Section 4.2) with the blessing of the environment minister, Prakash Javadekar. And the 'offending' piece itself makes a strong case for advanced countries to come together to stop forcing a development-versus-environment trade-off on coal-dependent countries and contribute instead to cleaning and greening coal. This was, and remains even today, my view on how to provide energy without aggravating climate change.

The other piece reproduced here (Section 4.3) was my Darbari Seth Memorial Lecture delivered at The Energy and Resources Institute (TERI) in New Delhi in June 2017. In this lecture, my colleagues and I spelt out India's energy dilemma, the problem of balancing the imperative of using coal against the desirable shift towards renewables, which the prime minister boldly initiated by setting an ambitious renewables target of 175 gigawatts by 2022. That there are so many stranded assets in the thermal-power sector, which have given rise to so many NPAs in the PSBs (the cost of which the government has eventually to foot), creates a real policy challenge.

For example, how much should we subsidize renewables, when this leads to less thermal use and hence greater power sector NPAs, creating a sort of double bill (subsidies plus bailout) for the government? The dilemma raised by the analysis and the implications of it are reflected in the title of the lecture: 'Renewables May Be the Future but Are They the Present?'

Determining the right balance between renewables and coal is overdue for another reason. If coal has a limited future (unless it can be significantly greened), the window for reforming the coal sector—still under a public-sector monopoly—to maximize output and efficiency is a very narrow one.

A final piece in this chapter—a public lecture delivered in Chennai—discusses how cooperative federalism can be harnessed to address challenges in the power sector. Cooperation is needed because the power sector is deeply afflicted at all levels—generation and distribution, Centre and states. The analysis in this lecture built on a chapter written for the Economic Survey of 2015–16.

One solution, which I have emphasized, learning from the experience of the GST which created one market, is to create one national market for power. It is a travesty that seven decades after independence we still do not have one market for power, and states can erect barriers—often substantial—to the purchase of power from other, more efficient, sources or states.

One of the key points my team made was to highlight just how complex electricity tariff schedules are, a fact that few had previously known, let alone acknowledged. In most markets we want one price for one product. But here we have many, many prices for the exact same product, depending on the activity, sector, size, timing and magnitude of use. Some of the sub-categories are worth noting. 'Mushroom and rabbit farms'? 'Floriculture in greenhouses'? The wildest imagination cannot make these categories up. Clearly, our fiction writers have some catching up to do.

The (Deliberately?) Bewildering Complexity of Electricity Tariffs

Consumer Category	Energy Charge (Rs /Unit)
LT-I:DOMESTIC (Telescopic)	1.45
LT-I(A):Upto 50 Units/Month	
LT I(B):>50 and upto 100 Units/Month	1.45
First 50 Units	
51-100 Units	2.60
LT I(C):>100 and upto 200 Units/Month	
First 50	2.60
51-100	2.60
101-150	3.60
151-200	3.60
LT I(D):Above 20 0 Units/Month	
First 50	2.60
51-100	3.25
101-150	4.88
151-200	5.63
201-250	6.70
251-300	7.22
301-400	7.75
401-500	8.27
Above 500	8.80
LT II:NON DOMESTIC/COMMERCIAL	
LT II(A):Upto 50 Units/Month	5.40
LT II(B):Above 50 Units/Month	
First 50	6.63
51-100	7.38
101-300	8.54
301-500	9.06
Above 500	9.59
LT II(C):ADVERTISEMENT HOARDINGS	11.58
LT-III:INDUSTRY	
Industry (General)	6.38
Seasonal Industries (off season)	7.09
Pisciculture/Prawn culture	4.63
Sugarcane crushing	4.63
Poultry farms	5.63
Mushroom & Rabbit Farms	5.63
Floriculture in Green House	5.63
LT-IV:COTTAGE INDUSTRIES & OTHERS	
a) Cottage Industries upto 10 HP	3.75
b) Agro Based Activity upto 10 HP	3.75

Consumer Category	Energy Charge (Rs /Unit)
LT-V:AGRICULTURE **	
LT-V(A):AGRICULTURE WITH DSM	
Corporate Farmers & IT Assesses	2.50
Wet Land Farmers (Holdings >2.5 acre)	0.50
Dry Land Farmers (Connections > 3 nos.)	0.50
Wet Land Farmers (Holdings ≤ 2.5 acre)	0.00
Dry Land Farmers (Connections ≤ 3 nos.)	0.00
LT-V(B):AGRICULTURE WITHOUT DSM MEASURES	
Corporate Farmers & IT Assesses	3.50
Wet Land Farmers (Holdings >2.5 acre)	1.00
Dry Land Farmers (Connections > 3 nos.)	1.00
Wet Land Farmers (Holdings ≤ 2.5 acre)	0.50
Dry Land Farmers (Connections ≤ 3 nos.)	0.50
LT-V(C):OTHERS	
Salt farming units upto 15HP	3.70
Rural Floriculture Nurseries upto 15HP	3.70
LT-VI:STREET LIGHTING AND PWS	
LT-VI(A):STREET LIGHTING	
Panchayats	5.64
Municipalities	6.16
Municipal Corporations	6.69
LT-VI(B):PWS SCHEMES	
Panchayats	4.59
Municipalities	5.64
Municipal Corporations	6.16
LT-VI(C):NTR Sujala Padhakam	4.00
LT-VII:GENERAL	
LT-VII(A):GENERAL PURPOSE	6.86
LT-VII(B):RELIGIOUS PLACES (CL ≤ 2 KW)	4.70
LT-VIII: TEMPORARY SUPPLY	9.90
HT-I:INDUSTRY	
HT-I(A): INDUSTRY GENERAL	
11 kV	6.02
33 kV	5.57
132 kV & Above	5.15
INDUSTRIAL COLONIES	
11 kV	5.96
33 kV	5.96
132 kV & Above	5.96

Consumer Category	Energy Charge (Rs /Unit)
SEASONAL INDUSTRIES (off season Tariff)	
11 kV	7.25
33 kV	6.59
132 kV & Above	6.33
TIME OF DAY TARIFFS (6 PM to 10 PM)	
11 kV	7.07
33 kV	6.62
132 kV & Above	6.20
HT-I(B):FERRO ALLOY UNITS	
11 kV	5.68
33 kV	5.23
132 kV & Above	4.81
HT-II:OTHERS	
11 kV	7.25
33 kV	6.59
132 kV & Above	6.33
TIME OF DAY TARIFFS (6 PM to 10 PM)	
11 kV	8.30
33 kV	7.64
132 kV & Above	7.38
HT-III:AIRPORTS, BUS STATIONS AND RAILWAY	
11 kV	6.91
33 kV	6.31
132 kV & Above	6.01
TIME OF DAY TARIFFS (6 PM to 10 PM)	
11 kV	7.96
33 kV	7.36
132 kV & Above	7.06
HT-IV; Govt., LIFT IRRIGATION, AGRICULTURE	
Govt. Lift Irrigation & Agriculture	5.64
Composite Water Supply Schemes	4.61
HT-V:RAILWAY TRACTION	6.68
HT-VI:TOWNSHIPS AND RESIDENTIAL COLONIES	5.96
HT-VII:GREEN POWER	11.32
HT-VIII:TEMPORARY	
RURAL ELECTRIC CO-OPERATIVES	
Kuppam	0.24
Anakapally	1.38
Chipurupally	0.22

When I went to see Chief Minister Nitish Kumar of Bihar in 2016, I challenged him to guess the number of electricity rates that were contained in Bihar's schedule. He did not know; he guessed five. His officials did not know either; they first guessed between ten and fifteen, and then over the course of my conversation changed it to about forty. Two years later, when I met Nitish Kumar again, the first thing he said was, 'Thank you for pointing out the messiness of our tariffs. It turned out that there were closer to 150 electricity rates in Bihar.'

After some initial resistance, the power ministry embraced the message from our analysis and made simplification of tariff schedules a reform priority in the forum of state electricity regulators. I don't know how much progress they have made. But I wish the power of having simple and transparent policies— issues that also came up in the GST discussions—could be better understood, so that stronger political convictions would form around them.

4.1

India's Approach to Paris

This note was written in 2015 and provided some thoughts on how India should approach the COP-21 negotiations on climate change in Paris (hereafter referred to as 'Paris') in December 2015.

1. Tone and Narrative

Paris offers a serious opportunity for Prime Minister Modi to score another major foreign policy success and cement his emerging reputation as an international leader. For that to be possible, India's tone and narrative must change.

First, India must convey that it truly cares about a successful conclusion in Paris because it is acutely aware that climate change will affect India seriously and disproportionately. All the studies on the impact of climate change—health, agricultural productivity, extreme events, rainfall and water—confirm this.

In fact, India's stakes in climate change mitigation are perhaps even greater than those for rich countries who will both be less affected and will be better able to cope with the consequences. Simon Kuper of the *Financial Times* noted these differential incentives astutely in 2011:[1] 'We in the West have recently made an unspoken bet: we're going to wing it, run the risk of climate catastrophe, and hope that it is mostly faraway people in poor countries who will suffer.' Fundamentally, the dynamic whereby the rich are the demandeurs—a term used in international relations to describe a party that seeks to prevent non-compliance of international laws and treaties—and countries such as India are the responders needs to be altered. Out of self-interest, we should be pushing the others proactively for a global deal.

Second, our tone can and must be less defensive. India has undertaken a series of very positive actions (de facto carbon pricing via petroleum taxes, incentivizing afforestation, taxing coal, setting ambitious renewables' targets, making transparent and monitoring local carbon pollution, and investing in public transportation and infrastructure), which can make us credible protagonists of a climate-change deal.

A key point to highlight is that in response to the recent setback to climate change—in the form of reduced global prices of energy and oil—India has reacted by increasing petroleum taxes, while the rich world, especially the US and Canada, has passed on these price declines to consumers, undermining climate-change mitigation efforts. Indeed, even as oil prices have climbed up in recent months, India has stuck to its deregulation commitments and allowed prices to rise nearly commensurately.

Third, we should signal our constructive spirit by being willing to condition our actions on those of others: that is, we will do more if others behave similarly.

2. India's Vital Interests: What We Should Ask of Others (the 'Rich')

India's vital interests are twofold: to get the rich world to act immediately and ambitiously to price carbon, and to finance research and development into clean coal energy.

Our demand should be that rich countries back up their emissions' targets with concrete actions to price carbon, starting with an immediate price of $25 per ton, and rising to $50 per ton within a short duration of time (to be specified later). They could achieve this either through a carbon tax or emissions trading, or some combination of the two.

Second, we must aim to get the rich world to finance (both public and private) on a war footing, research and development, and other investments that will clean and green coal, which aim at reducing the hazardous emissions and effects from coal burning. Here, India must counter a disturbing development. The rich world has become enamoured of renewables, indeed so much so that greening coal has become a casualty. This is reflected in the latest G-7 declaration to phase out fossil fuels. This would be a disaster for India, which will and must rely on coal for the foreseeable future.

Under any plausible scenario going forward, coal will provide about 50–60 per cent of India's energy. Coal will, and should, remain India's primary energy source because it is the cheapest fuel. So, the only way that India can meet its energy requirements efficiently while also minimizing the damage to the environment is if coal becomes clean.

It is worth reminding the world that in the last few years, India has made significant contributions to climate-change mitigation in the form of a highly inefficient coal sector with near-stagnant production, which has kept emissions below what they would otherwise have been. As coal-sector reforms improve efficiency and raise production, that contribution, by default, to climate change will increase dramatically with adverse effects on CO_2 emissions, unless coal is greened and cleaned.

3. India's Less Vital Interests

In following the discussions surrounding India's climate-change policies, it seems that India places great emphasis on three issues:

seeking climate change financing, retaining the distinction between Annex 1 (broadly advanced) and non-Annex 1 (broadly developing) countries, and emphasizing adaptation. For reasons elaborated below, I would argue that these issues should not be considered vital for India.

Regarding finance, three questions should inform our stance. First, is finance a binding constraint in achieving India's core objectives of climate-change mitigation? Second, are the commitments of cash-strapped advanced countries plausible? After all, the United States cannot muster the will and ability to contribute a few hundred million dollars (chump change really) to increasing the IMF's resources even though it has led to a serious loss in America's international standing and influence. Third, even if this will can be mustered, will finance be additional, real and from official sources (rather than private ones, which are not relevant to the official international effort)? The answers to all these questions suggest that obtaining finance cannot be a vital interest for us. In pressing this issue, India might score polemical victories but not substantive ones.

On the Annex 1/non-Annex distinction, it is important, even sacrosanct, to retain the principle that contributions will and should be commensurate with a country's development status. Here too, while historic responsibility is an argument that remains important, India should emphasize the need for development space and energy access for the vast majority of Indians going forward as the critical argument for differentiated responsibilities.

However, it is the substance, not the form in which it is expressed, that matters. The Annex 1/non-Annex 1 distinction is one form of expressing the principle of differentiated responsibilities. But it is a rigid one and, to be fair, is one that is less reflective of the circumstances today as compared to twenty-five years ago. We must be consistent here. If we correctly seek a seat on the United Nations Security Council on the grounds that the world has changed and that existing arrangements have been overtaken by current realities, that applies to climate change too. Hence, finding alternatives to the current rigid dichotomy—which also has been overtaken by the dramatic changes of the last twenty-five years—is not something that we should vehemently oppose.

A third non-vital interest is adaptation. India should be clear that in Paris our vital interest is climate-change mitigation, not adaptation. Mitigation is an issue that requires collective action and cooperation while adaptation does not, except insofar as it leads to more official financing. In Paris, the adaptation-is-important idea will be embraced by the poorest countries for whom financing is an important issue; it will also be peddled by the donor community which sees adaptation as a new raison d'être to justify and perpetuate itself. We need have no commonality with either of these camps.

In sum, India should not consider seeking financing, retaining the Annex 1 distinction, or adaptation as our vital interest in the negotiations. These issues can be used as bargaining chips in the final negotiations.

A strategy that focuses on these non-vital interests reduces the pressure on advanced countries to deliver on the really critical commitments—carbon taxation and public investments in greening coal—for climate-change mitigation.

4. Bargaining Issues

In the past, especially in trade negotiations, India's bargaining has been affected by a false sense of security stemming from being part of bigger coalitions. In Paris, though there are like-minded groups such as BRICS (Brazil, Russia, India, China, South Africa) and BASIC (Brazil, South Africa, India, China), India should be realistic about the unity and utility of these coalitions. For example, in its new climate plan, the 'intended nationally determined contribution', or the INDC, China has expressed a strong commitment to maintaining the Annex-based distinctions. In its actions, including in its agreement with the US, it has behaved differently. India cannot rely on or take comfort in the fact that China today is canvassing for the retention of this distinction. It is more than likely that in the end, China will abandon it. India must be prepared for this eventuality and, in fact, plan for its bargaining strategy accordingly.

Similarly, India might be tempted to make common cause with the poorer countries in Africa in pressing for financing. But as argued above, getting financing is not a vital interest for India, rendering that coalition less important.

The one group that India should make common cause with, because of its critical value, is coal-producing countries such as China, Australia, Poland, and even the United States. Greening coal is important for all these countries. But as mentioned, the rich world has become enamoured of renewables, which has made research and development in coal energy suffer greatly. It will take extra effort on India's part to keep the cleaning of coal centre stage in and after Paris, which might require creative coalition-building.

5. What Should India Offer?

India's INDC should reflect all the actions that it has undertaken and intends to follow through on. There is a really positive story to tell, especially in relation to the recent global oil price decline, where India has been as responsible as the others have been recklessly passive. The question is whether India should be willing to do more and commit to doing more. Although China's targets are substantively not significant, it did manage to win the narrative by strengthening its emissions' intensity target and adding a peak emissions' target in its agreement with the United States. Should India do the same?

The core of India's INDC should be its actions—actual and planned. But offering targets, and conditional ones, may help India change the narrative. One possibility here would be that India makes a conditional offer, saying it would take actions beyond the baseline if others were willing to do so as well. The conditioning variable would not be financing but rich country actions on carbon pricing and the effort to clean coal.

Such a conditional offer would signal India's cooperative spirit while at the same time articulating clearly and strongly what it considers are vital to the Indian and global effort to combat climate change.

4.2

Combating Carbon Imperialism[1]

A decade or two from now, the world should be able to look back at the UN Paris climate conference in December 2015 and say with the wistfulness of the ex-lovers in *Casablanca*: 'We'll always have Paris.' But will we? There is real anxiety in countries such as India that the stance of advanced countries might in one vital respect stand in the way of successfully fighting climate change.

In the run-up to the conference, there was a growing call—first articulated clearly at the June summit of the Group of Seven leading nations—to phase out fossil fuels. The US and others have also vowed to vote against fossil-fuel energy projects in developing countries when multilateral development banks are voting on them. Meanwhile, the US produces at least 35 per cent more coal than India.

For India, a country struggling to provide basic electricity to 25 per cent of its population that lacks reliable access to energy, this smacks of 'carbon imperialism' on the part of advanced economies. And such imperialism would spell disaster for India and other developing countries.

In fact, rather than replacing coal, the only way India and other poorer countries can both meet its needs and minimize damage to the environment may be to find effective techniques to 'clean and green' coal. Under any plausible scenario, coal will provide about 40–60 per cent of India's energy. It will, and should, remain the country's primary energy source because it is the cheapest fuel as compared to available alternatives.

India is neither unaware of the social costs of coal nor is it lax in promoting renewables. It has started taxing carbon. The coal cess has quadrupled to Rs 200 per ton since 2014. This has resulted in an implicit carbon tax of $2 per ton of CO_2 on domestic coal and $1.4 per ton of CO_2 on imports. This may, of course, still not be enough to cover all the social costs of carbon use.

There has also been a substantial indirect tax on carbon. In response to the fall in the oil price, the government has eliminated subsidies on petrol and diesel, and increased taxes. India has therefore moved from a negative price—that is, a subsidy—to a positive price on carbon emissions. In contrast, the governments of most advanced countries have simply passed on the benefits of declining oil prices to the consumers, setting back the cause of curbing climate change.

It is encouraging, too, that the problem of pollution is becoming part of domestic political discourse. India requires monitoring mechanisms for pollution in a number of cities. The pressure on the government to take account of the domestic social costs of increased carbon-related pollution—for example, health, accidents and congestion—is likely only to grow.

India is committed to an ambitious renewables programme, ramping up renewables production from 35 gigawatts (GW) today to 175 gigawatts by 2022. But as Bill Gates, Microsoft co-founder and philanthropist, has pointed out, the prices of properly costed renewables are not competitive with coal today, and they are not likely to be any time soon. It is wishful thinking to imagine that renewables can replace coal in the foreseeable future.

So, although India is committed to curbing climate change and to promoting renewables, making coal clean is vital to the country's development. However, this cannot be done by Delhi, or anyone else in the country, alone.

Technologies that are already available, such as carbon capture and storage, have proved prohibitively expensive. But to discover truly effective techniques, the world needs to embark on a programme akin to the Manhattan Project that produced the first nuclear bomb. This will require investment from both public and private sectors, in advanced and developing nations, as well as a range of policy instruments. But the rich world's preoccupation with phasing out fossil fuels creates a risk that the private sector— already lukewarm about investing in cleaning coal—will read the signals and abandon the project altogether.

In the past few months I have met senior leaders from the US, the UK, France, Germany, Australia and Japan. All appreciated that the need to clean coal is a significant part of efforts to fight climate change. The time is ripe to create a global green and clean coal coalition. That, rather than calls to phase out coal, would best serve the cause of fighting climate change.

4.3

Renewables May Be the Future, But Are They the Present?

Coal, Energy and Development in India

It was a great honour to be at TERI to deliver the Sixteenth Darbari Seth Memorial Lecture, on 17 August 2017. Seth was, of course, one of the titans of the Tata Group and Indian industry, and a confidant of the legendary J.R.D. Tata. He had a strong streak of public service—not to mention a sneaking soft corner for socialism—reflected in his founding of this terrific institution, TERI. It was also a great honour to follow in the footsteps of so many illustrious previous speakers.

At the outset, I want to emphasize that this is the joint product of deliberations with my two young colleagues, Rangeet Ghosh and Navneeraj Sharma. Almost all that I know about the power sector is due to Navneeraj, who educated me on power even while enlightening me on Ramana Maharishi and Ludwig Wittgenstein.

In outlining the speech, I prioritized the scope of renewables and coal in the current Indian context. I believe there is inadequate understanding of the issues related to coal and renewables; in fact, I am myself confused about how to think about them jointly. So, in a sense, delivering this address was an opportunity to think aloud, to clarify issues, hopefully for the audience but definitely for myself. My apologies in advance: I am not an energy expert, nor a climate-change expert, but someone who is trying to put it all together into a public-policy framework.

To my understanding, three features define the background for having this discussion on renewables and coal.

First, under the leadership of Prime Minister Modi, India has become one of the leaders in the global effort to combat climate change. The prime minister, along with the then French President, Francois Hollande, and leaders of other countries, led the initiative to launch the International Solar Alliance (ISA) at the Paris meeting in November 2015. In turn, this was underpinned by an effort to dramatically increase the role of renewables in the domestic-energy equation. India is now committed to installing 175 GW of renewables by 2022, which would account for 20.4 per cent of electricity generated from all sources. (TERI and its director-general, Dr Mathur, also deserve kudos for the terrific and constructive role they played in Paris.)

Second, this emphasis on renewables comes against the recent history of a dramatic expansion, even overexpansion, in thermal capacity, predominantly in the private sector (218 GW of total thermal capacity at the end of FY 2017 with an 8x increase in private-sector capacity to 84 GW between 2007 and 2017). That overexpansion—fuelled by the growth optimism of the mid-2000s—combined with stresses in the DISCOMs and slowdown in the economy has led to plummeting plant load factors (PLFs), declining profitability, the spectre of large amounts of stranded power assets, and consequentially, stranded coal assets as well. As we've been discussing, all this can have a detrimental effect on the health of the banking sector, especially public-sector banks, in the country, which, in turn, can adversely impact the health of the Indian economy, already afflicted by the TBS challenge.

Declining Plant Load Factors   Increasing Power Sector Debt

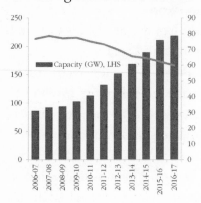
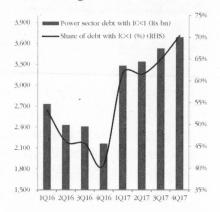

Third, discussions of renewables and coal must take into account India's regional and development realities. Coal is located predominantly in the poor, eastern hinterlands of India, while the potential of renewables is, with the exception of Rajasthan, in the richer, peninsular parts of India (Gujarat, Maharashtra and Tamil Nadu). Rohit Chandra, a bright, young academic, shows in his Harvard University PhD thesis that coal is both the source of livelihoods for millions and the locus of many communities[1] as well as an important source of fiscal revenues for many states. But coal is also the source of several development pathologies—corruption, crime, mafias, Maoist insurrection—captured in the term the 'resource curse'. (Economic Survey, 2016–17, vol. 1.) So, while the rise of renewables poses a threat to those livelihoods and communities, it may also afford an opportunity to escape from the attendant pathologies.

Monthly Per Capita Expenditure vs Per Capita Mineral Value

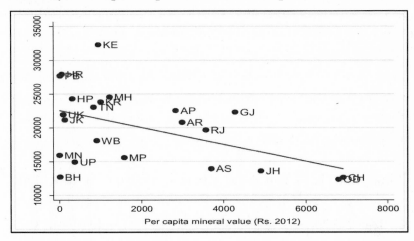

Ten Propositions in Brief

Let me summarize my talk in a few propositions, which I will elaborate on later. The overall theme and message can be captured in that famous remark made by St. Augustine: 'Lord . . . Grant me chastity and continence, but not yet.'

Proposition 1: Coal and renewables must be the joint focus of policy; they must be jointly decided, not separately.

Proposition 2: The social costs of coal should include its domestic externalities, but, at least for some time, not international externalities.

Proposition 3: Be abundantly cautious about claims on behalf of renewables. Properly costed, renewables will achieve true parity (in social terms) with coal only in the future.

Proposition 4: Beware of 'carbon imperialism' of advanced countries, which risks biasing our judgements about energy.

Proposition 5: Because coal is special, the social cost of renewables should include the costs of stranding thermal and coal assets.

Proposition 6: Current bids on renewables are not especially revealing or informative about the true costs of renewables because of extensive subsidies (implicit and overt) and strategic behaviour by renewables producers.

Proposition 7: There is a window, perhaps narrow, until renewables become truly viable, for accelerating the expansion of coal, and driving up capacity utilization sharply in thermal-power generation.

Proposition 8: Subsidizing renewables at a time when its social costs are above those of coal seems a double whammy for the government, which then also has to pick up the tab for the resulting stranded assets. (Not giving with one hand and taking with the other, but giving away with both hands.)

Proposition 9: This strategy will raise two dynamic implementation challenges, one on the political/social side, the other on the economic/financial side, which will need to be addressed.

Proposition 10: Rapid, organic growth in energy demand and technological progress in cleaning coal—for which there must be a collective international effort—will help minimize the tensions between coal and renewables.

Elaborating on the Propositions

Now allow me to elaborate on each of these propositions, some more than others.

Proposition 1: Coal and renewables have aspects of both substitutability and complementarity. In the future, renewable energy may substitute for coal-based thermal energy as a source of electricity but until the technology for energy storage improves dramatically, stable coal generation will complement (variable and volatile) renewable energy. Hence, coal and renewables must be the joint focus of policy; they must be jointly decided, not separately. And in some ways, by having a common minister for clean and 'dirty' energy—Piyush Goyal— we have institutionally recognized the Siamese-twins nature of the subject.

Proper Costing

Propositions 2 and 3 relate to the costing of renewables and coal, and here I specifically mean their true social costs. To these points, I will share some principles and then some tentative numbers.

Coal

For coal, the social costs must distinguish between domestic and international costs. The former include the negative impact on air pollution, and disease, water contamination, etc. These domestic costs must be added to the social costs of thermal generation. The most recent study[2] on India indicates that these costs are about Rs 0.34 per kWh or $5.4 per ton of CO_2 (total number converted into per unit number by dividing it by the total thermal-electricity generation). It is worth emphasizing that the social costs of thermal power may be overestimated to the extent that power will actually replace much worse forms of energy in large parts of India where households use kerosene and wood-fired stoves.

In principle, social costs also include international externality in the form of contributing to global warming. My view is that India would be entitled not to incorporate these costs in its domestic-policy calculations; only over time should India internalize, and progressively, the international marginal cost—the climate-change impact.

That is how I think equity in combating climate change should be addressed, how development and carbon space should be afforded to countries such as India by the advanced countries that have primarily and predominantly created the problem of climate change by occupying that space. If this is right, these international externalities would be small in magnitude for India—about $4 per ton or roughly Rs 0.14 per kWh (2017 prices)—according to the estimates in Nordhaus (2017).[3] Just for transparency, if India were to fully externalize the global externality, the comparable magnitudes would be $31 per ton or about Rs 2 per kWh.

On the other hand, there are other externalities related to coal which must be incorporated. One such externality is water, which is a scarce resource in India. For example, a 1000-MW coal-based power plant requires about 84 million litres a day.[4] Another is the displacement of people that occurs when a new coal mine is exploited.

Renewables

Turning to the costing of renewables, it is fair to say that the world has become enamoured of renewables, and for a lot of good reasons. Renewables offer the chance to strike at the problem of climate change decisively. As important, technological improvements in this area have been striking. There is a Moore's Law (stating simply that computer processing power doubles every two years) counterpart to Solar PV costs known as Swanson's Law, which states that Solar PV module cost falls by 20 per cent for every doubling in its capacity. These improvements are reflected in the dramatic decline in the price of photo-voltaic cells and in battery-storage costs. The holy grail here, of course, is that renewables achieve 'parity' with energy from fossil fuels.

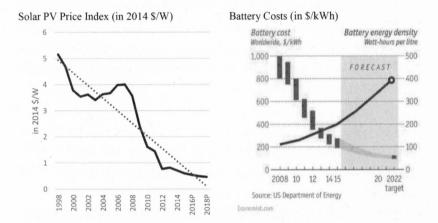

But I think there are also claims about renewables that one has to be wary of as Bill Gates said in the *Atlantic* in 2015.[5] As a country that is abundant in coal and where the political economy of coal and exiting gradually from it will be fiendishly difficult, a healthy scepticism about renewables would be in order.

Moreover, we must also consider that once capacity is created, the social costs of renewables—taking into account just variable costs—are almost zero, and hence considerably below the social variable costs of thermal power.

But we are concerned here with long-run decisions on solar power, which must account for investments already incurred in thermal power. Renewables, in this situation, must be properly costed:

- for intermittency—the fact that solar and wind are not available all the time—and storage costs;

- for the fact that greater solar capacity has to be installed to generate a unit of power equivalent to conventional sources; put differently, renewables have lower (equilibrium) capacity utilization;
- for land-acquisition costs, which could be high in India if political, regulatory costs are also included;[6]
- for the costs of building and upgrading grids to equip them for renewables;[7]
- so that all the hidden subsidies—and there are many of them[8]—are taken out.

One overlooked point is that while the price of PV panels has been plummeting—from about $3.50/watt in 2006 to $0.48 in 2017, they account for only a fraction of the total cost of solar energy.

Proper estimates of the full costs—not just levelized costs—of renewables are still elusive. But one thing is clear: recent prices bid at solar auctions in India are not a true reflection of the true cost, both because of the plethora of subsidies available and because there has been strategic underbidding in the reverse auctions as in the case of coal and telecommunications. (In fact, there is an important lesson here for renewables, namely, to avoid the experience of thermal power in creating excess capacity.)

But there are some useful pointers. Two recent papers offer some suggestive numbers that confirm that at least for India, true parity between coal and renewables is still a faraway reality.

One such reference is the updated paper by Charles Frank of the Brookings Institution (2016), who has a fuller analysis to take into account many of these costs for the US. His finding is that if emissions are valued at $50 per ton of CO_2, solar is marginally competitive, relative to thermal power. Recall that the social value of emissions in India is closer to $2.25 per ton, still far from the $50 suggested by the study. Recall too that India today has a tax ('cess') of Rs 400 per ton of coal, which is equivalent to about \$10 per ton of CO_2, still far from a state of true parity. And finally, recent market data (from the intercontinental exchange, or the ICE) suggests that the current global valuation of CO_2 emission is only about \$6.5 per ton.

Another paper by Gowrisankaran and others in 2017[9] is also instructive. Using the experience of Arizona, the authors calculate that solar achieves parity with coal if emissions are valued at \$139 per ton of CO_2 and if solar installation costs are \$1.5 per watt. This study used the data for 2011. Since then, solar costs must have declined but the broad relative assessment still holds.[10]

The other social cost of renewables relates to the energy form it will displace—coal. Given the current macroeconomic environment, with India afflicted by the TBS problem, any cost–benefit analysis of the impact of renewables must take into account the near-term impacts of the financial and economic costs of stranded assets in power and coal. And given the importance

Coal PLFs Distribution, No New RE and 100S-60W

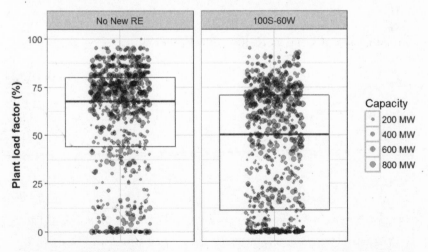

Source: GREENING THE GRID: Pathways to Integrate 175 Gigawatts of Renewable Energy into India's Electric Grid, Vol. I–National Study.

of coal from a regional and development perspective as discussed above, the social cost of renewables must include the social costs of affecting and dislocating communities that derive their livelihoods from coal.

Based on a study commissioned by the ministry of power, the chart below illustrates how much thermal generation might be displaced if the capacity of renewables rises sharply over time to reach 175 GW by 2022. For example, median plant-load factors decline from 63 per cent to about 50 per cent by 2022.

It is difficult to put precise numbers on the impact of declining PLFs, but they could be substantial. For example, the Economic Survey (Volume 2, 2017–18) estimates that the cost of stranded assets in power alone is Rs 0.7–0.8 per kWh. These numbers will surely rise if social costs are included.

Overall, the conclusion is that while there are considerable uncertainties about the social costs of renewables and power, we can make two judgements in increasing order of confidence. First, for India, today and at least for some time, the social costs of renewables are likely to be greater than thermal power. Second, today and at least for some time, it is highly unlikely for the converse to be true.

Social Costs of Coal vs Renewable Power Sources

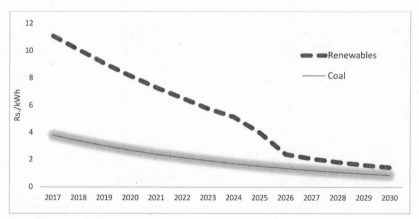

Carbon Imperialism

If coal is critical for India's energy needs, we must beware and resist what I have called 'carbon imperialism'. This terminology emanates from many sources and manifests itself in several forms. Not just G-7 countries, not just multilateral development banks but also bilateral agencies are targeting coal-based energy in poorer countries. The president of the World Bank, Jim Yong Kim, has said that new coal-fired plants would spell disaster for 'us and the planet'. I have discussed carbon imperialism in greater detail in Section 4.2 earlier.

Policy Implications

If the discussion above is reasonable, a few policy conclusions follow.

Implied Trajectory of Coal and Renewables

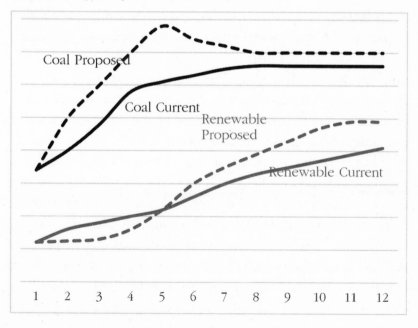

A plausible strategy going forward must be to accelerate coal and thermal in that window and then phase down thereafter sufficiently to provide at least the base load. The time we have before renewables become truly viable means that the reform of the coal sector and ramping up production and efficiency is vital.

The intuition mapped here is simple: maximize the use of national assets to the greatest extent possible and then gradually ramp up the use of free global assets—sunlight and wind—when it becomes advantageous to do so.

A corollary is to perhaps consider drastically reducing subsidies for renewables because it seems odd for the government to subsidize renewables while also picking up the tab for stranded assets in power and reduced coal consumption that will result from substitution of coal by renewables. The financial impact for the government arises from having to recapitalize the public-sector banks that have lent to power companies and from the reduced profitability of the coal industry. This seems to be an almost self-defeating ploy for the government to undertake at this time.

Advanced countries are seeing something similar, a perverse impact of the renewables revolution. As *The Economist* argued in an article (25 February 2017),[11] conventional power utilities face the threat of a 'death spiral' because their profitability declines from the scissors effect of falling demand and increasing renewables supply, some of it dictated by the 'must run' status of renewables because of their zero marginal cost.

However, this proposed strategy of subsidizing traditional utilities raises two challenges of dynamic implementation, one on the political/social side, the other on the economic/financial side, both of which will need to be addressed. On the former, the question is this: how do you ramp up coal in the short- to medium-term while simultaneously preparing for its phase-down beyond that? On the latter, how do you slow down renewables today while creating the right incentives for the private sector to prepare for its ramp-up later, when it achieves true parity?

Clearly, the first challenge will require careful planning to manage the gradual decreasing importance of coal, the impacts of which will be concentrated in a few areas geographically. But in some ways, virtue can be made of necessity and in the form of a credible threat. Analysis in the Economic Survey (2017–18) shows that coal and other natural resources do give rise to a form of natural 'resource curse' in India: Jharkhand, Chhattisgarh, Odisha, for example, have, on average, fared poorer than other states in terms of tax collection, institutional quality and size of manufacturing. Exiting from, or rather phasing down gradually, these resources is necessary for development. The long-term viability of renewables provides the credible threat to plan for this phase-down. At some point in the future, the incentives to use coal will diminish organically. Short of massive and indefinite support for coal—which will be inefficient domestically and counterproductive internationally—the sector will face existential threats.

Addressing the second implementation challenge will require some support for renewables even in the short run, if the sector is to be adequately prepared to take advantage of falling costs and become viable in the long run. There is also the argument that, because of learning-by-doing, costs themselves will be endogenous to the scale of operations and the financial and non-financial support given today.

So, a viable media is perhaps not to eliminate support for renewables today, but rather to reduce it from the high current levels with the aim of achieving the time path of coal and renewables shown in the figure on page 166.

Minimizing Tensions

In terms of dealing with current sustainability issues of the coal sector, rapid growth in demand and technological progress in cleaning coal will help minimize the tensions between coal and renewables.

A rapidly growing Indian economy—at close to double-digit—is the best guarantee of robust demand. But the move to electric cars offers another opportunity to shore up electricity demand in the long run.

On the second point. If India is committed to curbing climate change and to promoting renewables, making coal clean is vital to the country's development. However, this cannot be done by India, or anyone else, alone. Technologies that are already available, such as carbon capture and storage, have proved prohibitively expensive. To discover truly effective techniques, the world collectively needs to embark on a programme akin to the Manhattan Project that produced the first nuclear bomb. This would require investment from both public and private sectors, in advanced and developing nations, as well as a range of policy instruments. But the rich world's preoccupation with phasing out fossil fuels creates a risk that the private sector—already lukewarm about investing in cleaning coal—will read the signals and abandon this project altogether. Remember that even in the medium term, coal will provide the base load for power in India; for example, under India's Nationally Determined Contribution (NDC), fossil fuels will provide about 60 per cent of India's total power requirements. The time is ripe to create a global 'green and clean' coal coalition. That, rather than unconscionable calls to phase out India's cheapest form of energy, would best serve the cause of fighting climate change.

Concluding Observations

Rapid changes in technology are promising to help realize the promise of renewables. This is an eminently desirable development and one that India is attempting both to benefit from and accelerate. At the same time, these changes need to be seen in the context of India's current economic situation and its enormous endowments of coal, which is still a very cheap way of providing energy to hundreds of millions who are still energy deprived.

If there are a few key messages I would consider as a takeaway, they are the following: coal and renewables must be jointly decided because of their inter-connection—they are, in fact, Siamese twins. For example, declining prices of renewables is threatening to upend the thermal power sector, and as prices are renegotiated because power buyers—the DISCOMs—are themselves financially strapped, this threat will extend to the renewables themselves.

Second, India needs coal in the short–medium term; renewables are part of the energy answer but they also come with hidden costs, which must not be overlooked in our headlong embrace of renewables.

India cannot allow carbon imperialism to come in the way of rational, realistic planning for the future. On behalf and as an emissary, of coal, I want to say—both for policymaking and pointedly to TERI, and my reader—paraphrasing Rabindranath Tagore—'*Bhoola Na*' ('Don't forget or neglect me').

4.4*

Cooperative and Competitive Federalism to Further Reforms

The Case of the Power Sector

Along with the assistance of Rangeet Ghosh, Sutirtha Roy and Navneeraj Sharma, I presented a lecture at the Hindu Centre for Politics and Public Policy, which draws upon Chapter 11 on power in the Economic Survey of 2015–16 and our Sixteenth TERI Darbari Seth Memorial Lecture. The need for institutions such as the Hindu Centre for Politics and Public Policy in informing and guiding deliberation in the democratic policymaking process cannot be understated, as it has carved out a unique niche for itself in producing high-quality research on the burning public-policy issues of the day.

The topic of discussion was the challenges of reform in large federal polities such as India. This question assumes importance, and has particular salience, against the backdrop of the historic Goods and Services Tax, which despite the transitional challenges, is an extraordinary political achievement of reforms in a large and complex federal political structure such as India's. Bringing together the Centre, twenty-nine states and seven union territories, where all give up—or rather pool—their sovereignty is unprecedented. In fact, if one were to step back and see this against the resurgence of nativism and isolationism internationally—whether in the US, UK or Europe—the GST is a stark and salutary trend-defier.

But what can we learn from the GST experience for other sectors? The power sector offers an interesting case study. While it is a subject on the concurrent list, and while many decisions are taken by the state governments—for example, on power tariffs—there are important and rich interactions between the Centre and the states, both fiscally and politically. These interactions make the power sector an eminent candidate for harnessing cooperative and competitive federalism to further reforms in this sector. Why that is so and how it can be done was the subject of this talk.

Especially in the last few years, India has made great strides in boosting the physical infrastructure for power, comprising increases in generation and transmission capacity (Figures 1 and 2), which, in turn, have led to enormous improvements in people's access to power. Access to electricity has improved over time (Figure 3). Out of 18,452 un-electrified villages in April 2015, 14,885 have been electrified (80.5 per cent). Power for all under the Saubhagya scheme is a vital initiative to provide the basic amenity—of affordable and uninterrupted access to energy—to all Indian citizens. Since the industrial revolution, we have learnt that making life less 'dark' and less hot-and-cold are integral parts of escaping the Hobbesian State of Nature being 'nasty, brutish and short', according to which everyone has the right to liberty in order to act upon their lives in any manner to preserve it. Over the past few years, India's rank on the quality of power supplied (published as part of the Global Competitiveness Index by the World Economic Forum) has improved significantly (Figure 4). Energy shortages, including peak power shortages, have also declined (Figure 5).

Figure 1: Installed Capacity and Per Capita Consumption

Figure 2: Transmission Line Length

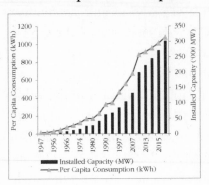

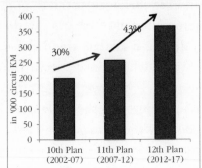

Figure 3: Electricity Access (per cent of population)

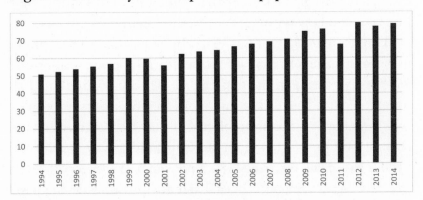

Figure 4: Quality of Electricity Supply

Figure 5: Energy and Peak Power Deficit (per cent)

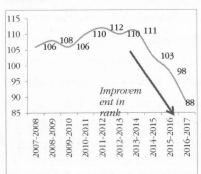

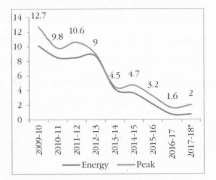

Sources: Ministry of Power, Central Electricity Authority (CEA), World Economic Forum and World Development Indicators (WDI).

More recently, the government, under the UDAY scheme, also launched a major initiative to address the perennial problem of financial losses in the electricity distribution companies— the DISCOMs. It is too early to say whether there have been substantial financial improvements over and above those resulting from the fact of replacing high-interest bank financing with much lower-interest government bonds (the initial numbers show that 65 per cent of the cost savings in UDAY are going to come from reduction in interest costs); and it is also too early to say whether the real reforms—in metering, in increasing tariffs—which are the real guarantor of durable success, have been effectively implemented.

What we can say is that, despite commendable ongoing efforts, the sector faces substantial challenges going forward, which makes it worthy of serious analysis.

Challenges: Macro Perspective

There are many challenges facing the power sector today, which I will go into detail about. But they can be summarized simply as: ensuring durable financial viability of the entire sector. In other words, as much emphasis has to be paid to financial and physical issues, as to reforming policies (to increase competition and choice), initiating schemes, correcting prices/costs and increasing quantities. Viability has to be achieved for the power-generating companies stuck with stranded assets in the aftermath of the GDP growth boom of the mid-2000s which are now facing competition from the renewables' sector, where technology is resulting in dramatically lower costs and prices. Viability—or a modicum of it—must also be achieved for the DISCOMs, many of which have seen a recurrence of the age-old problem of financial losses.

The sector continues to experience high transmission and distribution (T&D) losses (Figure 6 provides a cross-country comparison). Moreover, Aggregate Technical and Commercial

(AT&C) losses are around 22 per cent for 2015–16, which means that out of every 5 units of electricity produced, 1 unit of electricity 'leaks' or is not paid for. But it is difficult to precisely distinguish the losses arising from pure 'inefficiencies' on the part of distribution companies and those from political/social decisions to support poorer agents such as farmers and poor households.

Figure 6: Transmission and Distribution Losses (International Comparison)

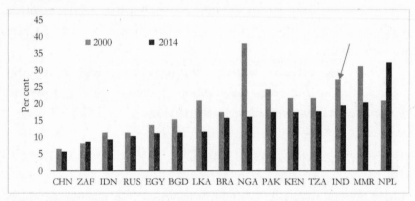

Source: From left to right, the countries are: China, South Africa, Indonesia, Russia, Egypt, Bangladesh, Sri Lanka, Brazil, Nigeria, Pakistan, Kenya, Tanzania, India, Myanmar and Nepal

Inefficiencies and helping the poor in turn necessitate cross-subsidization—charging much higher tariffs for industrial and commercial users—to salvage some of the lost financial viability. In turn, competitiveness of industry declines, undermining the 'Make in India' initiative. Indian industries continue to suffer the poor quality as well as higher electricity prices (not only relative to other consumer groups, viz., agriculture and households, also internationally). Figure 7 shows how India fares internationally in this regard. Back-of-the-envelope calculations suggest that some energy-intensive industries—textiles and chemicals—pay 25 per cent more on an average across states to produce a unit of their output, owing to elevated industrial tariffs.

Figure 7: International Comparison of Electricity Prices and Its Quality Supplied to Industry

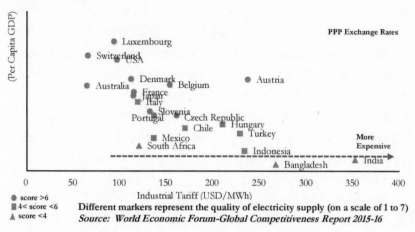

High prices of electricity, along with variable quality, has led towards creation of captive power generation (that is, when a medium-to-large industrial entity, say a steel plant, produces its own power) with consequences for costs. Figure 8 shows that the growth of captive generation since 2006–07 has been 9.2 per cent versus 3.7 per cent for electricity procured by industry from the utilities.

Figure 8: Acceleration in Growth of Captive Generation by Industry vis-à-vis Procurement from Utility

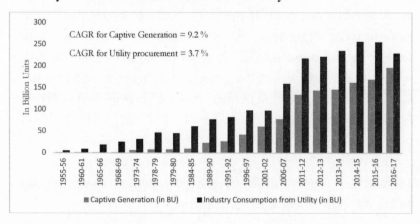

But even if financial viability and its collateral damage must now occupy centre stage, the question arises as to the role of the Centre and the attendant scope and need for cooperative federalism. After all, many of the issues in electricity are regulated by the states. The simple answer is that the Centre, as it has repeatedly discovered, is deeply implicated in the financial viability of the states. As we discussed previously, the power generators have borrowed heavily from the public-sector banks. Credit Suisse estimates that up to Rs 2.4 lakh crore of power generator debt that is under stress is owed to PSBs. It is the central government that has to pay for the attendant problems in the PSBs.

Similarly, the financial viability of the DISCOMs also affects the Centre both directly and indirectly. The DISCOMs too had borrowed tremendous amounts from the PSBs. In order to avoid a swelling of NPAs, their debts were taken over by state governments. In turn, state government finances affect the macroeconomic stability of the country, and state government bonds are seen to be implicitly guaranteed by the Centre. The Centre clearly has a critical role in ensuring the financial viability of the sector, which is the only manner in which the sector can fulfil its key aim of providing energy to all Indians.

Perhaps most importantly, the Centre has an enormous stake in ensuring that there is one market for power within India, which currently does not exist. If the GST has created one market, one tax, we must strive towards one market for power too. Power cannot be the cause of a Balkanized economic India, especially when the principal aim of the sector is to bring power and facilitate non-discriminated access to energy to everyone in the country.

Challenges: Specific Issues

In increasing order of difficulty, the following is a list of challenges facing the power sector in India today:

- bringing transparency and simplicity: 'One Market, One Price';
- addressing stress in power generation, including the challenge from renewables;
- reforming the fundamental structure of the power sector to increase competition and choice: 'One India, One Power Market'; and
- restoring long-term financial viability by making people pay for power, but equitably.

Bringing Transparency and Simplicity: 'One Market, One Price'

Figure 9 reproduces part of the 2016 tariff schedule for an Indian state. There are around ninety tariffs visible that vary by user, sector, type of activity and magnitude. In most markets we think of having one price for one product. Here we have multiple prices and in a manner that evokes the 'truth is stranger than fiction' dictum mentioned previously: separate tariffs for poultry and rabbit farms, for pisciculture, etc. But such multiplicity is a recipe for confusion, rent-seeking and various forms of distortions as it incentivizes consumers to game the tariff schedule and try to get themselves included in a lower tariff category.

What type of confusions may arise from complex tariff schedules? A recent survey (2017) conducted by the World Bank in Rajasthan provides some examples.

Noticing changes in electricity prices: Price awareness among residential consumers of electricity appears to be low in India. A recent World Bank survey in Rajasthan collected data on whether households noticed a change in price of electricity over a twelve-month recall period (during this period, the tariff schedule was known to be revised only once, in the month of September 2016).

Figure 9: Example of Complex Tariff Schedule

Consumer Category	Energy Charge (Rs /Unit)
LT-I:DOMESTIC (Telescopic)	
LT-I(A):Upto 50 Units/Month	1.45
LT I(B):>=50 and upto 100 Units/Month	
First 50 Units	1.45
51-100 Units	2.60
LT I(C):>100 and upto 200 Units/Month	
First 50	2.60
51-100	2.60
101-150	3.60
151-200	3.60
LT I(D):Above 20 0 Units/Month	
First 50	2.60
51-100	3.25
101-150	4.88
151-200	5.63
201-250	6.70
251-300	7.22
301-400	7.75
401-500	8.27
Above 500	8.80
LT-II:NON DOMESTIC/COMMERCIAL	
LT II(A):Upto 50 Units/Month	5.40
LT II(B):Above 50 Units/Month	
First 50	6.63
51-100	7.38
101-300	8.54
301-500	9.06
Above 500	9.59
LT-II(C):ADVERTISEMENT HOARDINGS	11.58
LT-III:INDUSTRY	
Industry (General)	6.38
Seasonal Industries (off season)	7.09
Pisciculture/Prawn culture	4.63
Sugarcane crushing	4.63
Poultry farms	5.63
Mushroom & Rabbit Farms	5.63
Floriculture in Green House	5.63
LT-IV:COTTAGE INDUSTRIES & OTHERS	
a) Cottage Industries upto 10 HP	3.75
b) Agro Based Activity upto 10 HP	3.75

Consumer Category	Energy Charge (Rs /Unit)
LT-V:AGRICULTURE **	
LT-V(A):AGRICULTURE WITH DSM	
Corporate Farmers & IT Assesses	2.50
Wet Land Farmers (Holdings >2.5 acre)	0.50
Dry Land Farmers (Connections > 3 nos.)	0.50
Wet Land Farmers (Holdings ≤ 2.5 acre)	0.00
Dry Land Farmers (Connections ≤ 3 nos.)	0.00
LT-V(B):AGRICULTURE WITHOUT DSM MEASURES	
Corporate Farmers & IT Assesses	3.50
Wet Land Farmers (Holdings >2.5 acre)	1.00
Dry Land Farmers (Connections > 3 nos.)	1.00
Wet Land Farmers (Holdings ≤ 2.5 acre)	0.50
Dry Land Farmers (Connections ≤ 3 nos.)	0.50
LT-V(C):OTHERS	
Salt farming units upto 15HP	3.70
Rural Horticulture Nurseries upto 15HP	3.70
LT-VI:STREET LIGHTING AND PWS	
LT-VI(A):STREET LIGHTING	
Panchayats	5.64
Municipalities	6.16
Municipal Corporations	6.69
LT-VI(B):PWS SCHEMES	
Panchayats	4.59
Municipalities	5.64
Municipal Corporations	6.16
LT-VI(C):NTR Sujala Padhakam	4.00
LT-VII:GENERAL	
LT-VII(A):GENERAL PURPOSE	6.86
LT-VII(B):RELIGIOUS PLACES (CL ≤ 2 KW)	4.70
LT-VIII: TEMPORARY SUPPLY	9.90
HT-I:INDUSTRY	
HT-I(A): INDUSTRY GENERAL	
11 kV	6.02
33 kV	5.57
132 kV & Above	5.15
INDUSTRIAL COLONIES	
11 kV	5.96
33 kV	5.96
132 kV & Above	5.96

Consumer Category	Energy Charge (Rs /Unit)
SEASONAL INDUSTRIES (off season Tariff)	
11 kV	7.25
33 kV	6.59
132 kV & Above	6.33
TIME OF DAY TARIFFS (6 PM to 10 PM)	
11 kV	7.07
33 kV	6.62
132 kV & Above	6.20
HT-I(B):FERRO ALLOY UNITS	
11 kV	5.68
33 kV	5.23
132 kV & Above	4.81
HT-II:OTHERS	
11 kV	7.25
33 kV	6.59
132 kV & Above	6.33
TIME OF DAY TARIFFS (6 PM to 10 PM)	
11 kV	8.30
33 kV	7.64
132 kV & Above	7.38
HT-III:AIRPORTS,BUS STATIONS AND RAILWAY	
11 kV	6.91
33 kV	6.31
132 kV & Above	6.01
TIME OF DAY TARIFFS (6 PM to 10 PM)	
11 kV	7.96
33 kV	7.36
132 kV & Above	7.06
HT-IV: Govt., LIFT IRRIGATION, AGRICULTURE	
Govt. Lift Irrigation & Agriculture	5.64
Composite Water Supply Schemes	4.61
HT-V:RAILWAY TRACTION	6.68
HT-VI:TOWNSHIPS AND RESIDENTIAL COLONIES	5.96
HT-VII:GREEN POWER	11.32
HT-VIII:TEMPORARY	
RURAL ELECTRIC CO-OPERATIVES	
Kuppam	0.24
Anakapally	1.38
Chipurupally	0.22

The proportion of households that reported to have noticed a change in price over the twelve-month period was just 37 per cent in urban areas and even less, at about 25 per cent, for rural areas (in Alwar and Jaipur). Furthermore, of the households that did notice a change in the prices of electricity, only 1.5 per cent correctly reported the month of price change to be September 2016.

Awareness of different charges and discounts available in the tariff schedule: The following table shows a typical household's understanding of various prices and incentives available in the tariff schedules.

Table 1: Household Awareness of Aspects of Power Tariffs

		Alwar		Jaipur	
Household awareness of		Rural	Urban	Rural	Urban
Application of fixed charges in the bill	Not aware	20%	18%	11%	9%
	Yes, aware	46%	61%	67%	64%
	Don't know/ Can't say	33%	21%	22%	28%
Slab-wise rates of electricity	Yes, aware	25%	47%	51%	62%
Discounts available for BPL card ownership	Yes, aware	32%	36%	60%	64%
Discounts available for rural areas	Yes, aware	31%	49%	48%	66%
Discounts available for solar panels/heaters	Yes, aware	7%	33%	12%	29%
Discounts available for installing prepaid meters	Yes, aware	4%	21%	5%	20%
Discounts available for paying bill before due date	Yes, aware	7%	16%	6%	24%

Source: World Bank.

The table indicates that most of the complex charges and incentives introduced by the regulators and the DISCOMs are not perceptible to the final user. These non-salient and complex tariff policies can therefore prevent consumers from responding to price signals. As shown in Chetty, Looney and Kroft's paper 2009,[1] if consumers are not able to understand complex price schedules, they don't respond to price signals, which makes changing behaviour difficult, which in India's power sector can be corrected by creating a simpler and intuitive tariff schedule.

Addressing Stress in Power Generation, including the Challenge from Renewables

In the power sector, a number of significant developments are affecting the short- and medium-term outlook. As shown in Figure 10, the price of renewables has been declining significantly. This is a positive, long-run development for India and the global effort to combat climate change. But it will pose a number of short-term challenges as well (discussed above in Section 4.3).

Figure 10: Fall in Solar Electricity Prices in Auctions

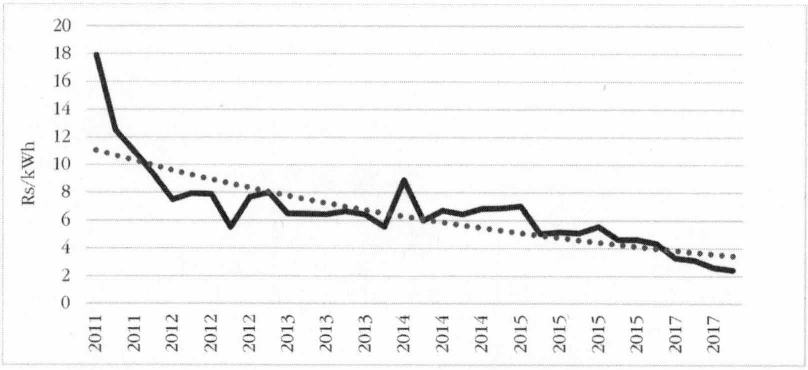

The bold line denotes actual prices while the dotted line denotes the underlying trend.

Figure 11 shows the increase in power-generation capacity (mostly in the private sector and that too mostly in the form of long-term power purchase agreements [PPAs] between generators and DISCOMs). Renewables becoming cheaper is only going to exacerbate the situation already made worse because of DISCOMs remaining under financial stress and the excess capacity created during the mid-2000s' boom. At present, there is reduced demand for private-sector thermal power. As a result, plant load factors have declined steadily, currently averaging around 60 per cent.

This implies that in the current distribution of plant capacity, a number of plants are operating at well below viable levels of capacity utilization. If a rough benchmark for the plant load factor of 60 per cent and above is deemed viable, then Figure 13 shows that nearly 50 per cent of current capacity is unviable. Reflecting this, Credit Suisse estimates that the proportion of companies in the power sector with an interest-coverage ratio of less than 1, referring to the ability to generate enough earnings to cover interest payments (a ratio of 2 is necessary for an investment grade rating), is still high at 50 per cent, with an associated vulnerable debt of over Rs 2.4 lakh crore (Figure 12).

Figure 11: Thermal Generation Capacity and Plant Load Factors (PLF)

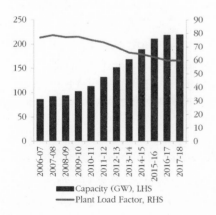

Capacity (GW), LHS
Plant Load Factor, RHS

Figure 12: Share of Debt with IC<1 and Total Stressed Debt in Power Sector

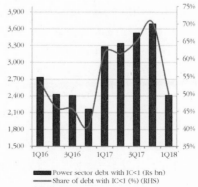

Power sector debt with IC<1 (Rs bn)
Share of debt with IC<1 (%) (RHS)

Figure 13: Unviable Private Sector Thermal Capacity at Different Plant Load Factors (PLF)

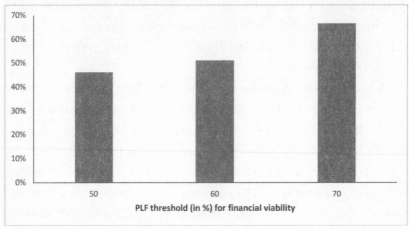

PLF threshold (in %) for financial viability

Source: CEA and Credit-Suisse.

It is fair to say that the world sees the future in renewables due to many valid reasons. It is a decisive strike against climate change. Technological improvements in this area have been equally striking. As mentioned in the previous chapter, there is a Moore's Law counterpart to Solar PV costs known as Swanson's Law, which states that Solar PV module cost falls by 20 per cent for every doubling in its capacity. These improvements have been reflected in the dramatic decline in the price of photo-voltaic cells and in battery-storage costs.

However, India has abundant coal resources and the political economy of exiting from it will be very complicated. Therefore, the issue of adoption of renewables in India is a tricky one (discussed earlier in Section 4.3).

Reforming the Fundamental Structure of Power Sector to Increase Competition and Choice: 'One Country, One Power Market'

The power sector has undergone significant changes at generation, distribution and transmission levels. The Electricity Act of

2003 was a landmark piece of legislation that envisaged more competition and choice, including via open access. Moreover, there are efforts afoot to increase competition at the retail level. Amendments to the Electricity Act of 2003 envisage opening up the retail-electricity sector to multiple players, including those from the private sector to introduce competition at the last mile of the value chain.

But it is worth understanding all the restrictions to choice that characterize the power sector at present.

The most egregious restriction, in our view, is that India is still not one market for power but instead a composite of multiple, fragmented markets. The evolution in the power market design has not kept pace with the transmission and generation capacity addition. The tenure and structure of contracts available to the generators still stay very limited. This alone is grounds for central government intervention. Figure 14 shows the cross-subsidy charges imposed by the various states on purchases of power from the power exchanges, which, in principle, is supplied by generators from all other Indian states.

The price of electricity for the industry turns out to be higher than the basic tariff chargeable to the industry. The reason they exist is simple: it is a form of protectionism practised by the states to sustain the basic tariff structure and cross-subsidization within them as well as to sustain the other inefficiencies of the DISCOMs. If firms or others were allowed to make purchases from other states, the DISCOMs will find it difficult to sustain the high tariffs imposed on industry, which itself results from the compulsion to charge lower rates for power in agriculture and households. Allowing purchases from the exchange would have a large effect on the revenue of the DISCOMs already suffering from a weak consumer base.

Similarly, there is a lack of choice in the wholesale markets. Until recently, much of the purchase of power in the exchanges emanated from industrial users. Recently, however, the share

Figure 14: CSS* + AS** Imposed by States for Purchasing Electricity from Power Exchanges

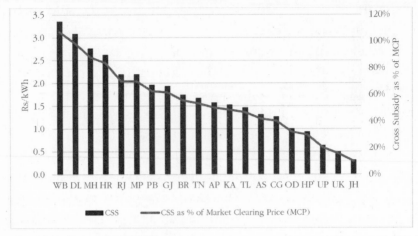

*Cross Subisdy Surcharge **Additional Surcharge

of DISCOMs in purchases from the power exchanges has been increasing while that from industrial users has been declining (Figure 15). The reasons are twofold: faced with their own financial problems, DISCOMs are choosing to buy cheaper power from the exchanges (which is linked to the cost of renewables) than from their suppliers under existing PPAs. In some cases, they are even reneging on their PPAs (which are typically of long duration and high cost relative to the spot market, or the cash market where immediate transactions take place).

Restoring Long-term Financial Viability by Making People Pay for Power but Equitably

Of course, at the heart of the financial viability issues in the power sector, for decades, has been the inability of state governments to make people pay market prices for power. In the past, there used to be a chicken-and-egg problem: consumers, even if willing to pay for power, wanted reliable power, and in its absence, were unwilling to

Figure 15: Share of Electricity Purchases on Power Exchanges (PXs)

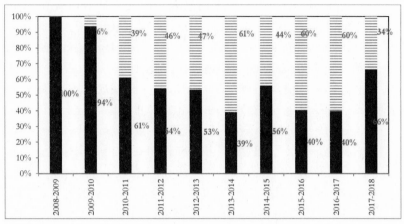

Open access share is on top (horizontal lines); DISCOMs purchase share is below (dark).

pay for it; the inability then to charge for power led to low or zero tariffs for a vast bulk of the population, and high tariffs for industry, which hurt the competitiveness of Indian manufacturing.

Under the UDAY scheme, state governments are required to raise and rationalize tariffs and to put in place the metering system that will allow for transition to a system in which consumers pay for power.

Solutions

How can these challenges in the power sector be tackled in order to ensure durable financial viability of the entire sector? Here are some points to consider:

Transparency

First of all, tariff schedules need to be drastically simplified. The ministry of power has made a commendable effort in starting this process of getting regulators together to convey this message. This is relatively easy but extremely important. State regulators must be instructed—and state governments must come on board—that there should be no more than, say, five rates in every tariff schedule. We are discovering even in the context of implementation of the GST that unnecessary complexity is costly.

But there are more areas where transparency must be improved. For example, the magnitude of subsidies received by the renewables sector—from the Centre and states, by direct and indirect means, on- and off-balance sheet—is a black box. Unless we estimate these subsidies, it is very difficult to make considered assessments about the costs and benefits of coal and renewables, and hence, on the broader policy approach to these sources of power.

Despite best efforts under UDAY, it is still quite difficult to derive information on tariff increases by the states and DISCOMs. DISCOMs publish financial data with a three-year lag. To address this issue, the accounting practices and reporting requirements of DISCOMs need to be rationalized to equip policymaking with more timely and reliable inputs.

The ministry of power has taken several steps to make data on different indicators of the power sector available to the public. With the increasing penetration of renewables, load dispatchers need to publicly share the transmission line utilization data, how often they are congested and what direction power is flowing in as this helps the distribution and generation companies plan more effectively. Proliferation of apps and websites notwithstanding, perhaps there is a need to consolidate the data in one master website, available in easily usable formats.

Stresses and Coal versus Renewables

As DISCOMs realize that there are cheaper, alternative sources of power than those that can be availed as per their current PPAs with generators, there will be a growing rush to renegotiate tariffs downwards. Nascent signs are evident already as states like Uttar Pradesh and Rajasthan have announced that they will renege on their existing contracts. The Supreme Court's recent rulings that contracts are sacrosanct will further complicate matters. Apart from the fact that India does not quite have a workable framework for contract renegotiations, the future workouts should be done in a manner so as not to render more capacity unviable and more debt unsustainable.

Moreover, stressed assets in the power sector need urgent attention. But there is also a need for a fundamental relook at PPP contracts. These are, by their very nature, incomplete contracts. While preserving the sanctity of contracts is important, it is unreasonable to expect DISCOMs—or any other government agency—to buy power at Rs 5–6 per kWh when the price of alternative power is a fraction of that. There must be a mechanism to inject some reasonable pragmatism into this. After all, there is considerable international evidence showing that PPP projects do get renegotiated.

So a major difficulty is the lack of clear and workable processes for renegotiating contracts. Rather than adopting a stance that rules out renegotiations, designing negotiating mechanisms with ex ante triggers and clear guidelines on how they will be settled might be necessary. To this end, and in line with the recent Kelkar Committee recommendations, there is a need to examine this issue in all its new dimensions.

Consider next the challenge from renewables. Based on a study commissioned by the ministry of power, if the capacity of renewables rises sharply over time to reach 175 GW by 2022, the median plant load factors in thermal generation may decline from 63 per cent to about 50 per cent by 2022. This is the challenge that the emergence of cheap renewable sources of power poses in that it could lead to a significant surge in stranded assets in the power sector with adverse consequences for the banking system and the government's finances.

The Economic Survey of 2016–17 (Volume 2) estimates that the cost of stranded assets in the power sector alone is Rs 0.7–0.8 per kWh (Figure 16). These numbers will rise if the social costs are included. There are considerable uncertainties about the social costs of renewables and power, but two judgements can be made in increasing order of confidence. First, for India, today and at least for some time to come, the social costs of renewables are likely to exceed that of thermal power. Second, today and at least for some time, it is highly unlikely for the converse to be true.

On the coal and renewables issue, our sense is that a plausible strategy going forward must be to accelerate the use of coal and thermal power within the next ten years (Figure 17), after which renewables become operationally and financially—and truly— viable. At that point, thermal power can be phased down to provide base load power. So, in the short run, the aim must be to increase PLFs in thermal plants to between 75–80 per cent so that they are viable.

Figure 16: Social Cost Comparisons

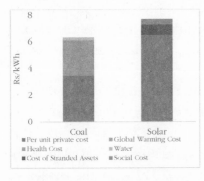

Figure 17: Suggested Future Path for Renewables and Coal

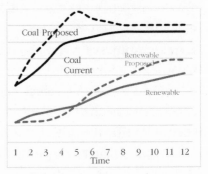

A corollary of the above is to perhaps reduce subsidies for renewables. This is because it seems odd for the government to subsidize renewables on the one hand and then also pick up the tab for the stranded assets in power and reduced coal consumption that result from these subsidies. The financial impact for the government arises from having to recapitalize the public-sector banks that have lent to power companies and to the reduced profitability of the coal industry.

Competition and Choice

It is a travesty that India is not a single market for power. To begin to actualize this vision, we need to increase choices for all stakeholders in the power sector. However, increased choices for consumers and hence competition at the retail end is essential, but this must be supported by competition upstream as well.

Increasing Choices for Industry and Power Exchanges (PXs)

First and foremost, we must rationalize, and even aim to eliminate, the cross-subsidy surcharge to promote open access and choice. The cross-subsidy surcharge sustains competitive populism or uncompetitive federalism. How? It allows a state government to not have to pay the consequences of being populist and providing free power; the cross-subsidy allows the state to make up for the loss in revenue from poorer segments by charging a higher price to other segments. Open access would not allow the latter. The threat of losing industrial consumers under an open access regime will also incentivize DISCOMs to ramp up efficiency.

We must also provide industry and the power exchanges the authority to negotiate contracts which suit their needs and are of longer duration than the day ahead market (DAM) for electricity available on power exchanges.

Increasing Choices for DISCOMs

It is increasingly untenable—in a world of rapidly declining costs—to insist that DISCOMs negotiate very long-term PPAs. They must be helped and encouraged to enter into more flexible PPAs of shorter durations so that they have the flexibility and room to do viable financial planning.

If industry buys more of its power from the exchanges and turns to the DISCOMs only to satisfy unmet needs, it does impose uncertainty on the DISCOMs. Therefore, they must be allowed to charge a reasonable risk premium on the industry for the uncertainty they face in their demand management; at the same time, it has to be ensured that the DISCOMs have an incentive to optimize their portfolio and not pass on their inefficiencies to industrial consumers.

Finally, electricity should be brought under the ambit of the GST, as proposed in an earlier chapter. This will allow the embedded taxes on manufacturing to be reduced, which will, in turn, help the sector's competitiveness.

Paying for Power and Direct Benefit Transfers

The Achilles heel of the Indian power sector and the perennially parlous state of the DISCOMs is, of course, the inability to charge for power from all segments of society. But there is some potential great news here, along with long-run implications. The good news is that since the cost of power—thanks in part to the renewables revolution—is declining precipitously, it must be less difficult to charge users for power. The experience of the telecoms sector is instructive. India solved the problem of phone connectivity in large part due to a technological revolution that both decreased costs of communication dramatically and at the same time rendered redundant monopolistic and centralized ways of delivering telecommunications services.

In the case of power, the cost reduction is happening, although the same impetus towards decentralized provisions is still not present. Politically too, it is more motivating to charge people Re 1 per kWh than Rs 4 per kWh. Of course, the transitional challenges of creating viable power generation must be addressed but reasonable prices for consumers, along with financial viability of the DISCOM sector, is perhaps less elusive.

At the same time, direct benefits transfer, in lieu of the power subsidy, offers hope. The exact architecture of the DBT needs to be worked out in consultation with stakeholders after pilots are conducted and the appropriate lessons drawn.

Our sense is also that there is much greater scope for making tariffs more progressive even within consumer categories. For example, in the Economic Survey 2015–16 (Chapter 11),[2] we found that the ratio of highest to lowest tariffs for consumers is lower in India (Table 2) than in other emerging market categories. There is also some evidence that the poorest households—for various reasons—spend more of their budget on electricity than richer households.

Table 2: Progressivity of Tariff (International Comparison)

Country Name	Ratio (Highest Category to Lowest Category Tariff)	ABR (for 30 units in US Cent/kWh)
Bangladesh	1.9	4.5
Representative Indian State	1.2	4.8
Sri Lanka	4.2	4.2
Korea	5.3	7.1
Vietnam	1.7	7.0
Brazil	2.9	6.4

Source: Economic Survey 2015–16, Chapter 11.

Strengthening Regulatory Capacity

Last but not the least, tackling these challenges will require regulators in each state to be ahead of the curve, not only in terms of being aware of the issues that plague the sector—which they already are to a significant extent—but also in terms of the technical expertise needed to diagnose and solve problems. Regulators in a few states have already seen value in state-of-the-art technical analysis to study some of the challenges highlighted above and this experience can move to other states in the spirit of cooperative, or perhaps competitive, federalism, sooner rather than later. The quality of regulation supported by improvements in institutional capacity will be critical.

Cooperative and Competitive Federalism as a Technology for Reform

Considerable progress has been made in providing greater energy access to Indian households and in increasing power generation and transmission capacity. However, considerable challenges still lie ahead, which require a unifying vision of reform; to reiterate: ensuring durable financial viability of the entire sector.

But in democratic politics, the *how* of policy change is an equally important question. As discussed earlier, even though many of the issues in power fall within the scope of state government policy and regulation, there is both a stake for and ability of the Centre to pursue reform in a cooperative federalism framework; in some cases, there is need to prevent uncompetitive federalism.

The Centre can deploy both sticks and carrots as it did under the UDAY initiative to nudge states into reform. By insisting on one market ('stick'), it can nudge states away from competitive populism; by providing a forum for regulators, it can build capacity and opportunities for mutual learning; by providing a political forum, it can foster policies in the collective interest (for example, bringing electricity into the scope of the GST); and by highlighting and rewarding best practices, it can incentivize competitive reform.

What the Centre did for the GST in creating the GST Council can be done for the power sector as well. For example, the prime minister envisaged the raison d'être of the Niti Aayog—in contrast to that of its predecessor, the Planning Commission—as a forum for fostering cooperative and competitive federalism.

Indeed, the Niti Aayog can become to all development issues in which the Centre and the states have an important stake— power, direct benefit transfers, e-NAM, water sharing, etc.— what the GST Council is now to domestic indirect taxes. In the virulent spread of cooperative and competitive federalism, with the experience of the GST as the harbinger, lies India's future.

Chapter 5

Agriculture

5.0

Agriculture, Agricultures, 'Terminal Values of Livestock'

Agriculture is critical for India in so many ways, not least in its ability to hold the entire economy back via inflation, agrarian distress and political restiveness, as well as the policy responses necessary to address them. In the last four years, agriculture has played a prominent role in shaping both Indian economics and politics. The first two years of the NDA government were marked by droughts and the following two years by reasonably good monsoons. Yet—and this is one of the unanswered, recent puzzles of Indian economics—under both conditions of scarcity and surplus, farmers' fortunes remained mediocre.

Agricultural incomes—outside of the cereal sector—have been stagnant regardless of the monsoon and agricultural production. Typically, of course, good monsoons should correlate positively with farmer incomes but they have not, especially from 2016 onwards. What we have seen instead is good agricultural production resulting in such sharp declines in farm prices that farm incomes have not been boosted. An interesting research question to pursue is whether demonetization has affected the rural cash economy in a manner that has structurally reduced the demand for farm products.

There is so much to be written on Indian agriculture and even though each of the economic surveys during my tenure contained full analytical chapters on agriculture, I feel I've barely scratched the surface. The first piece in this section—a speech I delivered to the National Academy of Agricultural Sciences— is my big-picture take on Indian agriculture. I argue that India has two agricultures—a pampered cereal sector and a neglected non-cereal sector that includes pulses, dairy and livestock. They merit very different policy approaches, which are elaborated in the section.

Regarding one of the non-cereal crops, namely, pulses, I had written an official report on ways of boosting production. That report encouraged me to think more about the use of transparency and better analytics in pushing reforms forward— and how specifically the Commission on Agricultural Costs and Prices (CACP) could incorporate the social costs and benefits of growing different crops in achieving better agricultural and environmental outcomes (Section 5.2).

Another non-cereal sector merited attention during the last four years because of the series of socially and religiously motivated actions—related to the vigilantist implementation of the beef ban—that affected the livestock sector. Sticking to the dictum that 'politics was above my pay grade', I did not express any public views on these actions but did want to draw attention to their economic consequences. (Actually, on one public occasion I was asked about the beef ban and joked that if I responded I would lose my job. That statement made it to the front page of the *Indian Express* and did not earn me any brownie points.) In a piece of verbal circumlocution, I hinted that their effect would be to reduce the 'terminal values of livestock as assets'.

In simpler terms, reducing the terminal values of livestock as assets means that bans on internal trading and exports of livestock would not only reduce the income from such activity directly, but also indirectly, because additional costs would have to be incurred from having to maintain unproductive livestock. They could also affect social returns. Stray cattle, and a lot of it, will have to be looked after; otherwise, diseases (foot and mouth) could spread, leading to health hazards. All of this would mean a smaller dairy and livestock sector with serious consequences for livelihoods.

Having immersed myself in the minutiae of agricultural policy, I am increasingly convinced that direct benefit transfers—even a quasi-universal basic income—has to be the future of farmer-income policy. The last piece in this section shows how a few states are making tremendous progress in this regard, but also how much more needs to be done.

As I wrote in the introduction, one of my disappointments and failures regarding the agricultural sector is the limited progress on fertilizer policy. I often joke that India is one country where the fertilizer sector is actually a macroeconomic issue because of the size of the fertilizer subsidy (about 0.6 per cent of GDP). In addition to its many costs, it is also one of the most complex interventions because it distorts consumption, production and trade, all at the same time, and the subsidies given to domestic firms are perverse because the more inefficient they are, the greater the subsidy they receive. Instead of closing down about one-third of existing urea plants which are irretrievably unviable, we have been attempting to rehabilitate moribund, inefficient ones in the public sector. Only an Indian interventionist mind of the feverishly imaginative variety with skills finely honed in the licence–permit–control raj could have willed the fertilizer subsidy policy with all its variations over time into reality.

There are many holy cows of untouchable policies in India and the fertilizer subsidy appears to be one of them, despite the overwhelming evidence against its damaging effects. The UPA-2 government started reducing the subsidy for petroleum products (petrol and diesel) through the astute means of small-but-frequent changes which lessened the psychological impact on the consumer and hence made it more acceptable. But that government did not dare to try the same reform for the fertilizer subsidy. Alas, pigs will sooner fly, and kaliyuga more likely to end, before the fertilizer subsidy is eliminated and replaced by more direct support.

In the first few months of my tenure, I joined an outstanding IAS officer Jugal Mahapatra, who was then the fertilizer secretary, in an effort to eliminate one of the many distortions in this sector. 'Canalization'—another relic of the license–permit–quota raj—involves an oligopoly on imports of urea, one of the most important and most highly subsidized fertilizers. Only three companies (two of them in the public sector, with chequered records) are allowed to import urea. Jugal and I were trying to make the simple case that imports of urea should be freed up to allow more companies to import urea and increase competition in the market and thereby reduce corruption and inefficiency, all of which would help farmers.

But in the bizarre world of controls and distortions, once some distortions are taken as a given, follow-up distortions such as oligopolies can seem normal. Even after Jugal's departure, my team and I worked for three years trying to marshal more facts and evidence to secure de-canalization. Four secretaries, one Cabinet secretary and one minister were all immune to my schmoozing skills, and de-canalization proved impossible to achieve. As a policy wonk-cum-persuader, I continue to wonder what more we could have done to move the needle.

One of the small consolations is that the complexity of the fertilizer subsidy makes it a great case study. Another consolation: one of my young colleagues, Siddharth Ravinutala, who worked with me on this issue, won the best thesis prize at Harvard's Kennedy School of Government for his work on the fertilizer situation in India. Convincing Harvard professors is evidently less 'hard work' compared to persuading Indian policymakers!

Transforming Indian Agriculture

By Loving Some Agriculture Less
and the Rest More[1]

It was an honour to deliver the Foundation Day Lecture at the National Academy of Agricultural Sciences (NAAS) on 5 June 2017 which was also, appropriately, World Environment Day. The topic I chose did not need any justification either in terms of its contemporary or historical importance: the government has made doubling farm incomes one of its top policy priorities. To this end, it has taken a number of important policy actions to boost agriculture: instituting soil-health cards, emphasizing efficient irrigation, strengthening government procurement of pulses, introducing neem-coating of urea, building more assets under MGNREGS, expanding crop insurance for farmers and building a common agricultural e-market via e-NAM (National Agriculture Market).

The historical salience derives from the fact that this was the hundredth anniversary of the Champaran movement of 1917, or the first satyagraha organized by Mahatma Gandhi during the British Raj. The first salvo of satyagraha was fired by the Father of our Nation on behalf of farmers—indigo farmers oppressed and exploited by colonial rule. Perhaps, as a result, the farmer has acquired a mythic status in Indian legend: pure, unsullied, hard-working, in harmony with nature and yet poor, vulnerable and a victim, first of the imperial masters and then of indigenous landlords and middlemen. Bollywood (and Kollywood and Tollywood) has, of course, played a key role in creating and reinforcing the mythology of the Indian farmer (I have in mind movies such as *Mother India*, *Do Bigha Zamin*, *Upkaar* and more recently, *Peepli Live* and even *Lagaan*).

To support and protect the farmer is also a professed ideology and mantra of politicians of all stripes and all times, reflected, for example, in the periodic granting of loan waivers and the perennial lure of announcing free power.

But the question I want to pose is this: has this mythological status actually come in the way of really being good to the farmer?

Why Agriculture Matters: An Irony

The reasons that agriculture matters are well known: it provides sustenance and employment to so many and food to all. In addition to these intrinsic positive reasons to invest in agriculture, there are other instrumental reasons: poor agricultural performance can lead to inflation, political and social disaffection and restiveness—all of which can hold back the economy. Thus, there are intrinsic as well as instrumental reasons for prioritizing agriculture.

But we must be clear and honest about one important link. The Nobel Prize winner Sir Arthur Lewis showed that economic development is always and everywhere about getting people out of agriculture, and of agriculture becoming, over time, a less important part of the economy (not in absolute terms but as a share of GDP). But this must happen along with rapid productivity growth, ensuring rising farm incomes and adequate food supplies for the people. The reason why agriculture cannot be the dominant source of livelihood is that levels of productivity and hence living standards can never approach—and have historically never approached—those in manufacturing and services. That, of course, means that we must get our industrialization and urbanization right for the alternatives to agriculture to become meaningful and prosperous.

When Dr Ambedkar famously derided the village as 'a sink of localism, a den of ignorance, narrow mindedness and communalism', he was perhaps on to a deeper truth—an Indian social complement to the Lewisian economic insight—that in the long run, people need to move and be moved out of agriculture. Dr Ambedkar was warning about the patronization of agriculture masquerading as a romanticization of rural India.

So the irony is this: we must care deeply about farmers and agriculture today because we want fewer but more productive and prosperous farms and farmers tomorrow.

In other words, all good and successful development is about facilitating this transition in the context of a prosperous agriculture and of rising productivity in agriculture, not least because that will facilitate good urbanization and rising productivity in other sectors of the economy.

I would like to nudge us all into collective self-reflection on the state of agriculture and its future. It is easy for me, or for anyone, to list ten or twenty different things that need to be done to improve our agricultural performance: stem the deterioration in agricultural research, educational and extension institutions, improve resilience, incentivize drip irrigation, etc. But it is as easy to list them as it is perhaps useless. Because for any improvement or reform that all the experts recommend, we have to ask the simple question: 'If that is so obviously good for agriculture, why hasn't it happened already?' Or, put differently, 'What is it about today that will make these proposals successful when they have demonstratively failed to persuade in the past?'

Rather, I want to ask a question or tentatively pose a hypothesis: is it possible that we actually love some crops (cereals) and their farmers too much and—for all the pious professions and mythologizing—other crops and their farmers not enough? To put it more bluntly, perhaps we are now smothering cereals with too much government support, and other crops—pulses, dairy, oilseeds, livestock, and fruits and vegetables—not enough?

The Successes

Before I elaborate on the main themes of my argument any further, I would like to take stock of our achievements and shortcomings in agriculture. Given where we began in 1947, Indian agriculture has come a long way. We have achieved food security (at least on the major crops), rural poverty rates have declined substantially, agricultural incomes have risen and nutrition levels have also risen.

In terms of successes, I would highlight the following:

The green revolution transformed Indian agriculture by increasing yields of wheat and rice, especially in northern and then in southern India. Credit here goes to international research but perhaps even more so to Indian scientists, agronomists, researchers and extension workers in public institutions that completed the links from technology to actual farm output.

The white revolution transformed the Indian dairy sector, increasing milk production, reducing dependence on imports, creating vibrant and participating institutional structures in agriculture and founding a vibrant consumer goods industry based on dairy. Credit here goes, of course, to Dr Verghese Kurien, leader of the Kheda Cooperative Movement (a movement that began in Gujarat inspired by Mahatma Gandhi's campaign against high peasant taxes) and the enlightened leadership of the National Dairy Development Board (NDDB).

In addition to these sectoral successes, there have been other regional achievements—such as of cotton in Gujarat, maize in

Bihar, sugar in Uttar Pradesh, wheat in Madhya Pradesh, and potatoes in West Bengal.

Glass Less-than-half Full

But (and you probably guessed a 'but' was coming), despite these successes, the honest story here is one of the glass being less-than-half full. Two statistics support my assertion: the overall agricultural labour productivity is less than a third of that in China and about 1 per cent of that in the frontier countries. Land productivity (measured as yield per hectare) is also well below the frontier. For example, in the case of rice, Indian yields are about 50 per cent of those in China and one-third of those in the US.

Figure 1: Overall Agricultural Productivity: Still Very Far from Frontier

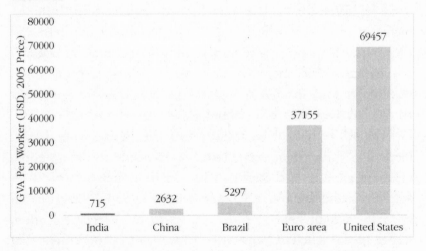

Second, agricultural incomes (as measured by income from cultivation, net of cost and unsold produce valued at local market rates) are still meagre.[2] The median household net farm income was about Rs 19,250 in 2012–13 or about Rs 1600 per month, which is not very far above the poverty line. To be sure, there is enormous variation, but the truth is it simply does not pay to be a farmer in India.

Figure 2: Agricultural Household Income

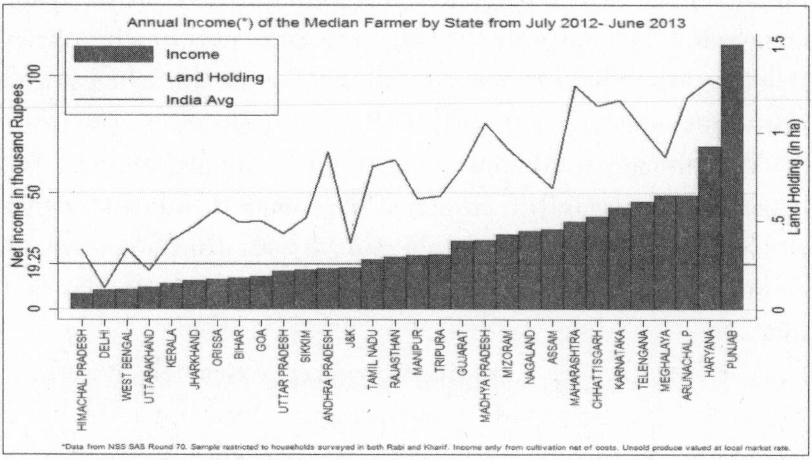

The New Malthusian Challenge

Before I elaborate on my central hypothesis, I would like to alert my readers to a new and serious challenge: raising agricultural productivity and reducing vulnerability are going to get harder because of what I call the re-emergence of the Ghost of Malthus (with auguries of looming scarcity). The four key agricultural resources: atmosphere, water, land and soil quality are all moving in very unfavourable directions. Climate change will reduce agricultural productivity and increase variability (all the models show a disproportionate impact on Indian agriculture); water is becoming perilously scarcer for climatic reasons and because of overuse and domestic misuse, especially in Punjab and Haryana; soil quality is depleting; and the pressures on land are mounting as population surges and alternative uses to farming are becoming more attractive.

Smothering with Love: Cereal-centricity

Think of how and how much we support cereal and especially rice production in the country. They are too numerous to exhaustively enumerate. The government helps the farmers through policies that affect the prices of outputs and inputs, through schemes and institutions.

We provide minimum support prices to farmers and the benefits accrue mainly to farmers who produce marketable output and that too mostly in cereals and wheat, which, in turn, is confined largely to a few states, notably in the north (Punjab and Haryana).

We then provide subsidies for power, water, fertilizer (now the second-largest subsidy), seeds, credit; we exempt agricultural income from income taxes; and we periodically grant loan waivers.

Look again at Figure 2 and see how clearly agricultural incomes in Punjab and Haryana exceed those in the rest of India to get a sense of this biased smothering with love.

Smothering with Love: Big, Not Small Farmers

There is a second aspect to this smothering with love: not only does it benefit cereal farmers, it also tends to favour larger farmers, or at least it does not adequately reach the smaller ones.

To explain this further, several examples come to mind. By definition, the exemption of agricultural income from tax favours those with larger incomes. In the case of fertilizers, we estimated in the Economic Survey (2015–16) that only about one-third of the total subsidy went to small and marginal farmers. On agricultural credit, there is now growing evidence that not all of this accrual goes to the farmers. On loan waiver, it is surprising how little the small and marginal farmer borrows from formal financial institutions (less than 50 per cent) and how much from informal sources, while the large farmer relies on formal sources to the extent of about 75 per cent. On power, we estimated in the Economic Survey that the bottom quintile received about 10 per cent of the total subsidy while the top quintal about 37 per cent, because of highly skewed electricity consumption.

But for a sector in which the aim is higher productivity and overall amelioration, is there something known as loving too much? The experience of Punjab is perhaps suggestive. Thanks to support, incomes are high, and amongst the highest, but there is growing evidence that this is proving to be counterproductive. Punjab has lost most of its earlier agricultural dynamism. Between 1971–72 and 1985–86, agricultural growth was 5.7 per cent compared to the all-India number of 2.3 per cent. Since 2005–06, its average agricultural growth has declined to 1.6 per cent compared to India's 3.5 per cent (Figure 3).

Figure 3: Agricultural Growth in Punjab and India (Average, Decadal, %)

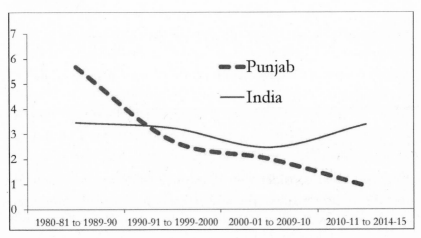

Consequently, the overall dynamism of agriculture in Punjab has suffered as its overall growth has slipped from being substantially above the Indian average to well below (Figure 4); consequently, Punjab has slipped from being the richest large state (excluding special category states) in 1984 to the ninth richest state by 2014.

Figure 4: Overall GDP Growth in Punjab and India (Average, Decadal, %)

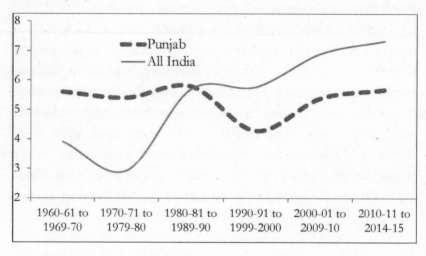

One can caution that Punjab's dynamism will only be restored if it weans itself off its agriculture that has taken a toll on its water resources, soil quality and human health (refer to the earlier mention of the 'cancer train'). Its fading dynamism may be in part due to the excessive support that its agriculture industry receives.

Loving Too Little

Next, we must consider that if we love some crops too much, perhaps we love many of the others too little. I have in mind here pulses, dairy and livestock, fruits and vegetables, and oilseeds.

In the case of pulses, commendable efforts have been made to increase procurement at the MSP (MSP without procurement, it must be emphasized, offers little comfort for farmers) and in the 2017 Kharif season (July–October cropping season), there was indeed a substantial increase to 2 million (out of a total output of 8.7 million). Despite this, it is estimated that about 60 per cent of the record Tur dal (a lentil) output was sold at less than the MSP, resulting in depressed income. Stock limits and export restrictions kept market prices low; had they been eased, the fortunes of farmers would have fared better.

I think we misunderstand an important economic insight here that we highlighted in the pulses report. Some of the loving-too-little occurs because of the perception of a tension between farmer and powerful, middle-class consumer interests. This leads to a response that creates policy volatility and pro-cyclicality, which increases price uncertainty for farmers. So, when prices go up, export restrictions are imposed, and when prices decline, import restrictions are imposed, and so on. But this perception and the consequent policy action do not adequately recognize a fundamental alignment of interests. Lower prices today will adversely affect future agricultural supplies (especially of crops that are predominantly produced domestically such as pulses, fruits and vegetables), which will increase consumer prices tomorrow. So, even over reasonable planning and political horizons, what is good for the farmer is good for the consumer.

On fruits and vegetables, restrictions on selling imposed via the Agricultural Produce Market Committees (APMCs) are perhaps taking a toll. Meanwhile, the government has created an electronic common market (called e-NAM) and the results are awaited.

Regarding dairy and livestock, two points are worth emphasizing. Governments have the right to choose their social policies. But in doing so, they must be fully aware of the economic costs of these policies. If social policies impede the workings of the livestock market, the impact on the economics of livestock farming could be considerable. A cost analysis must be undertaken for appropriate choices to be made.

Second, it must be recognized that the economics of livestock farming, and hence the fate and future of this source of livelihood, will depend critically on the terminal value of assets, in this case the no-longer-productive livestock. If social policies drive this terminal value precipitously down, private returns could be affected in a manner that could make livestock farming less profitable (and recent research by Anagol, Etang and Karlan [2013], titled 'Continued Existence of Cows Disproves Central Tenets of Capitalism?', suggests that returns to livestock farming are in any case very low and even negative). This declining terminal value arises both because of the loss of income from livestock as meat and the additional costs that will arise from having to maintain unproductive livestock. But there is more. It is possible that social policies could affect social returns even more adversely. Stray cattle, and a lot of it, will have to be looked after, otherwise diseases (foot and mouth) could spread, leading to health hazards and social costs.

Let me add, as an aside, that responding to changing consumer preferences for proteins, which Indians under-consume to the detriment of their health, needs both reduced cereal-centricity, and at the same time promoting, not hindering, alternative sources of protein from pulses, dairy and livestock.

Finally, there is the point of technology that again is especially important for pulses, oilseeds and dairy. Business author Harish Damodaran has written persuasively about the choices we face on genetically modified crops. To paraphrase him, it seems that the patronization of farmers masquerading as romanticization is rife. This must be addressed rationally, even beyond mustard. Any technology that offends both the left and the nativist right—

as genetically modified seeds and crops do—must be worth considering seriously.

If we want farmers to benefit from new technology, we must allow them these benefits regardless of the provenance of the technologies, just as we do in other sectors. Expropriating property rights retroactively and undermining the sanctity of contracts as sought by voices on opposing ends of the ideological spectrum could impede the flow of technology and thus end up hurting, not helping farmers. To be sure, we must absolutely ensure that there is no abuse of patent rights or other monopolistic practices but the right instruments must be chosen; moreover, there must always be an underlying cost–benefit analysis, but an analysis as farmers themselves would do it, rather than how it might be done for them.

Concluding Thoughts

Going forward, how do we redress this imbalance between the two sets of crops?

In terms of the loving-cereals-too-much challenge, it will be politically impossible to reduce current levels of support. Entitlements (for example, subsidies and high MSPs) have been created and exit from entitlements is fiendishly hard not just in India but the world over. The only possible way forward is to keep the magnitude of support and alter its form in order to change incentives. Professor Ashok Gulati of the Indian Council for Research on International Economic Relations (ICRIER) has recommended that support for fertilizers and power each be provided as a direct transfer than as a conditional subsidy. Perhaps this idea could be expanded into a quasi-universal basic income by combining some of the major support—power, fertilizer, even MGNREGA—into an unconditional basic support for all farmers, or farmers below a certain farm size. Our estimate is that if these three forms of support were replaced by direct support, the amount provided could be about Rs 1 lakh per year per cultivator.

In any event, as a minimum effort, ways must be found of reducing the addiction of agriculture in Punjab and Haryana to free up power and cheap fertilizer.

On the other category of crops that are loved too little, I think the challenge is equally daunting and, really, the flip side of the cereals' challenge. Here, one cannot help but come to the conclusion that policies can only seriously and sustainably be implemented if they—farmers in pulses, dairy, livestock, oilseeds, etc.—acquire more political voice to countervail other voices. Top-down efforts clearly have not been enough and, thus, pressure from below seems a necessary condition for redressing the balance.

A final and simple proposal. I have drawn a distinction—and I don't know how valid it is—between these two categories of objects of government 'love' for agriculture, and I have made some suggestions for rebalancing this love. To begin with, we could at least start highlighting and making clear this differential treatment. I would urge the Commission for Agriculture Costs and Prices in its MSP calculations to quantify not only the private costs and returns of various crops but also their true social costs. For example, the social cost of cultivating rice in north-western India far exceeds private costs because of damage to soil quality, depletion of water tables, damage to human health and spewing of pollution into the atmosphere. The disinfectant effect of more information and clarity might be a small technical step in creating awareness about the issues that could help in responding appropriately to the challenge.

In conclusion, I would suggest that perhaps more hard-nosed realism rather than woolly romanticization of the Indian farmer is what the doctor must order to transform the Indian agriculture sector.

5.2

The Arhar Solution to Pollution

Pollution, Paddy, Pulses and Pricing

The inferno of environmental pollution that the nation's capital and its surroundings have been witnessing has many causes, including weather conditions (thermal inversion), which facilitate the settling of particulate matter and other pollutants, dust on the streets generated in part from construction activity and vehicle-related emissions. Particularly critical is the burning of paddy after the Kharif harvest, which happens every year usually between April to October.

Multiple causes will require a broad-based response but one of the permanent solutions to the pollution problem is to address paddy burning. This is where pulses come in. In the Subramanian Committee report on pulses that was submitted in September 2016 to the ministers of finance, agriculture and consumer affairs, the possibilities created by a new variety of arhar (pigeon pea), developed by Dr K.V. Prabhu and his colleagues at the Indian Agricultural Research Institute (IARI), were discussed.

This variety (specifically, Pusa Arhar 16) has the potential to be cultivated in the paddy-growing regions of Punjab, Haryana and Uttar Pradesh, and eventually in all of India. Its yield (about 2000 kilograms per hectare) will be significantly greater than those of the existing varieties and because its size will be uniform, it will be amenable to mechanical harvesting—an attractive feature for farmers in northern India that currently use this technology for paddy.

Most importantly, arhar straw, unlike paddy straw, is green, and can be ploughed back into the soil. In the case of arhar, the farmer, even after combine harvesting (a machine that can simultaneously harvest a variety of crops) just needs to run a rotovator (a tiller used to dig in the earth) to cut the leftover straw into pieces, which can be ploughed back into the soil and will decompose relatively faster. In the case of paddy straw, the problem is the high silica content, which does not allow for easy decomposition nor can it be reused. Farmers, therefore, choose the easiest option of burning it.

But replacing paddy with pulses (in over half-a-million hectares or more eventually) will have other social benefits, in addition to reduced pollution levels. Our calculations suggest that pulses will use less fertilizer, less water and incur fewer emissions, and in addition, will replenish the soil with nitrogen, unlike paddy, which depletes the soil (see table below). Together, pulses' production would provide social benefits that we estimate at Rs 13,240 per hectare. On this basis, we had suggested a minimum support price for pulses over the medium term of close to Rs 9000 per ton so that pulses could become competitive with paddy, and naturally also preserve the incomes of farmers.

Social Benefits of Tur Compared with Paddy (Rs./ha)

	Fertilizer Subsidy (S)	Ground Water Subsidy (S)	Nitrogen Benefit (N)	GHG Cost (G)	Total Social Cost (S-N+G)
Tur	2878	1500	3883	0	495
Paddy	6897	5000	0	1838	13735
Net Benefits	4019	3500	3883	1838	13240

In the report we had highlighted that there would be additional benefits, but, of course, we had understated the social benefits of growing pulses: specifically, the reduced environmental pollution because less paddy would be burnt. But we were unable to quantify these benefits for lack of data. This needs to be rectified immediately to make public and transparent the causes and consequences of current policies.

Meanwhile, the broader policy lessons outlined in the pulses report have acquired new salience in light of the pollution problem. These lessons bear emphasis.

First, the future of sustainable agriculture must be based on encouraging agricultural science and research especially where India's scientists have done the hard and creative work. Agricultural research institutions must be free from political interference, must be accorded autonomy and must reward proven talent.

Second, making the fruits of science commercially viable will require price incentives to be re-evaluated. In the case of pulses and paddy, a complicating factor that determines the relative incentives is risk. Because of guaranteed MSPs in paddy, it is less risky to grow than pulses. The Subramanian Committee estimated that pulses production was about six times riskier than paddy production. To compensate this, the required MSP for pulses would have to be about Rs 1100 per ton, greater than otherwise.

Third, pricing in India must increasingly take into account the externalities, both positive and negative. In the case of agriculture, that means adapting the current methodology of setting MSPs used by the Commission for Agricultural Costs and Prices that focuses exclusively on private costs and benefits. This tends to encourage socially wasteful production and specialization such as excessive paddy production in north India with all the attendant consequences to which we are grim witnesses. As argued by Professor Ramesh Chand of the Niti Aayog and recommended by the Subramanian Committee report, the setting of a minimum support price must also incorporate social costs and benefits. At present, only private costs and benefits matter.

The burning of rice stalks affords an opportunity to implement a major shift in policy that can reduce pollution while also promoting indigenous research and science, incentivizing pulses production and rationalizing pricing more broadly. After all, converting crises into opportunities is the hallmark of good public policy.

5.3

Adapting Rythu Bandhu as the Future of Social and Agricultural Policies

One question I am increasingly asked is this: yes, the Economic Survey of 2017–18 (titled 'A Conversation With and Within the Mahatma') raised the profile of universal basic income (UBI) as a serious option, but has it had any resonance in policy circles? Or, more starkly, is the UBI actually being implemented anywhere in India? My answer is a qualified yes. Telangana's Rythu Bandhu (literally farmer's friend) policy is an embryonic UBI, or rather embryonic QUBI (a quasi-universal basic income, pronounced 'kyoo-bee'). And it could potentially also be the future of agricultural policy in India. Let me elaborate why.

As the Economic Survey made clear, India will never provide basic income that is literally 'universal'. Our politics will never countenance government cheques being sent to the rich. But government transfers to everyone except those at the top is a serious policy contender. Hence, instead of striving for a UBI, such a scheme, both more practical and politically sound, results in what we call the QUBI.

More generally, QUBIs are schemes in which transfers are given to everyone who meets an easily identifiable criterion. That is, they are universal within a clearly identifiable category. In the Rythu Bandhu scheme that category is all farmers who own land. This criterion can be applied because Telangana has titled nearly all landholdings, and has done so in an impressive fashion, without serious controversy or contestation within a short span of time.

Rythu Bandhu has, however, one undesirable property as social policy. Because payments to households are based on farm size, they can become regressive, that is the more land the farmers have, and hence the richer he/she is, the more is the payment (hence, the pressures to exclude large farmers from the scheme). In contrast, a pure UBI in which the same rupee amount is given to all households will be progressive because the effective subsidy rate (transfers as a share of household income) will be greater for the poor and decline with rising income.

Karnataka has been contemplating a scheme similar to Rythu Bandhu and it seems that other states could also follow. The key administrative challenge lies in establishing land titling, but states are beginning to make progress on that.

Of course, Rythu Bandhu is mainly intended as an agricultural rather than a social policy. In fact, viewed from this perspective, it could be the future of agricultural policy. Think of the current system of support for agriculture. Right now, there are schemes for every possible state of the world. There are schemes for bad harvests (monsoon failures) such as crop insurance and loan waivers. There are schemes for good harvests (bumper crops that depress prices) such as MSP-plus-procurement and price-deficiency schemes. And then there are schemes independent of outcomes, such as the various subsidies on inputs (fertilizers, seeds, power and water).

Today the Rythu Bandhu scheme is provided in addition, that is, over and above, to these schemes and hence can become fiscally unsustainable over time. However, if Rythu Bandhu is used instead to replace some or all of these schemes, critical advantages would ensue.

The surfeit of state capacity/administrative apparatus as well as financial resources—and all the patronage and corruption and inefficiency—devoted to administering the plethora of schemes for good, bad and all states-of-the-world could be economized on.

Farm income could be decoupled from production, avoiding the serious distortions that have been created, especially from overproduction of cereals (for example, rice stocks are becoming pest-infested mountains) and the overuse of water and fertilizers.

The magnitudes that can be transferred via DBT can be increased so that farm incomes can be augmented substantially and quickly. One illustrative calculation is as follows: eliminating the fertilizer and power subsidy in Punjab would finance an annual transfer of about Rs 92,000 to every cultivator or Rs 50,000 to every agricultural worker. This compares with a median agricultural household income of Rs 1,50,000 in Punjab, according to official estimates for the year 2013.

That said, it will take some time and effort before schemes like Rythu Bandhu can be adopted in other states. First, they will have to introduce comprehensive land titling. Second, a decision will need to be made whether the scheme should be more social policy or agricultural policy. As agricultural policy, the per-acre payment has a rationale. But as social policy, Rythu Bandhu will have to be rethought and replaced by something more progressive: for example, a common payment to all households just conditional on being a farmer.

It will be important to bring cultivators into the fold, as not all those who derive their income from agriculture are landowners. Under Rythu Bandhu, the hope is that market forces will lead to landowners sharing some of their benefits with agricultural labour. But that might not be effective.

The usual pressures to cater to various groups—such as providing differing amounts of assistance to different types of farmers or different types of agriculture, irrigated versus rain-fed, etc.—will lead to demands for finer targeting. This will result in complexity of implementation as was seen with the GST. Thus, this temptation must be avoided.

The final challenge—or rather an opportunity—is that schemes like the Rythu Bandhu must be done within a cooperative federalism framework, not least because of a fundamental complementarity: states control the implementation apparatus (namely, the land titling) while the Centre can provide resources.

A kind of grand bargain is thus possible between the Centre and the states. For example, the Centre could offer to finance part of the scheme, say, finding the funds by reducing the fertilizer subsidy. Alternatively, the Centre could convert some of its tied transfers (transfers allocated to particular schemes and projects) into untied ones, giving states the freedom to use them for schemes of their choice, including the QUBI to farmers.

The UBI offers an opportunity to eliminate poverty in one stroke or rather one click (for cash transfers). A QUBI like Telangana's Rythu Bandhu scheme—with some modification, preparation and cooperation—affords a similar opportunity: it could augment farmers' incomes and reduce agrarian distress in a way that makes for good social and even better agricultural policy. Where Telangana leads, other states such as Karnataka are bound to follow.

Chapter 6

The State's Relationship
with the Individual

6.0

JAM, UBI, QUBI and the Mahatma

In my first Economic Survey (2014–15), I came up with the acronym JAM—Jan Dhan, Aadhaar and Mobile—to refer to three technologies and developments that could transform the lives of the poor in India. The combination of financial inclusion, biometric identification and digital access is revolutionary in its possibilities. JAM first appeared in a section called 'Wiping Every Tear from Every Eye', the very evocative phrase from Pandit Nehru's 'Tryst with Destiny' speech. JAM is now an acronym that is so entrenched in the policy lexicon in India that it can be used on its own without explanation or clarification.

Here I must give credit to the finance minister, Arun Jaitley. When he read the first draft of this first survey, he offered one substantive comment, which proved to be both tactically brilliant and substantively acute. The chapter on JAM, based on some new research that my team had done, could well have been written by a Washington Consensus-inspired economist, deserving today's damning sobriquet 'neo-liberal'.

The draft focused on the efficiency benefits of JAM, and how replacing subsidies would reduce the price distortions in the economy. Mr Jaitley asked for it to be reframed so as to better achieve equity objectives, highlight leakages under existing schemes and show how JAM could lead to better targeting so that poor beneficiaries are not excluded from the coverage of public programmes. The whole tone and content of the chapter changed and for the better. The subsequent spread of the term 'JAM' owes in no small measure to the way that chapter was rewritten, thanks to his comments.

This chapter contains two sections on JAM, one of which appeared (in 2015) in the *New York Times*. The second section was written in response to subsequent criticism that we received, claiming that the piece overstated the benefits of the direct benefit transfer scheme that had been implemented for cooking gas, which at the time was the world's largest such scheme. The criticism was that the estimated benefits hadn't actually been realized—at least not so far, since the programme was only rolling out and had not yet reached all districts.

Throughout my tenure, I was very keen—indeed adamant—to ensure that our public pronouncements were rigorous and empirically robust, and that we didn't fall into the trap of overselling the impact of government policies and programmes. So in our response we explained the careful methodology we used to come up with our saving estimates, discussing in particular how the programme's gradual rollout enabled us to identify the programme's 'treatment effect'. I had to admit, however, that we did not make sufficiently clear in the *New York Times* piece that our savings estimate was for the future, when the programme was fully implemented. We should have been more careful, and I learnt from that experience.

In addition to JAM, another contribution of the survey that generated (and still generates) intense debate is the concept of Universal Basic Income. A chapter in the Economic Survey of 2016–17 was devoted to it and was one of the few detailed and data-based analysis of the issue. In writing this chapter, I was able to 'stand on the shoulders' of many illustrious Indian economists, including Vijay Joshi, Debraj Ray, Pranab Bardhan and Maitreesh Ghatak who had previously written on UBI. Pratap Bhanu Mehta helped me understand better the underlying political and ethical appeal of UBI. And a conversation with Abhijit Banerjee of MIT, who pointed out that a large number of poor, deserving beneficiaries were being excluded under the employment guarantee scheme, MNREGA, shaped some of the analysis on targeting in the chapter.

I think one of the reasons the UBI chapter struck a chord—and is now shaping the debate in India—was because it was written up as a conversation with and within the Mahatma (which was also the title of the chapter). I maintain a strong view that good, accessible and catchy writing is terribly important in public policy debates and formulation. So, the manner in which it was written, I believe, was important to the dissemination and acceptability of the idea itself.

But how did that idea strike me? In the middle of 2016, prompted by Indian historian and writer Ramachandra Guha, Tridip Suhrud, a great Gandhi scholar and translator of Gujarati fiction, invited me to give a talk at Sabarmati Ashram on Gandhi Jayanti (2 October). The general topic that was assigned to me was 'Gandhiji and Poverty'. As I was mulling over what I should speak about, I thought of the framework of UBI and then a light bulb went off in my head—what would Gandhiji have thought of the idea? Somewhere in my subconscious, the scene from *Lage Raho Munnabhai*—which I had watched with my youngest son Rohan—in which 'Bapu' Mahatma Gandhi carries on a conversation with Sanjay Dutt's character, Munna, was etched. I thought I could do the same with the Mahatma on UBI.

The fact that Gandhiji would be seriously conflicted by the idea did not occur to me until one of my bright, young colleagues, Sutirtha Roy, emailed me a quote from *Young India* emphasizing his opposition to anything that smacked of reward without effort. This is what economists, especially on the right side of the spectrum, call 'moral hazard', which leads to incentives for bad behaviour on the part of individuals. Such a recognition of conflict, stemming from the possibility that UBI carried both risks and benefits, made the UBI discussion a rich one.

At the ashram itself, I delivered a speech which was later elaborated into the chapter of the survey. Owing to the predominantly Gujarati-speaking audience, Tridip had to translate my speech. But it turned out to be memorable because he was a brilliant, animated communicator, and I could feed off the energy that he had established with the audience. Alas, it was not a musical jugalbandi à la Pandit Ravi Shankar and Ustad Ali Akbar Khan, but even as verbal jugalbandi, it proved to be thrilling. But then, just being in Sabarmati Ashram itself is a goose-pimply, soul-tingling experience.

I am also frequently asked whether the UBI has any serious prospects of being implemented in India. My response is: we will never see a strict UBI in India because the notion that the rich would ever get a pay cheque from the government would be fatally flawed as a political proposition. At the same time, it seems obvious that India will see increasing numbers of policy experiments in which direct transfers are provided to a large part of the population. And this could lead, over time, to a Quasi-Universal Basic Income (QUBI). Indeed, the larger the population covered under direct transfers and the clearer and broader the criteria for including people in them, the more such schemes will start resembling a QUBI.

QUBI was actively discussed in Jammu and Kashmir when Haseeb Drabu was the finance minister of the state. And in Telangana, the chief minister, K. Chandrashekar Rao, is now providing direct benefit transfers to all farmers based on their landholdings (Section 5.3). This is the kind of scheme that is very close in spirit to—and an embryonic version of—a QUBI. Had the invitation from Sabarmati Ashram not come, I doubt I would have thought about UBI, let alone written extensively about it. As in so many cases, and like so many Indians, I owe a debt to the Mahatma.

India's Distinctive Demographic Dividend

How Much More, for How Long and Where?

Andrew McAfee, the techno-optimist, tweeted in January 2017 that the world had reached 'peak children', which is to say there will never be more of them than there are now. Encouragingly, this is not true for India, which is poised to reap the so-called demographic dividend, which refers to the increase in a country's growth potential due to a young population. One-fifth of India's population is under twenty-five and will reach 35 per cent by 2020. Using new projections of population and age structure, provided by Professor Irudaya Rajan and Dr Sunitha for the Economic Survey (2016–17), here are some new findings on India's demographic dividend.

1. **India's demographic profile is distinctive:** India's demographic profile is unique in three ways, with key implications for the growth outlook of India and the Indian states. Figure 1 compares the UN's projections of the ratio of the working age (WA) to non-working age (NWA) population between 1970 and 2050 for India, Brazil, South Korea and China. This is an intuitive

number because a magnitude of 1 essentially means that there are as many potential workers as dependents.

Figure 1: Ratio of Working Age to Non-Working Age Population

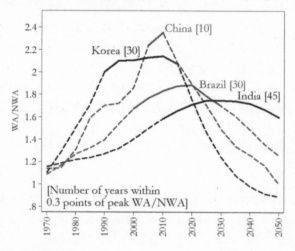

First, India's demographic cycle is about ten to thirty years behind that of the other countries, indicating that the next few decades present an opportunity for India to catch up to their per capita income levels. In addition, India's WA to NWA ratio is likely to peak at 1.7, a much lower level than Brazil and China, both of which sustained a ratio greater than 1.7 for at least twenty-five years. Finally, India will remain close to its peak for a much longer period than other countries. The broad implication is that the magnitude of the surge and the decline in India's demographic dividend will not be as strong as China's or Korea's but it will endure for longer.

2. India's demographic sweet spot is rapidly closing: Younger populations are more productive, tend to save more—which may also lead to favourable competitiveness effects—and have a larger fiscal base because of higher economic growth and fewer dependents. Countries with a large share of WA population appear to benefit from greater economic dynamism. However, the real demographic sweet spot arises not only from a large WA/NWA ratio but also a growing one.

Extending the work of Ashoka Mody and Shekhar Aiyar done at the IMF, we estimate the demographic dividend for India (the additional growth in per capita income due to demographic factors alone) for the next few decades in Table 1. It is striking to note that the dividend is projected to peak in the next four years. This does not mean that the demographic dividend will turn negative; rather, the positive impact will slow down.

Table 1: Additional Average Annual Growth Due to the Demographic Dividend (in Percentage Points)

Decade	Additional Growth
2001–10	1.44
2011–20	2.62
2021–30	1.81
2031–40	1.92
2041–50	1.37

3. India's demographic profile is highly heterogeneous: These aggregate projections mask considerable variations in the states' demographic profiles and the timing and magnitude of their demographic dividend. There is a clear divide between peninsular India (West Bengal, Kerala, Karnataka, Tamil Nadu and Andhra Pradesh) and the hinterland states (Madhya Pradesh, Rajasthan, Uttar Pradesh and Bihar). In contrast, there is much greater uniformity in demographic profiles across the provinces in China.

The peninsular states exhibit a pattern that is closer to countries such as China and Korea, with sharp rises and declines in the working-age population. The difference, of course, is that the working-age ratio of most of the peninsular states will peak at levels lower than seen in East Asia (West Bengal comes closest to Korea's peak because of its very low total fertility rate). In contrast, the hinterland states will remain relatively young and dynamic, characterized by a rising working-age population for some time, plateauing towards the middle of the century.

Figure 2 Per Capita Income in 2011 and the Demographic Dividend (2011–31)

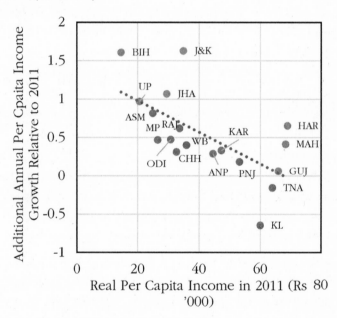

Demographically speaking, therefore, there are two Indias, with different policy concerns: a soon-to-begin-ageing peninsular India, where the elderly and their needs will require greater attention; and a young India, where providing education, skills and employment opportunities must be the focus. But the heterogeneity also offers possibilities of mutual help through migration. Aravind Adiga spoke of the ocean as India's light and the river (the hinterland) as India's darkness. But migration offers the possibility of retirees by the seas being helped and cared for by the young from river-land.

4. Heterogeneity is on balance an equalizing force with some exceptions: We compare the growth boost due to demographics for different states in India with their current level of per capita incomes. Figure 2 plots the two variables. The negative relationship signifies that, on an average, the poorer states today have a higher growth dividend ahead of them. Therefore, the heterogeneity in the states' demographic profiles offers an advantage. The demographic dividend can help income levels across the states to converge, and hence act as an equalizing force.

But the encouraging overall pattern described above hides some interesting outliers. Bihar, Jammu and Kashmir, Haryana and Maharashtra are positive outliers (they are far above the line of best fit) in that they can expect a greater demographic dividend over the coming years. This extra dividend will help Bihar catch up with the more developed states, while the already rich Haryana and Maharashtra will pull further away from the average level of income per capita in India. On the other hand, Kerala, Madhya Pradesh, Chhattisgarh and West Bengal are negative outliers: their future dividend is relatively low for their current level of income. This will make the poorer states fall back unless offset by robust reforms, while the relatively rich Kerala will probably converge to the average as its growth momentum declines rapidly.

In sum, demography affords India a unique opportunity, though it is, by no means, destiny. But this window will not be available indefinitely. The time to strike, to reform, to transform, is now.

6.2

Transforming the Fight against Poverty in India[1]

Transferring cash to poor families, on the condition that their kids attend school and get vaccinations, has been shown to be an effective way to reduce poverty and improve human health and well-being. Latin America is widely recognized as the pioneer of large-scale conditional transfer programmes, starting with Mexico in the late 1990s and expanding across Brazil over the past decade.

Similarly, these programmes have the potential for making a serious dent in poverty in India. Under the acronym JAM, a quiet revolution of social-welfare policy is unfolding. Jan Dhan is Prime Minister Narendra Modi's flagship programme to give poor people access to financial services, including bank accounts, credit and insurance. Aadhaar is the initiative to issue unique biometric identification cards to all Indians. Together with mobile money platforms, they will enable the state to transfer cash directly to those in need, without the money going through intermediaries that might take a cut.

India, the world's largest democracy, is also the world's largest poor country. The legitimacy of any elected government turns on its ability to provide for the poor. As such, both our federal and state governments subsidize a wide range of products and services with the expressed intention of making them affordable for the poor: rice, wheat, pulses, sugar, kerosene, cooking gas, naphtha, water, electricity, fertilizer and railways. The cost of these subsidies is about 4.2 per cent of India's gross domestic product, which is more than enough to raise the consumption level of every poor Indian household above the poverty line.

Sadly, government provisions for these subsidies are associated with significant leakages. For example, as much as 41 per cent of subsidized kerosene, which poor families use to light their homes, is 'unaccounted for' and is probably lost to the black market. Dealers sell it on the side to middlemen who mix diesel into fuel and resell it, which is bad for both health and the environment.

Furthermore, some subsidies benefit those who do not need them. Power subsidies, for example, favour the (generally wealthier) two-thirds of India who have access to regular grid-provided electricity and, in particular, wealthier households, which consume more power.

Why, then, do product subsidies form such a central part of the Indian government's anti-poverty policies? Subsidies are a way for states that lack implementation capacity to help the poor; it is easier to sell kerosene and food at subsidized prices than to run effective schools and public health systems.

Thus, the three elements of JAM are a potential game changer. Consider the mind-boggling scale of each element. Nearly 118 million bank accounts have been opened through Jan Dhan. Nearly 1 billion citizens have a biometrically authenticated unique identity card through Aadhaar. And about half of the Indian population now have a cell phone (while only 3.7 per cent have landlines).

Here's one example of how these three elements can be put to work. The Indian government subsidizes household purchases of cooking gas; these subsidies amounted to about $8 billion last year. Until recently, subsidies were provided by selling cylinders to beneficiaries at below-market prices. Now, prices have been deregulated, and the subsidy is delivered by depositing cash directly into the beneficiaries' bank accounts, which are linked to cell phones, so that only eligible beneficiaries—not 'ghost' intermediaries—receive transfers.

Under the previous arrangement, the large gap between subsidized and unsubsidized prices created a thriving black market, where distributors diverted subsidized gas away from households to businesses for a premium. In a new research by Prabhat Barnwal, an economist at Columbia University, we find that cash transfers reduced these 'leakages', resulting in an estimated fiscal savings of about $2 billion.

The scope for extending these benefits is enormous. Imagine the possibility of rolling all subsidies into a single lump-sum cash transfer to households, an idea mooted decades ago by the economist Milton Friedman as the holy grail of efficient and equitable welfare policy. JAM makes this possible.

To realize the full benefits of JAM, the government needs—and has begun—to address both 'first-mile' and 'last-mile' challenges.

The 'first-mile' challenges are identifying eligible beneficiaries and coordinating between states and central government departments. To deliver means-tested benefits via cash transfers, the government will need a way of identifying the poor and linking beneficiaries to their bank accounts. Further, eligibility criteria and beneficiary rosters vary, and technology platforms, where they exist, may not be seamlessly interoperable. Hence, the need for an extensive coordination exercise under the national government, which can incentivize states to come on board by potentially sharing fiscal savings with them.

The 'last-mile' challenge arises because cash-transfer programmes risk excluding genuine beneficiaries if they do not have bank accounts. Indeed, even if they have an account, they may live so far away from a bank—India has only 40,000 rural bank branches to serve 600,000 villages—that collecting benefits is arduous. Extending financial inclusion to reach the remotest and poorest will require nurturing banks that facilitate payments via mobile networks, which has achieved great success in countries such as Kenya. India can then leapfrog from a bank-less society to a cashless one, just as it went from being phoneless to cell phone saturated.

Overall, JAM offers substantial benefits for the government, the economy and especially the poor. Government finances will be improved because of the reduced subsidy burden; at the same time, the government will also be legitimized and strengthened because it can transfer resources to citizens faster and more reliably. Experimental evidence from the world's largest workfare programme—the Mahatma Gandhi National Rural Employment Guarantee Act—found that delivering wages via a biometrically authenticated payment system reduced corruption and enabled workers to receive salaries faster. With the poor protected, market forces can be allowed to allocate resources with enormous benefits for economy-wide efficiency and productivity enhancement. The chief beneficiaries will be India's poor; cash transfers are not a panacea for eliminating their hardship, but can go a long way in improving their lives.

6.3

Clearing the Air on LPG

The Impact of DBT in LPG and Beyond

A recent article titled 'LPG Subsidy Transfer: Centre's Savings Not More Than Rs 143 Cr, while It Claims Rs 12,700 Cr', published on 7 October 2015, cited our work—Siddharth George's, a PhD student at Harvard University, and mine—raising questions about how we estimated the benefits of delivering liquid petroleum gas (LPG) subsidies via direct benefit transfers. This article affords an opportunity both to respond to the specific claims and to discuss some broader issues relating to DBTs, and the larger JAM vision embraced by the government.

Cash transfers are increasingly seen as an effective anti-poverty tool in many developed and developing countries. Harvard University's Dani Rodrik, in his latest book, *Economics Rules*, says, 'A central tenet of economics holds that when it comes to the welfare of the poor, direct cash transfers are more effective than subsidies on specific consumer goods.' But all such general propositions must be tested against what the dynamics are of particular settings. This is what we attempted to do in the case of the LPG subsidy.

Our research, which was presented at a UNDP round-table discussion on cash transfers in early July 2015, aimed at identifying in a rigorous manner the effects of delivering LPG subsidies via DBT. Here, an important methodological point is worth stressing. Assessments of government programmes and projects often rely on a simple before-and-after comparison. Such comparisons can be problematic because it can be difficult to isolate the programme's impact from those of other events that occurred around the same time as the programme. In this case, one cannot simply compare LPG consumption in districts before and after DBT was introduced, because other things that affect LPG consumption—such as market prices, changes in the limits on number of cylinders eligible for the subsidy and the number of LPG consumers—also fluctuated during these months.

To address this problem, we relied on a 'natural experiment' afforded by the fact that DBT was introduced in phases; first implemented in certain districts in late 2013, then surprisingly suspended in early 2014 before being reintroduced in late 2014.

We were motivated to compare the change in consumption in the 'treated' districts (which saw DBT introduced in a particular month) as against the change in the 'control' districts (which operated as per normal). This comparison isolates the impact of DBT from other factors, as mentioned, that could affect LPG consumption as well. We expect that DBT will reduce consumption in the treated districts because, for example, it enables the ministry of petroleum and natural gas (MoPNG) to eliminate ghost beneficiaries. Using this approach and data on sales from over 12,000 LPG distributors from January 2013 to April 2015, we estimate that DBT will reduce sales of subsidized household cylinders by 24 per cent.

A key finding of our research is that DBT reduces the consumption of subsidized LPG cylinders—and thus the fiscal expenditure on LPG subsidies—by, on average, 24 per cent. This tells the government how much it can roughly expect to save due to DBT in any given fiscal year. To convert this percentage number into an absolute fiscal-year–specific rupee number, we need to know how much the actual subsidy amount will be in any year, which depends, in turn, on how many cylinders households buy and the per-cylinder subsidy, which varies with market prices.

For illustrative purposes, if one were to use FY 2014–15's average per-cylinder subsidy and total sales as an indicative benchmark, the annual savings from introducing the DBT could be estimated at about Rs 12,700 crore per year, which was the number attributed to our research in the newspaper article. Note that this is an estimate of how much a fully implemented DBT scheme *could* save—i.e., DBT introduced for all districts in all months.

This is not, as has been noted, the amount that DBT actually saved in FY 2014–15 because of the unusual circumstances of the year; also, as mentioned above, DBT was introduced in a phased manner—so many districts only implemented the programme very late in the fiscal year.

Moreover, in our study we focused on an estimate of prospective savings for a future fiscal year, because we believe that it is what policymakers taking decisions on the DBT and LPG programmes would like to know. In retrospect, we should, perhaps, have been more explicit in making clear that the fiscal-savings calculation— translating the 24 per cent savings number into absolute rupee terms—was not for any particular year, not least for FY 2014–15 given its peculiarities, but a prospective estimate of the impact of a fully implemented DBT. To reinforce the conditional nature of the savings calculation, we also suggested that savings would be lower if one used this year's lower prices (and hence per-cylinder subsidy). Our method is also not the only way to estimate DBT-induced leakage reductions. Another plausible approach is to multiply the number of deactivated 'ghost' connections in a year by the average annual subsidy per household.

Having established the substantial benefits of DBT in LPG, we further considered what the lessons might be for extending it to other sectors such as kerosene. But here, we urged caution because the LPG experiment had several special features that made the DBT scheme relatively successful.

First, implementing DBT in LPG proved easier because the oil marketing companies (OMCs) controlled distribution networks, which made it easier for the central government to drive the programme; the kerosene distribution network, on the other hand, is much larger and is controlled by the states via the public distribution system. Moreover, the LPG is a universal programme unlike subsidized kerosene, which is officially available only to the poor; targeting, therefore, becomes a much bigger challenge for kerosene.

A crucial second difference is that the LPG beneficiaries were largely urban consumers with bank accounts. The infrastructure for administering transfers was therefore available. Research by Prabhat Barnwal and the International Institute of Sustainable Development (IISD), among others, shows that risks of excluding genuine beneficiaries have been mitigated by these factors in the LPG case. In contrast, kerosene consumers are relatively poor, a large proportion are located in rural areas, and they are much more weakly connected to the financial system. Making direct transfers may therefore be difficult, and in some cases where they have been tried, the experiment has proven less than successful because beneficiaries either did not have bank accounts, or even when they did, could not easily access them. With regard to kerosene, there is still considerable scope for reducing waste, duplication and corruption but policy design and implementation must be carefully planned and coordinated amongst a number of stakeholders.

In conclusion, improving the quality of the economic analysis of government programmes is imperative, and our research methodology to estimate the benefits of the DBT programme in LPG was a step in that direction. Our analysis suggests that the benefits of implementing DBT specifically, viz., by way of the LPG subsidy, are substantial. And our drawing attention to the implementation challenges of extending the LPG experiment to other areas should provide reassurance about our intent: responsible analysis as researchers rather than as glib advocates of government policy.

6.4

Universal Basic Income from a Gandhian Perspective[1]

I was greatly honoured to deliver a speech on Gandhi Jayanti, on 2 October 2016, at Gandhi Ashram in Ahmedabad. Of perhaps India's greatest man, Albert Einstein had once said, 'Generations to come will scarce believe that such a man as this ever in flesh and blood walked upon this earth.' I myself am an avid consumer of Gandhi literature; one of my favourites, set in Ahmedabad, is Erik Erikson's biography of Gandhi, Gandhi's Truth, *which is all about the Ahmedabad mill workers' strike.*

Pandit Jawaharlal Nehru, in his famous 'Tryst with Destiny' speech had this reference to Gandhiji's ambition: 'The ambition of the greatest man of our generation has been to wipe every tear from every eye. That may be beyond us, but so long as there are tears and suffering, so long our work will not be over.'

And Gandhiji himself spelt out how this ambition was to be realized by the actions of every individual:

I will give you a talisman. Whenever you are in doubt, or when the self becomes too much with you, apply the following test.

244

Recall the face of the poorest and the weakest man [woman] whom you may have seen, and ask yourself, if the step you contemplate is going to be of any use to him [her]. Will he [she] gain anything by it? Will it restore him [her] to a control over his [her] own life and destiny? In other words, will it lead to *swaraj* [freedom] for the hungry and spiritually starving millions? Then you will find your doubts and yourself melt away.

As an aside, I have not seen this obvious point made but Gandhi's talisman embodies, and anticipates by more than three decades, the American moral and political philosopher John Rawls's Theory of Justice and the Difference Principle, namely, that the welfare of the poorest person in society must be the decisive factor in social-welfare judgements.

So, speaking of Gandhiji and his fight against poverty, specifically a new idea that is gaining currency, the first question I have is: how much progress have we as a country made towards the goal of eliminating poverty and empowering the poor?

Poverty and empowerment are multi-dimensional concepts, encompassing not just economics but social, political, cultural and spiritual realms. But we economists are crude and reductive partly because we want to measure everything that is both blessing and a curse.

In India, per capita GDP adjusted for purchasing power parity was just $840 per capita in 1950 and now it is $5200. For China and the US, during the same period, it increased from $950 to $12,500 and from $14,700 to $52,000 respectively.

Rural poverty, which was as high as 65 per cent in 1956–57 and probably around 70 per cent around Independence, today stands at 25.7 per cent, while overall poverty in country is at 21.9 per cent.

Our human development index (HDI), which ranks countries on the basis of life expectancy, education and per capita income levels, has also improved from 0.428 in 1990 to 0.609 in 2014. However, our overall ranking was still 130 out of 190 countries in 2014. So, we have come a long way especially since 1983, but we have by no means wiped out poverty, ignorance, disease and inequality of opportunity.

That said, amidst all the difficulties and challenges we face it is clearly the case that in economic terms the average Indian today is far better off than many years ago. When middle-class people complain that 'these days it is very difficult to get domestic help'—a very anti-Gandhian sentiment— it is undoubtedly a great sign of progress because, evidently, opportunities have improved, leading to fewer people willing to do domestic work.

However, this improvement has been uneven across regions, class, gender and social groups. I suspect that greater progress has been made by groups that have acquired greater political power. I also suspect that amongst the most challenged groups have been the tribals of peninsular India who are afflicted by geographic isolation, the 'resource curse' and conflict.

Since Gandhiji was unusually concerned with the plight of the Dalits, it is worth mentioning a positive story, as an aside. Based on surveys conducted in western and eastern Uttar Pradesh, my friend Professor Devesh Kapur (University of Pennsylvania) finds that growth and democracy have led to seismic social transformations in our country, affecting Dalits. The table below highlights this. Not only materially but also socially, their lives are being transformed. For example, instances of only Dalits lifting dead animals have declined by 67.3 percentage points in western Uttar Pradesh between 1990 and 2007.

Growth and Democracy Have Led to Seismic Social Transformations (Kapur et. al. 2011)

	Western Uttar Pradesh			Eastern Uttar Pradesh		
	1990	2007	Change	1990	2007	Change
Dalits not seated separately at non-Dalit weddings	26.9%	82.1%	55.1%	22.7%	91.1%	68.3%
Non-Dalits visiting Dalit homes eat/drink tea/water if offered	4.1%	62.6%	58.5%	1.1%	72.6%	71.6%
Government non-Dalit midwifes come to Dalit homes to deliver babies	0.0%	2.2%	2.2%	5.7%	54.3%	48.6%
Only Dalits lift dead animals	72.6%	5.3%	-67.3%	19.1%	5.6%	-13.5%

I want to move on to discussing an idea that is not only gaining currency around the world but could also, in one stroke, eliminate poverty in India. As briefly touched on before, this idea is of a universal basic income. The UBI would involve giving every Indian a sum of money sufficient to get all those who are poor today out of poverty. Current estimates suggest that this number would vary between Rs 4000 and Rs 10,000 per person per year, costing the government between 5–8 per cent of our GDP. (Central government expenditure today is something like 15 per cent of the GDP.)

UBI has been embraced both by thinkers of the left (Debray Ray, Pranab Bardhan, Maitreesh Ghatak) and of the right (Vijay Joshi). The left considers it as an antidote to poverty whereas the right thinks it will help in eliminating wasteful government expenditure. But what I'm interested in is to ask how the Mahatma would have reacted to this idea.

At one level, I believe the UBI would meet Gandhiji's objective when he said, 'There are people in the world so hungry, that God cannot appear to them except in the form of bread,' as well as, 'Poverty is the worst form of violence.'

But this would elicit at least four strong reactions, two of which would resemble a right-wing critique, and the other two a left-wing one. The first is what the right would call a 'moral hazard', or, as raised before, bad incentives that are created through so-called handouts.

In his book, *India of My Dreams*, Mahatma Gandhi writes:

> My ahimsa would not tolerate the idea of giving a free meal to a healthy person who has not worked for it in some honest way, and if I had the power I would stop every Sadavarta where free meals are given. It has degraded the nation and it has encouraged laziness, idleness, hypocrisy and even crime. Such misplaced charity adds nothing to the wealth of the country, whether material or spiritual, and gives a false sense of meritoriousness to the donor. How nice and wise it would be if the donor were to open institutions where they would give meals under healthy, clean surroundings to men and women who would work for them. I personally think that the spinning-wheel or any of the processes that cotton has to go through will be an ideal occupation. But if they will not have that, they may choose any other work, only the rule should be: no labour, no meal.

(In fact, there is evidence from a pilot UBI scheme run by the Self-employed Women's Association [SEWA] in 2011 in Madhya Pradesh, which shows that people actually worked more and made more investments.)

The second critique would be about Gandhiji's position as the good bania, the fiscal hawk who believed in sound personal and public finances, to live within one's means and avoid profligacy, including fiscal profligacy. Since the basic UBI scheme would cost anywhere between 5 and 10 per cent of the GDP, effectively putting a strain on public finances, especially if it were politically difficult to see the UBI as replacing rather than adding to existing schemes, Gandhiji perhaps would have been against the UBI.

Left-wing critiques of UBI would be the following. First, if cash transfers were, say, to replace food subsidies, the argument would be that the beneficiaries of the UBI would be exposed to the vagaries of the market on food availability and this would leave at least some who are more isolated, geographically and economically, worse off.

Then there is the complication that arises from Indian patriarchy and intra-household behaviour. If men control the wallet, as they often do, cash transfers would be imprudently used—and used more in line with the preferences of adult males than the real needs of the family—which would make women and children worse off. Dominant, domineering men cannot do the same with food, fuel and other commodities that are physically provided by the government.

There is also the critique by Jean Drèze, a development economist and activist, which goes along the following lines: We are making good progress on building a social safety net via the MGNREGA, PDS, pensions, maternity benefits, etc. Why not just follow through on these initiatives instead of getting distracted by a new scheme?

In my opinion, these are all very important arguments, which would have been familiar to and resonated with Gandhiji. Nevertheless, we should ask whether they can be addressed and overcome, and indeed much more work needs to be done to determine how important they truly are. Still, I think there are a number of countervailing arguments that need to be considered.

Could the UBI be a better way of reaching the poor than existing schemes? Currently, the government spends a lot of money to help the poor through a variety of schemes such as the MGNREGA, Janani Suraksha Yojana, PDS, fertilizers, MSPs, electricity, Integrated Child Development Services (ICDS), MDDS, Indira Awaas Yojana, National Livelihoods

Mission, Ujjwala, Swachh Bharat, to name a few. In 2014–15, we conservatively estimated that there were more than a thousand central schemes, and many have been in place for a long time. (There is even one that is ninety-six-years-old.)

In the Economic Survey (2016–17), we calculated that these schemes were not very well targeted. For example, about only one-third of the fertilizer subsidy reaches small farmers; nearly 40 per cent of the PDS kerosene was lost to leakage and about half the remainder reached the poor; most water subsidies were allocated to private taps. Even the MGNREGA, which is self-selecting, has an issue: expenditures are not highly correlated with places with the most extreme poverty. So, shouldn't we be asking whether there are better ways of targeting those in need and whether the UBI might actually help? (There is the famous Rajiv Gandhi estimate that only about 10 paise out of every rupee in social schemes reaches the poor.)

Second, there is something fragile about the conditions of the poor. World Bank research shows that even though people have moved out of poverty, they remain vulnerable ($2 a day, nearly 50 per cent). Sonalde Desai, a professor at the University of Maryland, has documented using India Human Development Survey (IHDS) panel data that 9 per cent of the non-poor households in 2004 became poor in 2011. She argues, 'Our public policies have historically focused on individuals who are poor by virtue of the accident of their birth—Dalits, Adivasis and individuals based in poor states and backward districts. But with declining poverty, the accident of birth has become less important than the accident of life. People fall into poverty due to illness, drought, declining opportunities in agriculture and urban blight.'

Desai's study of IHDS data shows that only 13 per cent of the population was poor in both 2004–05 and 2011–12, and this is the population most likely to be served by the present policies; 53 per cent of the people were poor in neither of the two periods and 25 per cent moved out of poverty between 2004–05 and 2011–12. The worrying finding, however, is that 9 per cent of the population fell into poverty during these years. This suggests that if we had provided safety nets in 2011–12 based on a below poverty line (BPL) card issued in 2004–05, 65 per cent BPL card holders would have already moved out of poverty (reflecting an error of inclusion), but of those poor in 2011–12, 40 per cent would not have BPL cards since they fell into poverty after the BPL survey (reflecting the errors of exclusion). The vulnerability of this last group has, unfortunately, received little attention. Desai further notes, 'As Latin American countries have found, moving to middle-income levels also means fostering a middle-income mindset for drafting social policies, with a greater focus on vulnerability instead of concentrating solely on chronic poverty.'

UBI can provide social insurance against such shocks. The poor have limited access to credit. For example, in Udaipur, those who live on less than a $1 a day pay about 3.84 per cent per month or nearly 60 per cent per year interest rate on their borrowings. They rely mostly on informal channels for jobs and social protection.

Most importantly, I believe getting out of poverty is as much a mental project, and is as psychological as anything else. If you look at decisions made by the poor, it may be as much because poverty and scarcity affect their psychological ability—cognitive bandwidth—to make decisions. A lot of evidence suggests that they make surprising choices: not saving enough, spending on non-essentials, taking up multiple jobs, etc. And, as a professor of economics at Harvard University, Sendhil Mullainathan, explains, those bad decisions abound. 'We're not just talking about shorter patience or less willpower,' he says. In the case of the poor, 'We're often talking about short-term financial fixes that can have disastrous long-term effects.'

A related insight comes from Katherine Boo in her book on the Annawadi slum in Mumbai, titled *Behind the Beautiful Forevers*.

Her important and depressing development insight is that the related pathologies we variously call weak public institutions, ineffective governance and corruption are especially costly, and most difficult to escape from, for the poorest. And her explanation of these costs is novel. It is not just that navigating, say, the Indian judicial system can be time-consuming, financially draining and livelihood-destroying; it's that the Indian system severs the link between effort and result, engendering deep despair. To this, she adds: '"We try so many things," as one Anganwadi girl put it, "but the world does not move in our favour."'

However, there are some challenges with UBI which also must be addressed for its successful implementation. Nearly a third of adults in India still do not have a bank account or access to a bank. Can the most vulnerable thus be reached with the greatest difficulty even through cash-based transfers? Can existing programmes really be eliminated (back to the 'exit' problem)? Can money be transferred to women instead of men?

As Gandhiji noted in his weekly journal *Young India* in 1925: 'From a pecuniary standpoint, in the initial stages at any rate, the cost of feeding people after taking work from them will be more than the cost of the present free kitchens. But I am convinced that it will be cheaper in the long run, if we do not want to increase in geometrical progression the race of loafers which is fast overrunning this land.'[2]

In conclusion, it is difficult to say how the Father of the Nation would have reacted to the UBI scheme. But we can be sure that the open-minded man he was, he would have given the idea a fair hearing. And who knows, he might even have agreed to implementing it.

Chapter 7

Speaking Truth to Power

7.0

Speaking Truth to Power
Being Karna and Arjuna

A chief economic adviser must be fully supportive of the government without spinning on its behalf. He must combine fidelity to the government with fealty to the larger good. In short, he must try and be both Karna and Arjuna. Especially in this post-truth, social media-saturated world, characterized by non-overlapping echo chambers of frenzied discussion, a CEA must engender public trust, which is achieved in part by speaking truth to power.

All this I understood when I accepted the job. What truly surprised me once I settled into the office was something I could never have imagined. I discovered that I, as an insider, had to be more critical of policies than outsiders.

The business, financial and analyst communities tend to be extraordinarily coy when it comes to commenting on official policies of the RBI and the government. I remember a prominent TV anchor telling me how at every post-budget show, industrialists and analysts would rave as cravenly about the budget on-camera as they would ferociously criticize it off-camera during the commercial breaks. There is also a research paper waiting to be written comparing analysts' commentary pre- and post-RBI monetary policy decisions, especially when decisions deviate from the consensus view. The contortions involved in the obligation to praise the RBI while also justifying its 'deviance' from their own analysis would be worthy of cataloguing.

Of course, they behave this way because their relationship to officialdom is not arm's-length. Bankers, for example, are careful not to get on the wrong side of the government or the RBI, because they worry about losing access and because they are regulated by them.

I often found myself a lone voice, questioning official policies. This section contains three other pieces in a similar questioning vein. My V.K.R.V. Rao lecture (Section 7.1) is an example of my role as a public dissenter vis-à-vis RBI actions. For several quarters, the RBI had made large, one-sided systematic errors in forecasting high inflation, which led to overly tight monetary policy. This lecture was directed not just at the RBI, but also at the financial and analyst community for not raising this issue more vocally.

The targets of my dissent also extended to the sovereign ratings agencies ('Poor Standards, Section 7.2) for their discriminatory treatment of India and China. And here we scored real victories because China was downgraded and India upgraded after our attacks. I was also a dissenter on another occasion, questioning the recommendations of a government-appointed committee. I disagreed with the N.K. Singh Committee's recommendations on fiscal targets, for three main reasons.

I believed that there was little justification for the serpentine fiscal deficit path proposed, there were too many targets that were not always internally consistent, and the numbers chosen for the targets were arbitrary. My solution was to offer an alternative, simpler framework in which the main objective was to place government debt on a gradually declining trajectory.

Eighteen months on, how do I feel about the committee's report and my own dissent?

I think my views have evolved, perhaps even significantly. I stand by my critique of the committee's report. I also think that my main recommendations of a simple commitment to steady declines in the debt and deficit ratios—rather than aiming for strict numbers—are still the way to go.

But I also think I made a strategic miscalculation in making the primary deficit the main target.[1] My dissent provoked some rich and interesting commentary in the press by Indira Rajaraman, Montek Ahluwalia and Pronab Sen. But in general the Indian economic ecosphere was not ready to embrace new concepts such as the primary deficit. Over the years, the public had become familiar with fiscal deficits, revenue deficits, effective revenue deficits, and so on. To add another ingredient to this deficit soup proved indigestible. Once that was seen as the main recommendation, the dissent note failed to gain the traction that it deserved. But I would say that, wouldn't I?

In addition, over the last few years, I have become less enamoured of the tremendous emphasis placed on targets, especially the fiscal deficit. Targets are indeed important. But process integrity is no less important. In fact, it is arguably more important.

I think the government made a commendable effort to bring back fiscal discipline after the profligate years following the global financial crisis. What is striking though is that while headline deficits have come down, debt–GDP ratios have been stubbornly high and rising. This is striking because deficit and debt ratios normally follow similar paths. If deficits are brought down to low levels, borrowing will be low, and nominal debt will rise by only a small amount. And if nominal GDP grows rapidly, the debt–GDP ratio should fall. The fact of rising debt despite healthy GDP growth warrants more attention.

Why didn't debt–GDP ratio decline? One reason is straightforward: the government has had to issue additional debt to finance bank recapitalization. But the deeper issue has to do with activities that aren't reflected in the budget deficit. To take one example, the LIC and the SBI are playing a quasi-government role in helping distressed public-sector and private-sector enterprises such as IL&FS. For the moment, these activities will not show up in the government accounts. But ultimately they may do so, for if the bailouts lead to losses, the government may need to step in to assume some of the debt that LIC and SBI have thereby incurred. Another reason is that financing of budgetary expenditures by the National Small Savings Fund (NSSF) or by the issuance of special bonds are not always reflected in real-time deficit numbers.

Firms must report their results according to established accounting principles. But things are different when it comes to government. Singer–songwriter Paul Simon once told us that there are fifty ways to leave a lover. Similarly, governments have more than fifty ways—policies and accounting—to meet a deficit target. The narrower the definition of government, the greater the scope for shifting things off-budget. And the more complicated the fiscal arrangements—as they are in India because of different layers of 'off-budget' activities and incurring of contingent liabilities—the more the scope for creative accounting.

This is where budgetary process integrity becomes invaluable. Institutions such as the CAG provide a useful check on fiscal integrity, but only after long lags, and often important matters can get obscured in the lengthy and dense reports. Moreover, governments are under no compulsion to restate fiscal results emerging from the CAG's findings. An independent fiscal council as the N.K. Singh Committee had recommended—and which I wholeheartedly supported—could play a constructive role, especially if it happens in real time. The challenge, of course, is to get governments to agree to such process integrity, which will act as a check on their behaviour—and to have people of integrity and credibility staffing such a council.

Ultimately, the only real external check on governments is vigorous, informed, real-time democratic discussions. Disappointingly, market participants have neither the incentives nor the ability to call out creative accounting, as my V.K.R.V. Rao Memorial Lecture points out. They also hedge and fudge. So, for the needed discussions to take root we will need more academic and policy institutions of high quality, independence and integrity (the Institute for Fiscal Studies in the UK is one such example).

The final piece in this section (7.4) is on fiscal federalism. The setting up of the Fifteenth Finance Commission provides an opportunity to think afresh about tax devolution. Southern states kicked up a fuss recently, arguing that the use of the latest population data in tax devolution would disadvantage them relative to the populous states of the Hindi hinterland; they see this as a penalty for their superior performance in bringing population under control.

Regardless of the merits of these arguments, there has been remarkably little analytical discussion of the broader issue of redistribution, even as the amount of devolution has multiplied several times over, leading some states to be consistently large net providers of resources to other states. The piece is based on a Business Standard Public Lecture that I gave in Mumbai four days before my departure. It has some controversial new estimates about how much tax redistribution takes place within India, and who benefits and who loses. It also has some ideas on how

India should design tax sharing in the new world of Indian fiscal federalism, a world in which India is getting more economically integrated but where both the states and the Centre are giving up some of their tax sovereignty. I hope that it can inform the ongoing debate and permeate the ecosphere for future debates.

7.1*

Competence, Truth and Power

Macroeconomic Commentary in India

I delivered the Sixth V.K.R.V. Rao Memorial Lecture on 11 May 2017 at the Institute for Social and Economic Change (ISEC) in Karnataka. Dr Rao was one of India's greatest economists. He was passionate about research not just for its own sake but for its application to policy and solving India's pressing challenges of poverty. He said, memorably, 'My passion was always to make my economics useful for the nation's economic growth and the welfare of its masses . . . economics should not be studied in isolation from the other social sciences . . . economics should be learnt and used to solve people's problems.'

Precisely for this reason, he was the pre-eminent builder of social science institutions. Dr Rao established three great national institutions—the Delhi School of Economics (DSE), the Institute of Economic Growth (IEG) and the Institute for Social and Economic Change—and was also instrumental in the creation of a number of international institutions. The idea for the Delhi School was hatched when he and Pandit Nehru were in the UK.

One of my favourite stories concerns Dr Rao's first recruit to the Delhi School of Economics. The DSE had advertised for an ordinary readership position, only to find that the great veteran economist K.N. Raj had applied. Dr Rao rejected the application and unilaterally offered him a prestigious professorship instead.

Given Dr Rao's abiding interest in research and his faith in its social values, the subject of this section is not altogether misplaced. As the title suggests, this addresses the state of macroeconomic policy commentary and research in the country.

Macroeconomics is central to the work we do at the ministry of finance and the RBI. Many key policy decisions are driven and underpinned by an assessment of the macroeconomic situation. So, whether the fiscal deficit should be higher or lower, whether public investment should be increased or decreased, whether interest rates should be increased or lowered, are all questions critically dependent on our assessment of the current state of the economy and where we think it is headed.

Formally, this assessment is made by the key policymakers: the ministry of finance broadly on fiscal policy; previously the RBI and now the Monetary Policy Committee (MPC) on interest and exchange-rate policies. Of course, sometimes they give advice to each other. (A small joke: the advice is almost always unsolicited and always the same—'CUT'—the RBI on fiscal deficits, the ministry of finance on interest rates, and they naturally savour their freedoms to ignore each other.)

In fact, the ministry of finance and the RBI are far from the only bodies that give advice. Assessments of the macro situation are, and must be, the result of a far wider process, in which inputs are also provided by experts in the private sector, academia and civil society. In each case, experts could be Indian or foreign. As an insider, I am an eager consumer of the opinions of outsiders. Indeed, when I was the CEA, I read a fair amount of commentary by analysts and journalists. But what I see from all my research is a clear pattern, and it is a worrisome one.

My central thesis is this: much of this expert opinion, and not infrequently, is liable to being compromised. In short, like the French novelist Émile Zola criticizing those who had unjustly framed a decorated soldier in nineteenth-century France: '*J'accuse!*'

What is my criticism? My claim is that experts often hold back their objective assessment. Instead, they censor themselves, and in public fora are insufficiently critical and independent of officialdom—whether the officials are in Mumbai or Delhi. To the extent they offer criticism, it is watered down to the point of being unidentifiable as criticism.

Let me immediately add two important caveats. First, what I am asserting is not unique to India; these 'misdemeanours' are widely prevalent across the world. Also, I am painting with a broad brush; there are some notable Indians who are consistent exceptions to my thesis/critique. Still, what strikes me is how few these exceptions are and how infrequently the experts are willing to engage in public debate about the macroeconomy.

Why do the experts do this? Why do they refuse to speak truth to power? If you ask them, they would likely say that they are just trying to be 'constructive'. But I feel something else is at work. For a variety of reasons, experts feel the need to stay on the right side of power—whether the RBI or the government. So, before policy decisions are taken, the experts tend to express the views they think the officials are likely to take. After policy actions, they try hard to endorse the decisions already taken. As a result, we in the government do not really benefit from their wisdom. This is a serious problem because high-quality policymaking demands high-quality inputs and high-quality debates.

The paradox is that in other spheres—such as trade policy or development policy—one sees a more vibrant, healthy and unself-censored debate. Why is there such little debate about macro policy? I would venture three explanations.

First, a major source of macroeconomic commentary is from the stakeholders, such as bankers and other financial-sector participants, whose relationship to officialdom is not arm's-length.

Second, when it comes to the more disinterested commentators—notably academics—there may be a certain intellectual diffidence. Macroeconomics is profoundly general equilibrium in nature, that is, it involves the interrelationships between several markets for goods, money and bonds both domestically and internationally, and these are inherently complicated. Because of these complexities, it is much more difficult to be sure of the optimal policy stance. All this might well discourage even independent commentators from standing out, from being contrarian to the conventional or official wisdom.

That said, I do believe something deeper is at work. On micro and development issues, India and Indians are on the global academic frontier. This is less true of macroeconomics. For example, while there are many Indian economists working abroad, there is very little research on Indian macroeconomics even in the US. Part of the explanation is that there isn't enough high-frequency data to make such work interesting. But surely this is only part of the explanation. This is a matter of sociological interest that needs greater investigation.

I want to illustrate some of these ideas with a few examples from recent Indian experience. The first example relates to the compromised analysis of the international ratings agencies which is discussed in Section 7.2.

Example 1: Fiscal Policy

Let me now turn to domestic examples. On the domestic side, there is a clear relationship between expert analysis and official decisions. Before policy decisions, the expert analysis is often illuminating. But once the decisions are taken, it is truly striking how the tune and tone of the analysis changes. Analysts fall over backwards to rationalize the official decision.

Some examples should make this point clear. Starting from the time the Fiscal Responsibility and Budget Management Act of 2003 (FRBM) was enacted, it had been an article of faith in the economic community that the government ought to abide by its strictures. About a decade ago, however, the government decided to conform to the letter of the FRBM while violating its spirit by issuing large sums of 'off budget' bonds to oil companies to window-dress the magnitude of the fiscal deficit. In that instance, I recall that the response of the experts was a whimper compared to the magnitude of the concealing actions. Once the decision was made, it was rationalized, rather than challenged.

A similar dynamic can be seen in the assessments of more recent budgets. Before the 2016–17 and 2017–18 budgets were announced, outside views spanned the spectrum. Some urged the government to stick to the pre-announced target, others to go slow on consolidation; some even asked for expanding the deficit, especially this year (2017–18), given the weakness of the economy after demonetization. Yet, whatever their initial view, once the budget was announced, commentators almost uniformly endorsed the actual government policy. One would have thought that they would at least be mildly embarrassed by their change of views. But they showed no signs of such embarrassment; indeed, they didn't even admit they had changed their views.

Example 2: Current Macroeconomic Assessment

Perhaps the epitome of the dynamic described above can be found in the assessments of monetary policy. Consider how expert assessments have evolved just over the past few months. After demonetization, a consensus had built up amongst the investor community and the economic analysts that the RBI would cut interest rates. This consensus was based on: (a) a declining trend in inflation from Q2 FY 2017; and (b) the projected short-term adverse impact of demonetization on growth.

It turned out that the Monetary Policy Committee of India (MPC) did not cut interest rates. Instead, in December, it signalled a more hawkish stance (going from accommodative to neutral), and since then has maintained that stance.

Yet, instead of criticizing the official decisions, as consistency would demand, analysts found ex-post logic to attribute merit to these decisions. That is, far from criticizing the central bank for holding rates constant over the past three announcements, analysts praised the policy stance as prudent and helpful in boosting the credibility of the inflation-targeting framework. While the RBI's decision may well be commendable, it is odd that before December, experts saw no inconsistency between a rate cut and the credibility of the central bank.

To be fair, some change in position could be warranted either if the official assessment revealed something about the economy that analysts did not previously know or if they learnt something new about the RBI's preferences or reaction function. Since December, there has been perhaps one new aspect of preferences that markets did reveal: after some ambiguity in September, the MPC has only subsequently (in February 2017) made clear that its target is 4 per cent, not, say, 5 per cent. Even allowing for this, the analysis and commentary have remarkably toed the official line post facto.

My second point is perhaps even more fundamental. I want now to present a macroeconomic update of the economy. Treat this as not my update or that of the ministry of finance's but that of a disinterested observer's who has just landed from Mars (say, brought home by our satellite Mangalyaan).

The following figures (1–9) lay out the update:

Figure 1: Falling Headline Inflation, Below Medium-term Target of 4 Per Cent

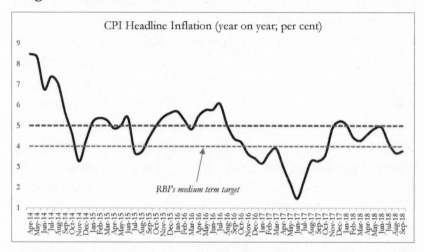

Figure 2: Easing Underlying Inflation Pressures: 'True' Core* Is Falling

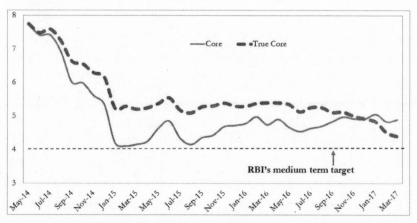

Core inflation excludes food and fuel. 'True core' also excludes transport services.

Figure 3: Easing Imported Inflation: Appreciating Nominal Exchange Rate

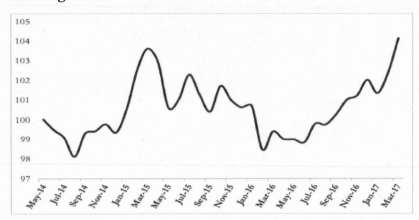

Figure 4: Slowing Underlying Growth: Real GVA Headline Flat, Sharp Dip in Core GVA

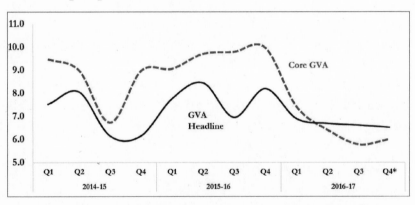

Core GVA is obtained by subtracting agriculture and government services from aggregate GVA.
*Q4 value is based on CSO's projection.

Figure 5: Sharp Decline in Credit Growth to Industry

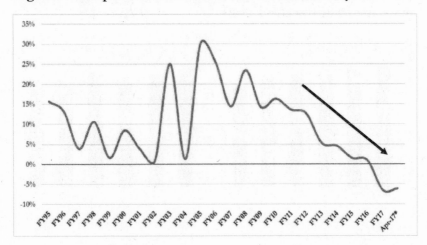

Figure 6: Deteriorating Competitiveness As Rupee Has Strengthened

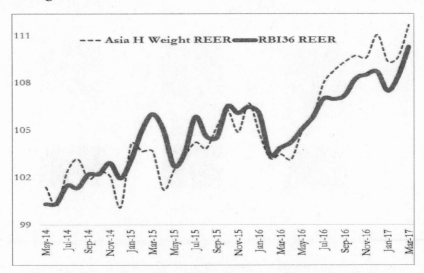

REER: real effective exchange rate; increase denotes deteriorating competitiveness. RBI36 REER based on trade with thirty-six countries, whereas the Asia H Weight REER assigns greater weights to India's Asian competitors (Economic Survey, 2016–17).

Figure 7: Further Fiscal Consolidation in 2017–18 at Central, State and Public-sector Levels

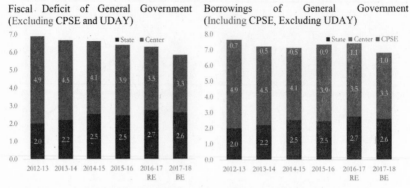

Fiscal Deficit of General Government (Excluding CPSE and UDAY)

Borrowings of General Government (Including CPSE, Excluding UDAY)

Data for 2015–16 to 2017–18 is for sixteen states (accounting for 80–82 per cent of GDP) for which budgets have been presented. CPSE stands for Central Public–Sector Enterprises.

Figure 8: Public-sector Investment

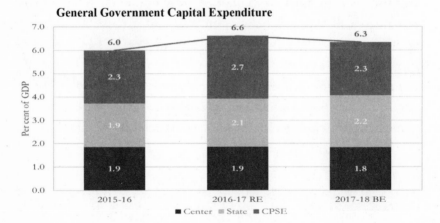

General Government Capital Expenditure

Figure 9: Monetary Policy: Increasing Real Repo (Policy) Rate

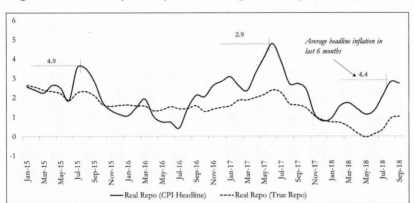

The bottom line from this analysis of the above charts is that inflation pressures are easing considerably, the inflation target has been overachieved, and the inflation outlook is benign because of a number of economic developments. Real activity remains weak and well below potential and the exchange rate is appreciating, thereby denting exports. Against this background, most reasonable economists would say that the economy needs all the macroeconomic policy support it can get. Instead, both fiscal and monetary policies remain tight. And on top of that, there are some officials who even think that the policies should get tighter.

Now here are my questions:

- Have they (and here I mean the thrust of opinion emerging from the analyst community) highlighted that we have overachieved on inflation well in advance of scheduled targets?
- Have they highlighted that core inflation—properly measured— has been declining steadily over the last seven months and is on target to achieve the medium-term inflation target?
- Have they highlighted that an appreciating exchange rate will dampen inflation going forward?

- Have they highlighted ritual invocations that oil prices could increase because geopolitical risks are less plausible today since oil markets have fundamentally changed, placing ceilings on oil-price movements?
- Have they highlighted that perhaps real activity could be recovering slowly, not rapidly, and hence that output gaps could be widening, moderating inflationary pressures?
- Have they highlighted that fiscal policy has been tight (and to borrow from American economist Paul Krugman's phrase perhaps even 'irresponsibly responsible'), and that public investment has not significantly increased at a time of weak private investment?
- Have they highlighted that even though liquidity conditions have eased (perhaps alarmingly), the real policy rate is at a recent high and at the previous high, inflation was much greater?

In sum, have they highlighted that inflation is under control and activity may be weakening, calling for all the fiscal and monetary policy support that the economy may badly need?

There is a famous joke about asking three economists for a view and getting four different answers. Today there are hundreds of economists outside the government and the RBI and several within. Instead of getting a hundred-plus views, we get about *one* view—the official view. It's even more interesting that about twelve months ago, when inflation was much higher and growth was higher as well, there were economists who called for a large cut in interest rates. Yet, today, they are silent.

The alternative view that I've presented—which is at variance with this consensus view both on the assessment and the policy prescription sides—is not necessarily my view, and may not even be the right view. But it is an eminently plausible view that must be part of the policy discussion—and yet we have not heard it, or even anything close to it. I find this a somewhat disconcerting state of the macroeconomic commentary in India.

Similar things happened in early 2015, when there were two successive rate cuts in-between monetary policy meetings. Inter-meeting cuts are supposed to happen exceptionally, and that too only in response to new and unforeseen developments, but the commentary was surprisingly incommensurate with the actions.

Another example relates to liquidity conditions in two episodes (the first in late 2015 and the second in the period following demonetization), when policy announcements and actual liquidity conditions have diverged in a manner that would have been the object of insistently serious commentary in other countries, but in India have been greeted by indulgent acquiescence on the part of commentators.

Concluding Thoughts

If what I have argued has some validity, some conclusions follow. We need more disinterested voices—especially universities and independent researchers that are distant from and not dependent upon the apparatus of power—to speak up. This may require us to beef up capability in macroeconomic teaching in our universities so that we can build up the intellectual confidence for people to express contrarian opinions. In substantiation of this point, look at the FRBM debate. I am really heartened by the debate emerging around the FRBM report. But note that this debate is gathering steam because of the thoughtful contributions of independent voices such as Professor Indira Rajaraman and Professor Pronab Sen. The investor community reported on the FRBM as if there was a unanimity of views, which there wasn't.

(An aside. Let me remark here that one of the interesting and potentially very positive developments about social media is that it has encouraged more US and UK academics to enter the realm of the macroeconomic policy conversation. In India, while social media is as omnipresent as elsewhere, it has not become a forum for serious macroeconomic debates as elsewhere.)

Another conclusion relates to the behaviour of officialdom. All officialdom wants validation for its actions. So, in the short run, it will want to shape opinion in its favour. But in the long run, that is perhaps not desirable. Public interest is better served by richer debate that encompasses critical views, including those of the officialdom. Officials should signal that clearly.

As I conclude, the opening line of a famous essay, 'Of Truth', by Francis Bacon—considered the father of the scientific method—comes to mind: 'What is truth? said Jesting Pilate, and would not stay for an answer.' In this post-truth world, with independent, self-created, self-validated realities, perhaps Pilate would have wearied of even asking the question.

But one thing is certain: truth, no matter how elusive that notion is—the discovery of which, no matter how hard that search is going to be—requires diversity of opinion. Such diversity will require both competence and capability. And above all, it will require voices that are not silenced, compromised or conveniently moderated by the lure or fear of power.

7.2

Poor Standards

China and India and the Dubious Assessments of Ratings Agencies

In recent years, the role of ratings agencies has increasingly come into question. After the US financial crisis, questions were raised about their role in certifying as AAA (the top rating, signifying the near-absence of risk) bundles of mortgage-backed securities that had toxic underlying assets (memorably described in Michael Lewis's *The Big Short*). In other cases, questions have arisen because they failed to sound the alarm ahead of financial crises—often ratings downgrades have occurred post facto, a case of closing the stable doors after the horses have bolted.

It is also worth assessing the role of rating agencies in more normal situations. In the case of India, American financial services company Standard & Poor's, in November 2016, ruled out the scope for a ratings upgrade for some considerable period, mainly on the grounds of the country's low per capita GDP and relatively high fiscal deficit. The actual methodology to arrive at India's rating was clearly more complex. Even so, it is worth asking: are these variables the right key for assessing India's risk of default?

Consider first per capita GDP. It is a very slow-moving variable. Over the last forty-five years, real per capita GDP has increased by just 2.5 per cent per year on an average in middle-income countries. At this rate, the poorest of the lower-middle–income countries would take about fifty-seven years to reach upper-middle–income status. So, if this variable is really the key to ratings, poorer countries might be provoked into saying, 'Please don't bother this year, come back to assess us after half a century.'

Consider next the fiscal variables. Ratings agencies assess fiscal outcomes by comparing a country's performance to that of its 'peers'. So, India is deemed an outlier because its general government fiscal deficit of 6.6 per cent of the GDP (2014) and debt of 68.6 per cent of the GDP (2016) are out of line with certain other emerging markets.

But India could very well *be* different from these 'peers'. After all, many emerging markets are struggling. But India is growing strongly, while its fiscal trajectory coupled with its commitment to fiscal discipline exhibited over the last three years, suggests that its deficit and debt ratios are likely to decline significantly over the coming years.

Even if this scenario does not materialize, India might still be able to carry much more debt than other countries because it has unusually low levels of foreign currency–denominated debt, and, in particular, because it has an exceptionally high 'willingness to pay', as demonstrated by its history of never defaulting on its obligations. As Jason Furman, chairman of President Obama's Council of Economic Advisers, has emphasized, debt sustainability is as much or more about the political willingness to pay rather than the economic ability to do so. The biography of former prime minister Narasimha Rao by Vinay Sitapati makes clear that India went to extraordinarily lengths as mentioned previously, including flying gold from the RBI's vaults to the Bank of England, to reassure creditors in 1991 that it would honour its debt obligations.

Figure 1: Credit/GDP and GDP Growth for China and India and Their S&P Ratings

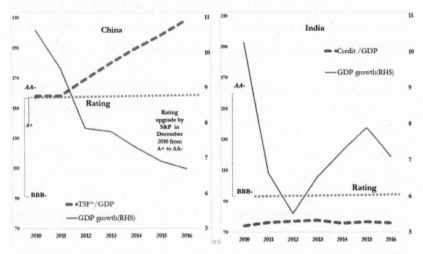

Source: WDI and S&P; for 2016, India's credit data are from the RBI and Credit Suisse; for 2016, China's credit number is obtained by adding flows of total social financing (TSF) from the Bank for International Settlements (BIS) to the 2015 stock.

India also compares favourably to other countries on other metrics known to be closely related to the risk of default. Consider the contrast with China. In 2008, in response to the global financial crisis, China launched a historic credit expansion, which has so far seen the credit–GDP ratio rise by an unprecedented 86 per cent of the GDP, much larger than the stock of India's credit–GDP (Figure 1) ratio. At the same time, Chinese growth has slowed from over 10 per cent to 6.5 per cent.

How did Standard & Poor's react to this ominous scissors pattern, which has universally been acknowledged as posing serious risks for China, and indeed the world? In December 2010, it upgraded China's rating from A+ to AA- and it has never adjusted it since, even as the credit boom has unfolded and growth has experienced a secular decline.

In contrast, India's ratings have remained stuck at the much lower level of BBB-, despite the country's dramatic improvement in growth and macroeconomic stability since 2014.

In other words, the level and change in the ratings received by China and India bear no resemblance to the dramatically different evolution in the level and change of the underlying risks.

These anomalies raise a question: does the fault, dear Brutus, lie in the objective economic circumstances of the 'beheld-ratees' or in the hard-to-decipher methodologies of the 'beholder-raters'?

7.3*

FRBM

A Dissent Note Outlining an Alternative Fiscal Architecture

It has now been fifteen long years since the Fiscal Responsibility and Budget Management Act was enshrined in law and the basic principles of prudent fiscal management were elaborated. Over this period, the situation in India has changed completely. Back in 2003, the economy was fairly small and still relatively closed to the outside world, generating per capita incomes that lagged far behind that of other emerging markets. Today, India has become a middle-income country. Its economy is large, open and growing faster than any other major economy in the world.

Amidst these dramatic changes, the fundamental insight of the FRBM has endured. The country should always endeavour to strengthen its fiscal position so as to ensure medium-term debt sustainability and contain macroeconomic imbalances. If this is done, credibility will be preserved, borrowing costs will be kept low, and most importantly, crises can be averted.

A strong fiscal position also supports growth. It generates the savings needed to allow high levels of private investment to be sustained over the medium term. It also provides room for counter-cyclical policies, allowing public investment to be stepped up when growth is temporarily weak.

These basic principles of fiscal rectitude are ever-enduring. At the same time, the transformation of India's economy means they will need to be translated into a very different fiscal framework from the one envisaged fifteen years ago. The broad objectives, longer-term targets and glide paths must all be rethought, as those that were appropriate for the small and vulnerable economy of long ago but surely are no longer valid for the large and strong economy of today.

The new framework will also need to take into account the experience gained during the first decade of the FRBM's operation. The FRBM has played a vital role in promoting the concept of fiscal discipline. It was also successful for a time in ensuring that fiscal discipline was actually maintained. But it failed in two important ways.

First, it failed in flow terms, in the sense that it couldn't prevent a build-up of dangerous fiscal imbalances. During the growth

Figure 1: Central Government (CG) Fiscal Deficit and Expenditures (Per Cent of GDP)

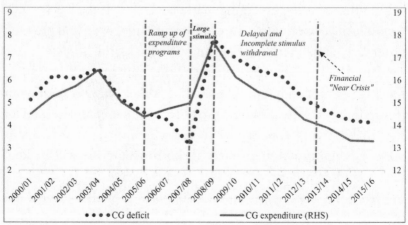

Source: International Monetary Fund.

and revenue booms of the mid-2000s, it allowed new spending programmes to be introduced, which could not be sustained when receipts fell back to more normal levels (Figure 1). Then, after the global financial crisis, the FRBM failed to prevent an excessively large stimulus, which was withdrawn neither adequately nor on time. The end result was the financial currency 'near-crisis' in the autumn of 2013.[1]

Second, the FRBM failed in stock terms, in that it couldn't place the country's debt securely on a downward path. To be sure, the stock of central and general (Centre plus all the states) governments' debt initially followed a declining trajectory (Figure 2). But after 2010–11, the trend was first interrupted, then actually reversed. This failure ultimately stemmed from the reliance on rapid growth rather than fiscal adjustment to do the 'heavy lifting' on debt reduction. Such a strategy worked well when the nominal GDP was increasing rapidly. But it proved unsuccessful when the nominal growth slowed.

Figure 2: General Government Debt, Primary Balance and Interest Rate–Nominal Growth Differential

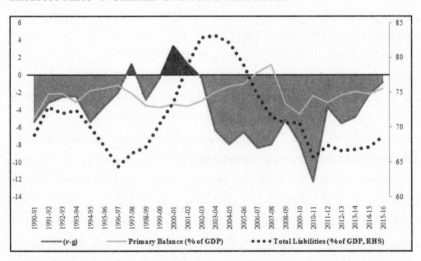

Note: 'r' is the average nominal cost of government borrowing, 'g' the nominal GDP growth rate, and primary balance is the total government revenue minus non-interest costs. Light grey (and dark grey) areas denote periods of favourable (unfavourable) debt dynamics.

From this particular experience of the FRBM's somewhat mixed success, two important lessons can be drawn. Fiscal rules need some flexibility so that large cyclical swings can be handled within the framework—rather than by abandoning them—thereby disciplining departures from fiscal rules during these swings. The rules need to be reformulated to ensure that this time around, debt is placed firmly on a downward trajectory.

The FRBM committee's report accordingly focuses on these issues. On the first, it proposes an 'escape clause' to deal with the cyclicality problem. Ideally, this problem should be handled by cyclically adjusting the deficit targets. But as the report points out, calculating such adjustments is not possible at the present time. So, instead, the committee has formulated an escape clause, with a number of carefully defined triggers, a bounded adjustment to the target and a sensible timeframe for returning to the adjustment path. Notably, and to address the flow problem described above, the clause is symmetric, curtailing spending in booms as well as curbing prolonged and unduly large fiscal expansions in response to downturns.[2]

The committee's recognition that the FRBM needs an escape clause is welcome. However, the formulation of this clause is problematic. The key trigger relating to growth would only be activated in exceptional circumstances, when growth departs by 3 percentage points or more from its latest four-quarter average. As a result, two distinct problems are likely to arise. The government will have no flexibility to relax the fiscal stance to combat ordinary recessions, yet it will simultaneously have too much room to expand spending during growth booms.

Some simple examples make the problem clear. If real GDP growth declined from 5 per cent to just above 2 per cent, causing revenue growth to falter, the government would be required to cut spending to achieve the fiscal-deficit target. Similarly, if growth increased from, say, 6 per cent to just below 9 per cent, all of the increased revenue could be spent. Such behaviour would produce a dramatically pro-cyclical fiscal policy, aggravating the slumps and booms, thereby running the risk of generating macroeconomic instability. To avoid such an outcome (especially to escape from the straitjacket of no flexibility even in the face of a serious downturn), the government would likely abandon the FRBM framework, as it did after the global financial crisis.

In other words, the design of the escape clause risks ignoring lessons from the Indian experience during the period 2007–08 to 2014–15 discussed earlier.

Now, on the basic architecture of the committee's recommendations—the proposed objectives and operational targets—I have serious reservations.

In effect, the committee is proposing three targets: stock (debt–GDP ratio), flow (fiscal deficit–GDP ratio) and composition (revenue deficit–GDP ratio, with the revenue deficit defined as current expenditures less current revenues). This is a problem, because multiple targets force policymakers to aim at too many potentially inconsistent objectives and analytical frameworks, running the risk of overall fiscal policy being difficult to communicate for the government and comprehend for market participants, and the risk of the government not achieving any of its goals.

Moreover, each of the targets is questionable. The debt target is set at an arbitrary 60 per cent of the GDP for general government. The medium-term fiscal deficit target is set at an equally arbitrary 2.5 per cent of the GDP for the central government. The revenue deficit target, whose very rationale is debatable, is nonetheless set at an extremely precise 0.8 per cent of the GDP for the central government. Perhaps oddest of all is the fiscal deficit path, which calls for a deep cut in the first year (2017–18) to 3 per cent of the GDP for the central government, then a pause for two years, then a resumption of deficit cutting, this time by moderate amounts.

No real rationale is provided for such a serpentine path, and it is difficult to find one.

In contrast, I would propose a simpler architecture, comprising just one objective: placing debt firmly on a declining trajectory. To achieve this, the operational rule would aim at a steady but gradual improvement in the general government's primary balance (non-debt receipts minus non-interest expenditures) until the deficit is entirely eliminated. This strategy would ensure that debt will remain on a downward path even over the longer term, when India's debt dynamics turn less favourable. I elaborate on these points below.

Objective: Debt Level or Trajectory?

The lodestar of this report is the level of government debt. In this respect, it echoes the reviews by rating agencies, which have repeatedly claimed that debt is India's main fiscal problem. Indeed, the level of concern expressed in this report is such that, while debt is invoked to be an 'anchor' for fiscal policy, this anchor hovers uneasily between being a 'ceiling' and a 'target'. Clearly, it cannot be a ceiling because in that case the government would be in violation of the FRBM from the moment the revised framework is introduced. So, it must be something more akin to a target.

But it has never been so obvious that the current level of debt is such a problem, much less such a pressing one that it needs to be brought down to 60 per cent of GDP within the next five years. To begin with, India has carried much higher debt ratios in the past, as much as 83 per cent of GDP, without encountering debt-servicing difficulties or finding that the debt posed obstacles to growth. In fact, the country experienced its greatest-ever period of growth in the mid-2000s when the debt was as much as 10 percentage points higher than it is today. So, the public might well ask why the debt ratio is suddenly considered such an impediment to India's aspirations that it merits a legal response taking the form of a 'debt ceiling' well below levels of the recent past.

The answer given in the report is that India needs to reduce its debt to a safe level, which is confidently asserted to be 60 per cent of the GDP. But increasingly economists doubt whether it is really possible to identify 'optimal' or even 'safe' levels of debt. Different studies have identified very different thresholds of debt danger, ranging from 20 per cent of the GDP to 90 per cent of the GDP. Moreover, all of these studies, most prominently C.M. Reinhart and Kenneth S. Rogoff's research from the National Bureau of Economic Research in the US, titled 'Growth in a Time of Debt', have been criticized as methodologically questionable. The negative relationship they find between the level of public debt and growth turns out to be sensitive to many factors, most importantly the direction in which that debt is heading.

Recent developments have only underscored the doubts. Earlier, it was assumed that debt levels exceeding 100 per cent of the GDP would surely be dangerous. Yet, after the global financial crisis, debt ratios in many advanced countries crossed this threshold and interest rates simultaneously fell to historically low levels. As a result, it is now unclear to policymakers whether debt in Europe really needs to be reduced to the 60 per cent of the GDP levels specified in the Maastricht Treaty. Certainly, EU authorities are no longer making any serious efforts to enforce this rule.

In the end, the safe level of debt is more a matter of the willingness of the political system to service its debt than any innate ability to do so. And India has always demonstrated exceptionally high determination to repay, most famously in 1991 when it shipped gold out of the country as collateral for foreign loans, to prove that it was committed to repaying them.

For India, indeed for any country, what matters far more than the precise level of debt is the *direction* in which the debt is heading. If investors see that debt is on a declining path, they are reassured. If it is instead rising explosively, they might worry that the commitment to fiscal discipline has been eroded. In that case, they would demand higher interest rates on government securities, which would quickly feed through into higher borrowing costs for the private sector, damaging investment and growth. In a worst-case scenario, markets might completely refuse to purchase government debt, forcing the government to default and triggering a financial crisis.

A loss of debt sustainability is extremely unlikely in India. But the country does have an underlying vulnerability, which needs to be addressed, lest such a scenario one day comes to pass. This vulnerability is the country's primary deficit. Put simply, India's government (Centre and states combined) is not collecting enough revenue to cover its running costs, let alone the interest on its debt obligations.

There is nothing extraordinary about running a primary deficit per se. Most of the other large emerging markets do so, having fallen into this situation after the global financial crisis when the GDP growth and revenues slowed, while stimulus spending was increased (Table 1). Even so, India stands out for the size of the deficits that it has run over the past decade, especially when compared with its rate of growth. At such rapid rates of growth, substantially greater than those of its peers, its primary deficit should have been much lower than others; instead it has been significantly greater (Figure 3).

As a result of running a primary deficit, the government is dependent on growth and favourable interest rates to contain the debt ratio.[3] In recent years, the growth–interest rate [g–r] differential has been just sufficient to keep the debt ratio stable. It follows that if one day growth were to falter and interest rates were to rise, the debt ratio could start to spiral upwards. A debt explosion would admittedly require a large, unlikely shock. But it is not just a theoretical possibility, either—it is exactly what happened to Greece.

Table 1: General Government Primary Balance (Per Cent of GDP) and Real GDP Growth (Per Cent)

	2007	2008	2009	2010	2011	2012	2013	2014	2015	2016	Average	Real GDP Growth (%)
Argentina	1.7	1.8	-1.1	-0.4	-1.4	-1.5	-2.4	-3.2	-5.4	-5.6	-1.8	2.3
Brazil	3.2	3.8	1.9	2.3	2.9	1.9	1.7	-0.6	-1.9	-2.8	1.2	2.0
China	0.4	0.4	-1.3	1.1	0.4	-0.2	-0.3	-0.4	-2.1	-2.2	-0.4	8.9
India	0.4	-5.3	-5.2	-4.2	-3.9	-3.1	-3.1	-2.8	-2.3	-2.1	-3.2	7.4
Indonesia	0.9	1.7	-0.1	0.0	0.5	-0.4	-1.0	-0.9	-1.2	-1.0	-0.2	5.7
Mexico	1.5	1.7	-2.3	-1.4	-1.0	-1.2	-1.2	-1.9	-1.2	0.1	-0.7	2.1
Russia	5.6	4.7	-6.2	-3.1	1.7	0.7	-0.8	-0.7	-3.2	-3.4	-0.5	1.5
South Africa	3.9	2.1	-2.5	-2.1	-1.1	-1.3	-0.9	-0.6	-0.6	-0.4	-0.4	2.1
South Korea	1.4	1.2	-0.7	0.8	0.9	0.8	-0.2	-0.3	-0.4	-0.3	0.3	3.3
Turkey	2.9	1.7	-1.4	0.3	2.1	1.1	1.4	1.4	1.2	0.3	1.1	3.5

Source: IMF Fiscal Monitor, October 2016.

Figure 3: Real GDP Growth and Average Primary Deficit (Per Cent of GDP), 2007–16

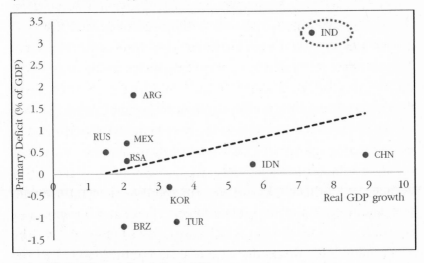

Source: IMF, World Economic Outlook, October 2016.

There is another consideration that needs to be kept firmly in mind. Both theory and evidence show that highly positive [g–r]—economic growth exceeding interest rates—is a feature of emerging markets. For advanced countries, the differential is typically close to zero; indeed, growth theory suggests that in the long run, there should not be a substantial wedge between the two. If [g–r] is zero, the primary balance must also be zero (or in surplus); otherwise, the debt will not be sustainable.

Since India is converging rapidly towards the West, it should prepare for the day when the growth–interest differential turns sustainedly unfavourable. It is certainly better to take pre-emptive action rather than wait until a problem arises. The central objective of the fiscal framework, consequently, should not be to achieve an arbitrary debt objective. Rather, the framework should aim at eliminating the primary deficit so that debt will continue to decline steadily, even in the longer run when favourable [g–r] dynamics fade away.

Admittedly, a primary deficit objective may sound unusual, for so far there has been little focus on this problem in India. But in other countries, particularly those in Latin America such as Brazil, it has long been the linchpin of the fiscal framework. Moreover, in recent years the primary balance has become quite a standard concept internationally. Over the past decade, there have been sixteen IMF lending programmes in which the primary balance—and not the overall balance—was the operational target, including important cases such as Greece and Ireland.

It will doubtless take some effort to accustom India to this framework. For example, the government would need to explain that adopting a primary-deficit objective does not mean that the bulk of the deficit is being ignored. Rather, it means the government is focusing squarely on the part of the budget that the government can control, as opposed to interest payments, which are largely predetermined. The government would also need to explain why eliminating the primary deficit is so important. This can be done simply by pointing out that a zero deficit is needed to end the current Ponzi-scheme–like situation in which the government is borrowing merely to pay its running costs, leave alone the interest on its debt.

In the meantime, until these principles sink into the public consciousness, a primary-deficit path can always be translated into the more familiar yearly objectives for the fiscal balance.

Path: Uneven or Smooth?

Any glide path needs to be grounded in India's past experience and its prospects for the future. Here, three distinct features must be kept in mind. First, over the medium term (the likely horizon for the revised FRBM), forces of convergence combined with steady reforms should deliver robust growth averaging around 8 per cent. By the same token, these forces may well lead to a slowdown thereafter. Consequently, the next decade should be viewed as a golden opportunity to 'fix the roof while the sun is shining'.

A second related point is that India, like most emerging markets, normally undertakes policy-related fiscal adjustment only gradually. Aside from crisis periods, the fiscal position has only improved sustainedly when it has benefitted from windfalls, arising from exceptional growth (as in the mid-2000s) or major declines in oil prices that allow for lower petroleum-related subsidies and higher excise taxes. For example, between 2014–15 and 2016–17, lower oil prices will have contributed about a percentage point to fiscal adjustment. Figure 2 illustrates the point, showing that the primary balance has remained relatively stable, apart from the growth boom around 2007–08 and the oil-related improvement more recently.

Third, there is no clear and present danger that demands a sharp response. On the contrary, the standard macroeconomic

indicators—growth, inflation, current-account balance, reserves—
are all at the best level they've been in years.

These three considerations suggest that that the fiscal
strategy should aim at modest but steady improvements that
over the course of this decade will gradually transform the
fiscal position. But this is not what the committee proposes.
Instead, it recommends a serpentine path for the Centre's fiscal
deficit, starting with an exceptionally large 0.5 percentage point
reduction to 3 per cent of the GDP in 2017–18, followed by no
further change for two years, then a further gradual reduction to
2.5 per cent of the GDP by 2022–23 (Figure 4). In other words:
cut sharply, pause, cut moderately. It is difficult to imagine a
path that is more uneven and more difficult to justify or explain
to the public.

**Figure 4: Fiscal Deficit: Committee's Recommendation and
Alternative Proposal** (Per Cent of GDP)

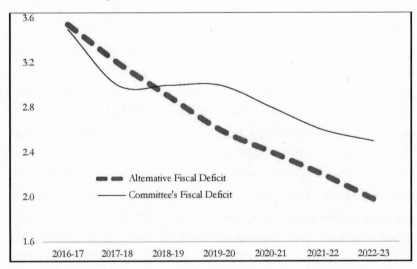

Instead, I would propose a trajectory much more consistent with
India's experience and prospects. The Centre's primary deficit

should be put on a gentle glide path, whereby it is reduced by 0.2 percentage points a year until a modest surplus of around half a per cent of the GDP is attained. If this path is followed, the Centre's fiscal deficit would have narrowed to 2 per cent of the GDP by 2022–23.

Strategy: Appropriately Ambitious?

The problems with the committee's proposal go far beyond the serpentine shape of the glide path. The deeper problem is that the envisaged strategy is at once excessively ambitious, and insufficiently so. Excessive, in the sense that there is no reason why such a large and disruptive adjustment would be needed next year (2018–19). Insufficient, in the sense that over the longer term, it fails to deal decisively with the true fiscal vulnerability, namely, the primary deficit.

Short-term Problems

Consider first the short-run problems. Not only is there no threat of imminent crisis, but such a large adjustment would be inappropriate from a cyclical point of view, as it would impart a contractionary impulse to an economy that remains in the early stages of a recovery, with export demand weak and investment and real credit actually falling.

Invocations of 7 per cent real GDP growth to justify a sharp fiscal contraction should be seen in light of the fact that growth remains below potential. Moreover, growth projections are subject to higher-than-normal confidence margins because the demonetization exercise in November 2016 was an unprecedented event. There are no guideposts from the past that allow one to confidently forecast the extent or duration of the impact of demonetization on the GDP.

Nor is it convincing to argue that credibility demands that the fiscal deficit be reduced sharply to 3 per cent next year. The government has already demonstrated its commitment to fiscal probity by continuing to cut the fiscal deficit even in the face of tepid economic activity.[4]

Medium-term Problems

Clearly, then, the committee's framework is not adequate to assess the desirability of the medium-term strategy. So, let's employ the one set out in the section where we examine the unviability of assuming a 'safe' level of debt and are thus better suited to examining the direction in which the debt is heading. From this perspective, one can see that the proposed path is insufficiently ambitious, as it manifestly fails to 'fix the fiscal roof'.

Over the next five years, the ratio of the Centre's interest obligations to the GDP is likely to fall by around 0.5 percentage points of the GDP, as high-cost debts from the previous decade are repaid. This will create considerable room for additional spending during the period when the committee calls for the fiscal deficit to be kept at 3 per cent of the GDP, meaning that for two years the primary balance would actually be deteriorating, rather than improving (Table 2). This deterioration would ultimately be reversed, assuming that the adjustment resumes as scheduled.

One may ask how this will affect the overall (general government) balance. Even assuming that the states succeed in curbing their deficit to around 2 per cent of the GDP,[5] it would not achieve the needful: the general government primary balance would remain in deficit throughout the medium term. In contrast, the alternative proposal would indeed eliminate, or come close to eliminating, the general government primary deficit by 2021–22.

Table 2: Medium-term Fiscal Deficit, Primary Deficit and Debt Paths for Central Government: Committee's Recommendation vs Alternative Proposal

	Primary deficit; Alternative	Primary Deficit; Committee	Fiscal Deficit; Alternative	Fiscal deficit; Committee	Debt; Alternative	Debt; Committee
2016–17	0.3	0.3	3.5	3.5	49.4	49.4
2017–18	0.1	-0.3	3.2	3.0	47.6	47.3
2018–19	-0.1	-0.1	2.9	3.0	45.6	45.5
2019–20	-0.3	0.0	2.6	3.0	43.3	43.7
2020–21	-0.5	-0.1	2.4	2.8	40.7	42.0
2021–22	-0.6	-0.1	2.2	2.6	38.2	40.3
2022–23	-0.7	-0.1	2.0	2.5	35.7	38.7

The committee's strategy may also fall short of its own debt objective. It may seem that adhering to fiscal-deficit targets could ensure achieving a debt target. After all, stocks (such as debt) are merely the sum of flows (such as deficits). But this is not true when the targets are expressed as ratios to the GDP, as they must be since the economy is growing. In this case, the precise relationship between deficits and debt depends on how fast the economy is growing.

Under the committee's identified scenario, growth is sufficient to ensure the debt target will be achieved as long as the deficit targets are respected. But in a slightly more adverse scenario, where real growth falls to 5 per cent for a few years before recovering—as indeed occurred a few years ago—the debt/GDP target at the end of the decade would be missed by no less than 3–4 percentage points. This alternative scenario underscores India's basic vulnerability: as long as the primary balance remains in deficit, progress in reducing the debt ratio will remain hostage to the vagaries of the growth–interest differential, factors which are outside the government's control.

The need for ambition in the medium term is reinforced by the situation of state government finances, which have been adversely affected by slower growth, the need to assume debt of the DISCOMs (under the Ujwal DISCOM Assurance Yojana [UDAY] scheme), and the need to implement the Seventh Pay Commission recommendations.

Consistency between Debt Objective and Operational Fiscal Deficit Rule

There is further a consistency problem between the debt objective recommended by the committee and the operational flow targets proposed. As mentioned previously, the debt objective hovers uneasily between a 'ceiling', a 'target' and an 'anchor'. In places, the committee refers to this objective as a 'ceiling'. But clearly this phrasing cannot be taken literally, for in that case the government would be in violation of the FRBM from the moment the revised framework is introduced because the current level of debt is above this ceiling.

Alternatively, the debt target could be interpreted as notional (an 'anchor'), something to be achieved 'one day', similar to the 60 per cent objective in Europe. In this case, it would not be adding much to the framework: the binding constraint would remain the fiscal-deficit path.

These considerations suggest a third interpretation, namely, that the debt objective should be seen as a 'target', meant to be achieved over the next decade. In this case, a number of serious questions arise. If debt is indeed a target, the operational rules for the fiscal deficit should have flowed from the debt objective. But they do not as the committee makes clear that the operational target instead flows from an alternative (and orthogonal) framework based on macroeconomic balances.

The well-known standard equation that relates the steady state debt ratio (D) with the constant fiscal deficit (FD) and constant nominal growth rate (g) is given by: $FD = D \text{ times } [g/(1+g)]$.

This was the equation that led to the famous Maastricht Stability and Growth Pact (SGP), which came into effect in 1999. In Europe, the objective of a debt target of 60 per cent of the GDP (arrived at because that was close to the average prevailing then in Europe) combined with a medium-term nominal growth assumption of 5 per cent, led to the choice of the fiscal deficit target of 3 per cent of the GDP (60 times 5).

Taking the committee's debt target of 40 per cent (for the central government) and the assumed nominal growth rate of 11.5 per cent, yields a central government fiscal-deficit target of about 4.1 per cent of the GDP (11.5/1.115 times 40). But the committee has proposed a resting place for the fiscal deficit of 2.5 per cent of the GDP by 2022–23, which is substantially lower than dictated by the debt objective. So, the operational target does not stem from the debt objective.

Where does the medium-term fiscal deficit target of 2.5 per cent of GDP come from? The committee has used a simple macro-balance equation to arrive at this number. The report assumes a current-account–deficit target, adds on the latest data for household financial saving to get a figure of 10 per cent of the GDP in available resources, then divides this amount equally between the government and the private sector, and divides the government share equally between the Centre and the states. Hence, the 2.5 per cent of the GDP.

There is some rationale for the last step, in that an equal division between the Centre and states follows a long-established precedent. But the other steps are arbitrary and the assumptions fragile.

It is not obvious that domestic saving should be predicted on the basis of the latest data. Saving fluctuates widely and is endogenous to growth: household financial saving was around 10 per cent of the GDP in the early years of the new millennium, then surged to around 11.5 per cent of the GDP during the boom, and fell sharply during the recent years to around 7 per cent of the GDP. So, the latest reading forms a slender reed on which to base legally binding, medium-term fiscal targets.

Finally, the division of resources equally between the public and private sectors is not only arbitrary but seems normatively wrong. Should the state really aim to take half the available household financial saving? On what basis?

Next, consider the implications of adding a hard debt (stock) objective to the fiscal deficit (flow) targets.

Consider how the government would need to respond if inconsistencies develop between the deficit and debt targets. Recall that the change in the debt–GDP ratio depends essentially on two factors: the fiscal deficit–GDP ratio, which measures the flow of new debt[6] and the rate of growth of nominal GDP, which effectively inflates away the old debt. To see this, imagine the case where the fiscal deficit is zero, real growth is zero, but inflation is 10 per cent. The debt–GDP ratio will shrink because the debt will stay the same but the denominator will increase by 10 per cent.

This situation creates a potential inconsistency between the deficit and debt targets. If inflation turns out to be lower than anticipated, the deficit targets would need to be tightened to ensure the debt–GDP target is respected. If these adjustments were to occur frequently (say every year), all predictability of the framework would be lost. But if adjustments were made infrequently, large and disruptive adjustments would be needed.

In fact, even if targets were adjusted frequently, the adjustments might need to be large if the deadline for achieving the debt target were approaching. For example, if the target were one year away, and debt still needed to be reduced by 1 percentage point, spending might need to be cut by 0.3–0.4 percentage points of the GDP in the middle of the fiscal year (about Rs 45,000–60,000 crore in today's terms) if inflation fell just a percentage point short of what was projected.

Such cuts would not only be disruptive and difficult to achieve, they would also be unwise. For, if inflation was falling short of the target, this could well be occurring because the economy was in a cyclical slump, which would be exactly the wrong time to be tightening the fiscal stance.

Summing up, a meaningful debt target requires the operational rules to flow from the target. But they don't. Instead, they flow from an alternative and orthogonal framework based on macroeconomic balances. And the numbers that stem from this framework are based on fragile assumptions about saving in the future and ad hoc choices on how that saving should be allocated between the public and private sectors.

Moreover, a hard target would quickly run into operational problems, forcing frequent reassessments of the fiscal-deficit path and occasional large, pro-cyclical spending cuts. At some point, many will begin to wonder why these adjustments are necessary and why it is so important to reduce debt to 60 per cent of the GDP. And when that happens, it will be impossible to give a credible answer, in which case the framework will be abandoned.

A Revenue-Deficit Target?

There is a valid reason to focus on the revenue deficit, namely, that capital expenditure should not be viewed in the same way as current spending. Capital spending is an addition to the nation's capital stock, which should bear future dividends that will counterbalance the interest costs of the debts incurred to finance it. Current spending yields no such future dividends. For this reason, the UK government attempted, until the global financial crisis, to follow a 'golden rule' of borrowing only for investment, and such a concept was built into the original FRBM as well.

That said, there are stronger reasons why the revised FRBM should eschew a revenue-deficit rule. The most obvious one is that it is simply not true that capital spending is always better than current spending. Both types of expenditure can be wasteful. At the same time, both types can be useful. There is a lot of context specificity to actual choices between the two which would be constrained by a blanket rule. There is a strong critique that India underspends dramatically on health and education, arguably to an even greater extent than on capital expenditure.

Moreover, one could argue that since future generations of Indians will be vastly richer than current ones, it would be optimal to borrow some consumption from the future for the benefit of those alive today. The way to do this would be by running a revenue deficit. Accordingly, it makes little sense to place arbitrary limits on the share of the revenue deficit in the overall deficit.

One could even go further. It might actually be counterproductive to establish a revenue-deficit target. The reason is that the greater the proliferation of targets, the greater the chance that the government will ignore some of them, thereby damaging the credibility of the entire framework. This is not just a theoretical point: it is exactly what has happened over the past decade. The existing FRBM already contains revenue-deficit objectives, but these have been routinely ignored, so much so that this objective has essentially been forgotten. The problem is not one of negligence; it is inherent to any framework where the objectives are many and potentially conflicting. So, adding a revenue deficit rule would further add to complications that already stem from having both a debt and fiscal-deficit rule, as described above.

Concluding Thoughts

The existing FRBM has served several important purposes. It has brought to the fore the vital importance of fiscal discipline, underscoring its central role in keeping the country on its rapid growth path, which is raising living standards towards those in the West. It has also provided a valuable framework for budgetary discussions. That said, India has changed substantially since 2003. The FRBM consequently needs to be updated in the light of the country's distinctive experience and its unique prospects going forward. After all, fiscal rules gain their force not so much from their legal strategy as from the consensus that lies behind them, in the economic, political and wider social communities. For such a deep consensus to be forged, the rules themselves need to be simple, consistent and broadly feasible.

Unfortunately, the committee's proposed architecture falls short on all these counts. There are multiple targets on stock, flow and composition, diffusing the focus, complicating communication and comprehension, and risking non-compliance. Further, the targets themselves are arbitrary. A 60 per cent debt–GDP rule cannot command broad consensus. Nor can a revenue deficit target of 0.8 per cent of the GDP. And the medium-term fiscal deficit target of 2.5 per cent of the GDP is based on a conceptual framework that is unrelated to the debt objective and based on calculations that are hard to justify.

Most critically, the fiscal-deficit path follows an odd sequence of 'cut-sharply, pause and cut again' that is difficult to explain or justify; inappropriate in the short run because of cyclical considerations; and insufficiently ambitious in the medium term in placing India's debt on a sustainable long-term trajectory.

Finally, the key trigger for invoking the escape clause (growth to exceed the recent trend by 3 percentage points) is so demanding that it would fail to provide enough flexibility during severe downturns and enough discipline during growth booms. In other words, the new architecture would be a corset on fiscal policy, resulting in extreme pro-cyclicality—aggravating booms and busts—with adverse effects on the economy.

Instead, I propose a simple and consistent architecture that reflects India's fiscal realities of the past and its prospects for the future. There should be one target: a steady glide path that eliminates the general government primary deficit within five years. This would ensure a declining debt trajectory, which would reassure investors and ensure that India's debt remains sustainable even when India's debt dynamics turn less favourable in the medium term. And the 'escape clause' should have a more reasonable growth trigger that allows for some relaxation of the deficit targets during recessions and some tightening of these targets during booms.

Such a simple, clear and consistent architecture would truly establish an FRBM for the twenty-first century.

7.4

Fiscal Federalism in India

An Analytical Framework and Vision[1]

India is changing: from many fragmented economic Indias to one integrated India; from a more centralized political India to many quasi-sovereign Indias. As a result, its fiscal arrangements, especially on tax sharing, need to evolve. But in what direction? That is the unenviably difficult question facing the Fifteenth Finance Commission (FFC) under the chairmanship of N.K. Singh.

Already, controversy has arisen. Initial salvos were fired by a number of southern states. Their concerns were expressed in technicalities, namely, the particular criteria the FFC should use, and their precise definitions. But the underlying issue is a serious one: how much tax revenue should prosperous states be expected to transfer to less well-off ones? The answer to this question is inevitably political. But economics can, and indeed must, help channel the debate by providing facts and a framework in which to think about them. Otherwise, the political debate may just generate heat and discord rather than light and comity.

Framework

What, then, is the framework that economics can provide?

Tax sharing in all federal systems needs to address three different objectives:

- redistribution (equalizing transfers);
- risk-sharing in response to shocks, especially within the framework of a political union with a single currency; and
- incentives for better performance—service delivery and revenue mobilization—at the lower tiers of government.

In the Indian context, these objectives are influenced by some hardy perennials. There is still a lack of 'convergence' in per-capita incomes amongst Indian states, making fiscal redistribution politically necessary for some states and burdensome for others. Then there is the excessive dependence of the lower tiers of government on transfers from higher tiers, potentially creating a bad dynamic of poor public-service delivery and weak accountability, which leads to poor tax effort, which feeds back into poor delivery.

This long-standing context has in recent years been impacted by three developments: the abolition of the Planning Commission, which implies that Centre–state transfers will now happen largely through the budgetary process and finance commissions; the verdict of the Fourteenth Finance Commission, which restored more autonomy to the states both on the tax and expenditure side; and the introduction of the GST, which has furthered economic integration, diluted fiscal autonomy and redistributed the tax base in favour of the relatively poorer and smaller states. The first two developments are well-known. Less appreciated is the impact of the GST.

Redistribution

The major task of FCs has been to come up with a formula for sharing taxes between the Centre and the states as a whole ('vertical devolution'), creating a pool of resources which is then divided amongst the states themselves ('horizontal devolution').

Successive FCs have deployed very different criteria for horizontal devolution. It is hard to discern any underlying method or pattern. We need to go back to first principles, and restore the primacy of the idea, implied in the Constitution, that the divisible pool comprises taxes that the Centre is collecting on behalf of the states. Accordingly, the default should be to give back to the states the taxes they have generated. Redistribution should then be understood as departures from this benchmark.

Based on this simple idea, we can calculate how much redistribution has been effected by successive FCs. When we do so, we find that the amount of redistribution has been rising steadily. After the Tenth Finance Commission, the share of the divisible pool used for redistribution was 22 per cent. After the Fourteenth Finance Commission, the share increased to 32 per cent. This translates as an increase from about 0.5 to 1.3 per cent of GDP, or a fivefold increase in real per-capita terms.

Figure 1: Share of Tax Resources that Involve Redistribution

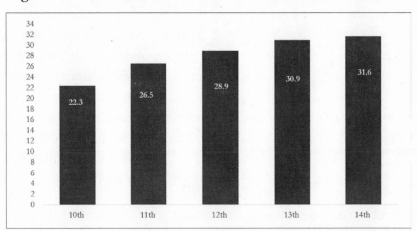

Second, as a result, some states have become large net contributors and others large beneficiaries. We measure contributions or benefits as a share of the notional amounts that states should have received had tax revenues simply been given back. On this basis, the fiscal impact of redistribution amounts to as much as 70–100 per cent, both for contributors and beneficiaries.

The pattern of these transfers is interesting. As expected, the largest receiving states are in the north-east and the interior. But contrary to popular impression, the large contributors are not all in the south. Rather, they are in the west, south and in the north (Figure 2). The Vindhyas are not the axis (metaphorical or geographic) distinguishing beneficiaries and recipients.

There have been important changes in the pattern of redistribution over time. The contribution of the southern states has been rising and the benefits to the north-east have been declining while those to some of the interior states—Uttar Pradesh, Madhya Pradesh and Bihar—have been rising.

Figure 2: Contribution/Benefit As Share of Notional Revenue (%)

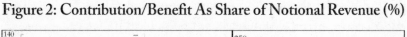
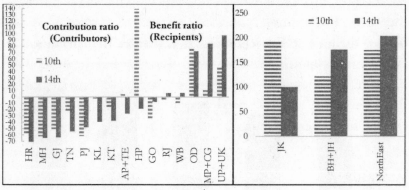

Fourth, some of these trends may reverse going forward, because of the introduction of the GST. Under the previous system, taxes accrued disproportionately to states that were major producers. But the GST is consumption-based. Preliminary research based on examining the first nine months of data suggests that this has indeed made a major difference, as the poorer and smaller states (that are broadly consumers) have seen a significant expansion in their tax base. Many of the net consuming states such as almost all the north-eastern states as well as Uttar Pradesh, Rajasthan, Madhya Pradesh, Delhi, Kerala and West Bengal have witnessed increased post-GST shares. As a result, their need for transfers may have correspondingly diminished.

Risk-sharing

We must all learn the lessons from Europe. Integration brings prosperity but it also allows shocks to be transmitted from one state to others. And if these states lack the monetary means to deal with the shocks and have limited fiscal manoeuvrability, serious economic and political tensions can arise.

The GST is transforming India into a common market. At the same time, the pooling of tax sovereignty that it has entailed has its counterpart in some loss of sovereignty for the Centre and the states. For example, the GST has subsumed around 31 per cent of the gross tax revenue of the Centre. It has subsumed an even larger proportion of the states' own tax revenue, around 47 per cent. This suggests that states, in particular, have lost some fiscal flexibility, and will need some help in dealing with major shocks, such as crop failures.

Rewards

Service delivery and own-tax raising by the states and third-tier institutions (urban and rural local bodies) remain a work-in-progress. Indian states collect much less own revenue (as a share of total revenue) than their corresponding tiers in countries such as Germany and Brazil. Also, both urban and local bodies in India are almost solely dependent on devolution from above. A common assertion is that not enough taxation powers have been devolved to the lower tiers. But this cannot be the explanation, for revenue collection falls far short of the potential already conferred.

For example, land revenue collection (for 2015–16 in three states—Karnataka, Tamil Nadu and Kerala) averages only around 7 per cent of potential, based on the market value of land. Even in states such as Kerala and Karnataka—ahead of others in devolution of powers to RLBs— the collection vis-à-vis potential is only around one-third.

This hints at the existence of a 'low-equilibrium trap'. Poor service delivery has led to weak own-tax revenue generation, weak accountability and resource-dependence, which has led back to poor delivery. This is a serious problem, for if urban governments are unable to meet the growing demand for services as population shifts to the cities, there will be a risk of social disruption.

Consequently, the issue facing the FFC is: can it provide credible incentives for second- and third-tier fiscal bodies to improve their own revenue performance, especially direct taxes, in order to facilitate better service delivery?

The Way Forward

Overall, the suggestion I've laid out above is that tax sharing should have four 'pots'.

First, a default pot, in which states get back their due based on their tax base (what might be called true 'devolution').

Second, a redistribution pot that balances the short-run need to equalize without denting the long-run incentive for revenue generation. Critically, the aggregate amount of redistribution and the contributions from the states need to be politically acceptable. Redistribution cannot permanently get ahead of the willingness of the underlying body politic to sustain it. Once the redistribution pot is decided, the allocation among states can be based on simple and parsimonious criteria, avoiding the complexity and arbitrariness that underlie current recommendations.

Third, there should be a risk-sharing pot to deal with both all-India (financial and currency crises) and state-specific shocks (monsoon and droughts). This could be done, for example, by setting aside a small share of the divisible pool (say 1 per cent) to be deployed in the event of shocks. The Centre and states have, of course, other fiscal instruments to deal with shocks but a common response could become more effective and a desirable feature of fiscal arrangements going forward.

The fourth (rewards) pot could be to break the 'low-equilibrium' trap at the lower tiers of government. For many reasons, this is not an easy task. One possibility might be to use matching grants so that a portion of the divisible pool is set aside and given to third-tier institutions conditional on their raising their own resources.

Finally, in the absence of the Planning Commission, a new institution may be needed to implement this 'vision'. The GST Council could be such an institution. Thus far, it has worked very effectively and demonstrated that cooperative federalism can work. It can now build on that experience to take on issues related to resource transfers and any other follow-up and implementation work which future fiscal federalism will necessitate.

India's future lies in cooperative federalism. Increasingly, the Centre and the states must come together to solve problems across the economic landscape. Therefore, its fiscal arrangements must be commensurate with the challenges ahead, and based on a framework and vision that are economically coherent and politically acceptable. The Fifteenth Finance Commission has an opportunity to design them as if it were the First.

Chapter 8

What Do They Know of Economics Who Don't Know Globalization and Tennis?

8.0

Globalization, Arrow, Federer and Nadal

'What do they know of cricket who only cricket know?' asked the Trinidadian Marxist historian and cricket writer, C.L.R. James. The same is true of an economist, especially a development economist, and even more so a practising development economist. But what must an economist know? Surely, he must know about globalization, the great economist–polymath Kenneth Arrow, and the tennis skills of Roger Federer and Rafael Nadal.

The first two sections (8.1 and 8.2) in this chapter are about globalization and the WTO. All economists who have been copious in their output will have said things that are either prescient or stupid—or prescient at some points and stupid at others. As Robert Solow famously said, 'Much of the change we think we see in life is merely the truth going in and out of fashion.'

In 2008, nearly a decade before the rise of Trumpism, I wrote a piece in the *Financial Times*, along with Professor Devesh Kapur of Johns Hopkins University and Pratap Bhanu Mehta, vice chancellor of Ashoka University, detecting a shift in the intellectual climate in the US away from openness and globalization. I pointed out that some very cosmopolitan and diverse American economists—Paul Krugman, Paul Samuelson,

Joe Stiglitz and Michael Spence—all Nobel Prize winners—had started expressing misgivings about globalization, intimating an intellectual climate change against global integration.

In 2013, I located the source of the problem in 'hyper-globalization', a new phase in the seemingly unrelenting onward march of global integration. Not everyone (to put things gently) has agreed with this claim, put forth in a paper with Martin Kessler. But I take some satisfaction in knowing that no less than Paul Krugman, who won the Nobel Prize for his work on trade, considers this paper one of the two most important recent papers on trade.

Section 8.1 was a public lecture delivered in New Delhi after the Brexit referendum and the Trump election. It is a coming together of the *Financial Times* and academic pieces. The title of the lecture sums up the argument: 'Hyper-globalization is dead. Long live globalization.' In other words, the lecture offers what seems today an optimistic view that only extreme forms of globalization—not globalization per se—are threatened.

In that piece, I also sketched out what India's response should be against this backlash. A number of Indians have argued that India should turn back to an inward-focused growth strategy, a view that in recent months seems to be acquiring new allure, judging from the spate of tariff increases. But an inward-looking strategy would be a folly given India's history—our bitter experience of poor performance under the closed and regulated environment of the pre-reform period.

That said, an outward-growth strategy will only work if international markets remain open, something that cannot be taken for granted in the current environment. India will need to engage in reciprocity (promising to open my market if you open yours), something which it has been hitherto unwilling to do.

Section 8.2 sets out a companion strategy, which aims at keeping markets open by reviving the WTO and multilateralism.

The onus will increasingly be on the non-superpowers, middle-sized countries such as India, to assume leadership in the international trading system. Whether that is possible or whether India will only be on the margins of influence and never occupy a seat at the high table remains to be seen.

Section 8.3 is an obituary of Ken Arrow, the great economist, Nobel Prize winner, and the father of social choice theory. It turns out that the brilliant economist and former US treasury secretary Larry Summers is the nephew of both Ken Arrow and the other great economist, Paul Samuelson.

At a party in Delhi in the winter of 2016, I was chatting with Larry and mentioned to him that I thought not only his uncles but his late father, Robert Summers, also deserved the Nobel. I said that his work with Irving Kravis and Alan Heston in developing the famous Penn World Tables which allowed cross-country comparisons of income to be made based on the famous purchasing power parity (PPP) concept provided a real empirical backbone to the entire field of development economics. Larry asked whether I could say this in an email to him so that he could pass it on to his mother, who he thought would be thrilled by the recognition of her husband's work. I found that very touching. It provided a clue as to why Larry inspires such fierce loyalty and affection in so many students, colleagues and friends.

For having waded through all the dense, turgid material in the first seven chapters the reader surely deserves some reward. That is why the last two sections (8.4 and 8.5) are on tennis, my true sporting love. They are paeans, respectively, to Federer and Nadal, the two greats of all time.

There is a sentence in my Federer piece: 'If there is one moment encapsulating Federer-as-Nureyev, it is when Federer has just struck his backhand: his legs are off the ground and both arms are fully extended in opposite directions, the metrosexual tennis ballerina (ballerino?) poised in mid-air, the long fingers splayed, sensitive and sensuous.'

My friend Rahul Jacob, a tennis connoisseur, who writes on tennis for the *Financial Times*, responded to this sentence by sending me the picture below with a message: 'Your very point, a year ago.'

For all the things I probably got wrong on economic policy, there is some consolation that I may have got this description right!

Hyper-Globalization Is Dead.
Long Live Globalization!

In July 2016 I delivered the keynote lecture at the India Policy Forum, where the leading questions on my mind were: What sense do we make of all that is happening around us—Brexit, the US elections, the refugee crisis, Brazil, China, Russia? How do we economically situate all that is happening around us? And what are the implications of these events for the globalized world and for India? How should India prevent the possible backlash against globalization which can, in some ways, derail India's long-term growth prospects? How does a country like India generate a growth rate of 8 to 10 per cent to catch up with advanced countries?

The Historical Perspective

Globalization has come in four phases. The first phase from 1870 to 1914 was the first great era of globalization. British economist John Maynard Keynes wrote a famous paean to this golden age of globalization in his *Economic Consequences of the Peace*:

What an extraordinary episode in the economic progress of man that age was which came to an end in August 1914! . . . The inhabitant of London could order by telephone, sipping his morning tea in bed, the various products of the whole earth, in such quantity as he might see fit, and reasonably expect their early delivery upon his doorstep; he could at the same moment and by the same means adventure his wealth in the natural resources and new enterprises of any quarter of the world, and share, without exertion or even trouble, in their prospective fruits and advantages; or he could decide to couple the security of his fortunes with the good faith of the townspeople of any substantial municipality in any continent that fancy or information might recommend. He could secure forthwith, if he wished it, cheap and comfortable means of transit to any country or climate without passport or other formality, could dispatch his servant to the neighbouring office of a bank for such supply of the precious metals as might seem convenient, and could then proceed abroad to foreign quarters, without knowledge of their religion, language, or customs, bearing coined wealth upon his person, and would consider himself greatly aggrieved and much surprised at the least interference.

The second phase was during the interwar years when there was a rapid reversal of global economy and a de-globalization of the world's economy.

The third phase began with the end of the war years, and was a period of re-globalization characterized by rapid technology developments and declining transport costs, combined with very aggressive trade liberalization by the advanced countries. Export to GDP ratios rose to around 15 to 16 per cent. After 1990, we see the birth of the fourth phase—the era of hyper-globalization. Trade to GDP ratios picked up enormously, reaching about 30 per cent just before the onset of the global financial crisis in 2008.

The question that faces us at this juncture is which of these trajectories will the future bring? More hyper-globalization, the policies of isolation that led to de-globalization, or a further continuation of the status quo? Luckily, current events can give us some clues.

The era of hyper-globalization coincides with the reversal of fortunes of the 'Rest' (which included countries like India) and the West. From the 1950s to the 1990s, the rates of economic growth in European nations, the UK and USA were very rapid, outstripping the growth rates of all other countries in the world. After 1990, this was reversed, when the poorer countries grew more rapidly as compared to the traditional Western economies. Consequently, the backlash against globalization has also seen a reversal over time.

Initially, the global South had anxieties surrounding the Washington Consensus (the neo-liberal view that globalization, deregulation and privatization were the recipe for economic development), and now it is the global North that has anxieties about globalization with a rising disenchantment clearly visible in the politics of both the USA and European countries. We must analyse where it comes from and how it affects us, recognizing that it is in the interests of the global South to ensure that hyper-globalization continues despite this backlash.

In 2011, what did Michael Spence, Joe Stiglitz, Larry Summers, Paul Krugman, Paul Samuelson and Alan Blinker have in common? One might hazard a guess and say that they were all Nobel Prize recipients in economics. But there's more. By 2010, they—all global cosmopolitans and part of the Davos jet set—were all prominent voices expressing misgivings about globalization, signalling the unspoken: just as India is arriving, the West wants to close down its markets.

The nature of this amorphous backlash, however, is different in the US and the EU. In the United States, there is a much broader disenchantment with the economy and not just globalization which I described in my book on the rise of China, titled *Eclipse: Living in the Shadow of China's Economic Dominance*.

Multiple shocks have hit the US—slowing productivity growth, the associated technological challenge of machines replacing humans, rising income inequality especially at the very top (the Piketty problem), stagnant median wages for the already beleaguered middle class, and the resulting decline in socio-economic mobility. The Harvard economist Larry Katz captures this beautifully: 'Think of the American economy as a large apartment block. A century ago—even thirty years ago—it was the object of envy. But in the last generation its character has changed. The penthouses at the top keep getting larger and larger. The apartments in the middle are feeling more and more squeezed and the basement has flooded. To round it off, the elevator is no longer working. That broken elevator is what gets people down the most.'

In the European Union, the disenchantment with globalization is different, in that it is directed at immigration and a disenchantment with the European project as it were. If anything, Brexit proved that millions of Britishers do not believe in the idea of European unity. The problem is much bigger than the question of economic expediency; it is of institutional erosion, a sentiment echoed by Ambrose Evans–Pritchard, business editor of the Conservative-leaning *Daily Telegraph*, when he writes, 'The Project bleeds the lifeblood of the national institutions, but fails to replace them with anything lovable or legitimate at a European level. It draws away charisma, and destroys it. This is how democracies die.' The irony here is that it was Britain's Margaret Thatcher who created the Single European Act, which established the Single Market.

An obvious solution to the globalization problem, at least in the West, is clearly a stronger, bigger state which cushions people against adversity and dislocation, and provides the wherewithal to make them more mobile so that their prospects improve. However, this solution has few takers. Ronald Reagan's 'Government is the problem, not the solution,' still resonates strongly in the US and UK. Obamacare is struggling to survive. In the UK, the people who benefitted most from the EU dole-out, the Brussels beneficiaries if you like, were more likely to vote to leave the EU than others who did not benefit as much.

It is important to analytically distinguish between disembodied and embodied globalization. Disembodied globalization is the free flow and exchange of goods, capital and technology, whereas embodied globalization is the immigration and emigration of peoples. Of the two, embodied globalization, i.e., immigration, creates issues beyond the scope of economics, and has become increasingly salient. Indeed, the 'threat' represented by immigrant labour and the ills of globalization it represents have been the subject of nativist rhetoric and identity politics of right-wing parties. However, in countries like Greece and Spain, where immigration is not an issue, we see the rise of a political left coalescing around austerity measures. Both in the EU and the USA, we see this strange melding of the conventionally far left and far right parties, united in their distrust of globalization.

The second aspect of globalization is the difference in the experiences of the US and those of Europe. In the US, there is more integration between dissimilars—the rich and poor—and relatively shallow forms of integration. In the EU, the integration is much deeper because of the Single European Act that all countries were made to adopt/be adopted, guaranteeing the free movement of goods, capital, services and labour, and of course, a monetary union. In the UK, the problem of immigration is not the cook from India or Pakistan, but the Polish plumber and the Slovenian waitress—fellow Europeans. Shallow integration among unequals and deeper integration among similars are both under attack, the threat being that of complete disintegration.

A critical test that will determine the fate of globalization is the integrity and longevity of the Eurozone. In the post-war period, the European Project was a lofty political one and sought to bury a century of animosity, but it also became the most ambitious trade project with the introduction of the Single European Act and then became the most ambitious project of monetary and currency union with the creation of the euro and the Eurozone. Let us consider a few new challenges to these projects.

The first is the role of Germany in helming the Eurozone, which has become unusually prominent since German unification, and now post Brexit. Incidentally, the UK is not part of the Eurozone. Germany's share of the EU population in 1985 was 17 per cent; this number went up to 31 per cent post unification, and post Brexit, will become 37 per cent. Europe is no longer a union led by three near-equals—Germany, France and the UK—it is now led by one hegemon, Germany.

The second is the big gap in the GDPs of various countries in the EU. This problem is even more salient in Europe because the Eurozone's legitimacy depended on being a vehicle for convergence. People signed up for the European Union to become richer and catch up with the bigger players. But instead they are seeing that the EU, instead of being a zone of convergence, has become a big-time zone of divergence.

As these income gaps widen, especially those between Germany and its neighbours—Portugal, Italy, Greece and Spain—it falls on Germany to act as a hegemon. According to economic historian Charles Kindleberger's 'hegemonic stability' theory, for there to be economic stability, the hegemon must provide open markets, stable currency and emergency finance. However, we see that this is not the case within the EU. Germany has become a huge net exporter such that other countries do not have a market. Germany is mercantilist—an economic policy aimed at maximizing the trade of a nation—in a system which needs it to be a buyer of last resort. Given this behaviour, the argument of economic expediency, the raison d'être of the Eurozone, stands undermined.

What does all this lead us to conclude about globalization and where does this analysis leave us? One is torn between predicting a doomsday scenario built on the heels of the optimism that 'this time it will be different', and believing that this exact scenario has been borne out in the past. One of the tentative conclusions I will draw is that disembodied integration is not under threat— ideas, technologies and capital are always going to circulate freely. Shallower forms of integration may still be extant but deeper forms of integration, however, are in trouble and could see a reversal in the future.

One may recall that globalization was driven by 80 per cent technology and 20 per cent policy. Even if we remove policy from the equation, the 80 per cent technology share will continue to drive globalization. Going forward, globalization may be impeded by the actions of governments, but technology, which is without provenance, will continue propelling globalization.

Globalization is not a one-way street. It has become a mesh that is difficult to untangle. China and India receive foreign direct investments, but they also contribute to FDI. The hypothesis is then that shallower forms of integration will continue, and that the flow of trade and capital will continue. We need not become overly pessimistic about that. However, prevailing anxieties about deeper forms of integration may be justified. The catch-up of developing countries is strongly associated with globalization. Think of China and India, but now anxiety in the global North should induce anxiety in the global South, especially for late convergers such as India.

To shield from the impacts of globalization (or de-globalization, as the case may be) in both the North and South, we will need to rethink the role of the state. This rethinking can be realized in the form of better social safety nets, wealth taxes on the rich, more public investment and reducing the role of finance.

Implications for India

India needs to answer three questions: Should India change its development strategy towards more consumption-led or domestic-market–led growth? If not, will the current econo-political climate allow India to have an export promotion strategy? And lastly, what must India do to make such an outward-facing strategy viable?

My answer to the first question facing India is that consumption-led or domestic market growth cannot deliver a sustainable annual growth rate of 8 to 10 per cent. It is theoretically doubtful and empirically unprecedented. An outward-oriented strategy is desirable because demand is infinite. If there is a productivity shock, we can sell without facing lower prices internationally. On the other hand, an inward-orientation strategy means that we can't sell as much, and if we do want to sell more, prices will fall and welfare will be affected. Empirically, no country in recent history has grown at about eight per cent or more for over three decades without being a major exporter. Why should India be different?

The feasibility of such a domestic market-oriented strategy is still questionable. Can the world absorb another China? China's share in the world GDP is 3.3 per cent, and India's share is 0.5 per cent. India can still achieve an export growth of 15 per cent along with a GDP growth of 8 per cent subject to China becoming a normal trader and rebalancing its economy. If China succeeds in rebalancing towards a consumption-led growth model, India can occupy the space vacated by China with its outward-oriented strategy. I also think that the carrying capacity for services is greater than that for manufacturing. If that is the case, India is well positioned. India's current share is only 0.2 per cent, but it could easily raise this number up to 1.5 to 2 per cent without running up against politically motivated trade barriers in advanced countries, where there are limits to how much they can absorb goods and services from the outside.

The fundamental argument, however, remains that India cannot achieve 9 per cent growth without an outward strategy. But India can achieve this outward-oriented strategy uniquely, via a different pattern than followed by the East Asian tiger economies, namely, through a combination of manufacturing and services instead of only manufacturing. Needless to say, if deeper forms of integration are going to be subject to barriers, India will be hurt because international labour mobility has served India well up till now. This remains a significant challenge for our future.

So, how should India position itself? India and other developing countries have a strong interest in keeping global markets open and preventing a reversal of globalization—our rapid growth depends on it. This requires assuming leadership on globalization, and revitalizing the World Trade Organization and multilateralism. What will also be required is engaging less unequally in international trade negotiations. In the new world, it will be increasingly difficult to expect less than full reciprocity by others. And given that global markets are very important for our growth going forward, we should keep FDI flows open, because FDI incentivizes people to keep international markets open.

My conclusion, thus, is 'Hyper-globalization is dead. Long live globalization'. The world has changed and it may be difficult to sustain deeper forms of integration even among equals. However, if shallower forms of integrations are going to be the way forward, this is the opening for revitalizing multilateralism and for Indian leadership in the WTO.

To paraphrase Keynes, we must ensure that the projects and politics of nativism and isolationism do not play serpent to the paradise of open markets and open borders because, as a late and precocious converger, India still has a lot of distance to cover, and an international open market is, for us, an existential necessity.

8.2

The WTO Reborn?

For too long, the World Trade Organization has languished—to lift a reference from T.S. Eliot in his seminal poem 'The Waste Land'—by the 'waters of Leman' (Lake Geneva). Once the world's pre-eminent multilateral trade forum, the WTO has been steadily marginalized in recent years, and recent rebukes of globalization, such as the United Kingdom's Brexit vote and Donald Trump's election as US President, suggest that this trend will accelerate. But these outcomes may actually have the opposite effect, owing to three key developments that could enable the revival of the WTO—and of the multilateralism that it embodies.

The first development is the decline of alternative trade arrangements. The WTO reached its peak in the early years of this century, a few years after the Uruguay round of global trade negotiations concluded, and a time when more countries—most notably China—were acceding to the organization.

But major trade players like the United States and the European Union subsequently shifted their focus from multilateral trade agreements to bilateral, regional and mega-regional deals. The mega-regionals deals—namely, the Trans-Pacific Partnership (TPP) and the Trans-Atlantic Trade and Investment Partnership

(TTIP)—posed a particularly grave threat to the WTO. Yet, those are precisely the kind of deals that the Trump administration is rejecting, or at least postponing.

European integration had a similar impact on the WTO, as it provided an alternative platform for managing intra-European trade. But the European Project has fallen on hard times, the most salient sign being the UK's impending departure from the EU. After Brexit, the WTO will probably become an important forum for Britain's trade relations with the world. Any further disintegration of the EU will only bolster that trend.

Of course, it is possible that regional trade agreements in Asia and elsewhere will continue to flourish. But new leadership would have to emerge. And no single systemically important country today meets the rigorous requirements of such leadership: internal political stability, economic dynamism, relatively contained risk and a steadfast commitment to open markets.

However counterintuitive that may sound, a second development that bodes well for the WTO's revival is voters' increasing rejection of hyper-globalization. Hyper-globalization is essentially 'deep' integration. It goes beyond creating open markets for goods and services to include increased immigration (in the US and Europe), harmonizing regulations (the ambitions of the TPP and the TTIP), intrusive adjudication of domestic policies (the investor-settlement procedures under the North American Free Trade Agreement [NAFTA] and the TPP) and, in the EU's case, common currency. For such integration, regionalism is much more effective than the WTO.

Now that 'deep' is out, as I've argued in the previous section, the WTO could once again become an attractive forum for trading countries to do business. Make no mistake: there will still be a lot of globalization for the WTO to facilitate and manage, not least because of the inexorable march of technology. The mesh-like structure of trade and investment connecting countries, embodied in global value chains—what Aaditya Mattoo of the World Bank and I have called 'criss-crossing globalization'—will prevent significant backsliding.

The third development that could reinvigorate the WTO is a more protectionist stance by the Trump administration. If the US raises tariffs or implements a border-adjustment tax favouring exports and penalizing imports, its trade partners are likely to turn to the WTO for adjudication, given the organization's demonstrated dispute-settlement capability.

The WTO could, therefore, become the place where US trade policies are scrutinized and kept in check. The universality of WTO membership, previously seen as an impediment to countries eager to move ahead with new rules and agreements, could be its main strength, as it implies a high degree of legitimacy, which is essential to minimize trade tensions and the risk of conflict.

In my book *Eclipse: Living in the Shadows of China's Economic Dominance*, I argued that multilateralism, or the participation of three or more parties and/or governments in decision making, organizations and such, offers the best means for ensuring the peaceful rise of new powers. But it seems that the same argument could apply equally well to the management of receding powers.

The WTO's revival will not happen automatically. Willing stakeholders must actively pursue it. The most obvious candidates for the job are the mid-size economies that have been the greatest beneficiaries of globalization, and that, unlike the US and some European countries, are not currently under pressure from a globalization-averse public.

The champions of multilateralism should include Australia, Brazil, India, Indonesia, Mexico, New Zealand, South Africa, the United Kingdom and, possibly, China and Japan. Since none of these economies is large (with the exception of China), they must work collectively to defend open markets. Moreover, they must open up their own markets not only in the traditional areas of agriculture and manufacturing, but also in new areas such as services, investments and standards. In doing so, these countries would also be responding to the increasingly transactional approach to sustaining openness that the larger traders are being compelled to adopt.

The world needs a robust response to the decline of hyper-globalization. Multilateralism, championed by mid-size trading economies with a strong interest in preserving openness, may be the answer. To the shores of Leman they must now head.

8.3

Kenneth Arrow

The Transcendental Economist

Almost everything that has to be said about the recently deceased Professor Kenneth Arrow has been said: gifted economist, the youngest recipient of the Nobel Prize for economics, extraordinarily generous human being, mentor of several subsequent Nobel laureates, and polymath. So, what is left to say, apart from the overlooked facial resemblance to another Nobel Prize winner, the author Saul Bellow?

At the risk of over-claiming and over-simplifying, it is probably fair to say that amongst twentieth-century economists, there were (with apologies to Sir John Hicks), John Maynard Keynes, Paul Samuelson, Kenneth Arrow, and then everyone else. These were the three gods of the economics pantheon, all theorists, each dazzling in his own way, each creating and/or shaping a whole discipline or disciplines both in content but also in basic framework and methodology.

Keynes created the discipline of short-run macroeconomics with profound implications for the conduct of macroeconomic policy. And unlike the other two, who confined themselves to academics (mostly), Keynes flitted between the ivory tower and the corridors of power frequently and formidably to show that economists could shape and influence economic policy and economic institutions directly. He was the exemplar of economist-as-policy-practitioner.

When Paul Samuelson, also a Nobel Prize winner, died, Paul Krugman famously wrote (drawing upon Isaiah Berlin) that there are foxes (who know many things), hedgehogs (who know one big thing), and then there is Paul Samuelson; meaning that he knew many things and many big things—a true intellectual colossus. Krugman then went on to list Samuelson's eight seminal contributions to economics.

Comparisons are, of course, silly and dicey, but one can hazard that Kenneth Arrow's achievements were in some ways arguably greater than Samuelson's. Samuelson's many contributions helped us think through the first principles of many issues in economics—public goods, taxation, savings, trade, consumer preference, pensions and finance. Arrow's two stunning contributions (both theoretical) in some ways both built and undermined all of politics and all of (market) economics. Samuelson made mega contributions, Arrow made meta contributions; Samuelson's related to one discipline, Arrow's transcended two.

Arrow's 'Impossibility Theorem'—the first contribution—questioned whether democratic politics itself was possible in any meaningful sense. If you start with individual preferences, it is very difficult (or impossible) to come up with a rule (say, majority voting) that aggregates these preferences and produces a societal preference that can satisfy some basic conditions. The only rule that satisfies these conditions, it turns out, is dictatorship, or rule by one person which would be abhorrent to all, Arrow included.

His work (along with Gerard Debreu's) on the General Competitive Equilibrium established the possibility of the market economy as a coherent, interconnected system. Adam Smith famously said, 'It is not from the benevolence of the butcher, the brewer, or the baker that we expect our dinner, but from their regard to their own interest.' The work of Arrow and many others showed how such self-interested individual behaviour could produce outcomes that had broadly desirable social virtues; prices and the information that they conveyed were at the heart of the mechanism for the transmission from individual selfishness to social good.

But this work showed how demanding were the conditions for the market system: for the price mechanism to work, undistorted markets needed to exist for all goods and services, for all future times, and for all contingencies ('states-of-nature') with full information available to all agents in the economy. And one of the major implications of his work was followed up on by Arrow himself. He showed how asymmetric information between the provider and the consumer of health services made the market for health fragile, requiring extensive government intervention to fix. Obamacare, coming several decades later, could be seen as inspired by Arrow's work.

Stepping back, one might say that Arrow's two contributions showed the inherent limits to, even the existential difficulties of, all politics and economics, which start from atomistic decision makers—voters in politics, and firms and consumers in economics. So, when Francis Fukuyama proclaimed the triumph of democratic politics and market economics as an empirical matter in 1989, Arrow—affirming the famous joke about the economist—could well have said, 'Sorry, Frank, they may work in practice but I showed forty years ago that they do not work in theory.' Post-Brexit and Trump, we are now discovering that perhaps they don't work in practice either.

Another contribution of Arrow's is worth mentioning. In the early 1960s, the two Cambridges (the one on the River Charles in the US and the other on the River Cam in England) were bickering viciously over the definition, description and measurement of capital as an input in production (the famous 'Capital Controversy'). Arrow (then very much in Cambridge, US) chose to stay above the fray, and in the very issue of the *Review of Economic Studies* (1962) that featured the controversy, wrote a piece on learning-by-doing which influenced the theory of endogenous growth developed years later by Paul Romer, acknowledged this year by the Nobel committee. The key insight of Arrow's being that the average costs of production decline with scale so that increasing returns were more likely to characterize most production technologies, leading to uncompetitive markets dominated by a few large firms rather than the competitive world of many small firms.

The Arrow–Samuelson comparison is interesting for another reason: family connections. Arrow's sister, Anita Summers, a well-known academic herself, was married to Robert Summers, an economist, whose brother was Paul Samuelson. Larry Summers is thus the nephew of both Arrow and Samuelson, and the lineage shows. The world needs reminding that in this stellar family, Robert Summers himself was deserving of the Nobel Prize. He, along with Larry Heston and Irving Kravis, created the famous Penn World Table (PWT), which allowed incomes and consumption—and hence standards of living—to be compared across countries using the concept of purchasing power parities. Without this PWT data, the rich and exciting field of empirical development economics may have not bloomed at all. Robert Summers, alas, is no more, but the Nobel committee—which does not grant the award posthumously—can still honour his work by awarding the Nobel Prize to Larry Heston.

It is surprising that Sylvia Nasar has not already mined this rich material for a family biography that might be titled, 'Two Brothers and a Brother-in-Law'. And that brother-in-law, Kenneth Joseph Arrow, may possibly have been the best and most impactful of them all.

8.4

Roger Federer: An Ending, Indefinitely Postponed

Roger Federer's Australian Open victory in January 2017, followed up by the 'Sunshine Slam' (wins at Indian Wells and Miami), raises this salivating prospect for tennis fans: a Grand Slam for Federer at the geriatric (in tennis terms) age of thirty-six. What lends plausibility is that this season Federer has worsted his nemesis—Rafael Nadal—three times already, including in two finals, the epic one and the trigger for the Roger revival being the Australian Open itself.

There was something very special about that victory not least because there was a lot at stake in the match, indeed Federer's very claim to being the 'Greatest Ever'. Losing to Nadal yet again, Federer fans would have had difficulty countering the assertion (first made by Mats Wilander) that no one can be considered the greatest of *all* times if he wasn't even the greatest of his *own* times. And the Rafa–Roger head-to-head statistics would have been devastating: 7–2 in Rafa's favour in Grand Slam finals, and 10–2 in Grand Slam finals and semi-finals. Roger–Rafa, in other words, was never a contest, making a mockery of Roger's 'Greatest Ever' claims.

But with that victory and especially the manner of that victory, history's verdict, might start, just about, looking a little different. Federer did in the Aussie Open and in the twilight of his career what he had never done in his prime: beat Rafael Nadal on a surface other than grass in Grand Slam matches; beat Rafael Nadal converting his weakness—the backhand, which was really only a weakness when playing Nadal—into his greatest strength; and beat Rafael Nadal in a five setter, displaying mental toughness in coming from behind to win the deciding fifth set. In short, Roger managed to vanquish all the demons of the past in this match.

Why the new Federer emerged from the ghost of the old one will probably never be satisfactorily answered. Perhaps it was because Roger felt he had little to lose having just come back from a major injury so that even reaching the final was a bonus, as his post-victory remarks (unconvincingly) suggested. Perhaps because Roger and Rafa had not played for a long time so that the demons of defeat were not on the surface of his psyche, playing tricks with his mind and hence muscle memory. Or perhaps Roger had genuinely achieved a mental equipoise about his place in history and about his long, post-peak tennis career.

Whatever the cause, the effect was unmistakable, manifested particularly in the new Roger backhand: less slices and more drives, and drives hit with power, fluency and uninhibited flourish. If there is one moment encapsulating Federer-as-Nureyev, it is when Federer has just struck his backhand: his legs are off the ground and both arms are fully extended in opposite directions, the metrosexual tennis ballerina (ballerino?) poised in mid-air, the long fingers splayed, sensitive and sensuous.

Edward Said, amongst others, has written about the Late Style of artists and writers, and Beethoven in particular. In a great piece, Brian Phillips of Grantland has similarly written about the distinctive Late Style of Roger. Roger, in his view, has managed athletic decline in surprisingly effective ways in sharp contrast to others such as Jordan or even Bjorn Borg. Despite no longer being a serious contender, Roger continues to play without evoking commiseration or condescension in his fans, the normal reaction to a has-been athlete. By showing that there can be a post-tennis life in and outside tennis and doing so on his own terms, Federer has achieved a freedom and grace rare among athletes. (Of course, there is also a real Late Style story waiting to be written on Nadal, bringing a battered body back to life for Grand Slam–level tennis, through sheer mental fortitude.)

With the Aussie Open final result, and the subsequent 'Sunshine Slam', the Brian Phillips view must be updated or even revised. Roger has once again scaled the summit, is today the best player in the world, and is arguably playing the best tennis of his career. The saga of rise and gentle, genteel decline needs to be rewritten because . . . Roger is *baaaack*.

So, a Federer Grand Slam? On current form and recent performance, Wimbledon and the US Open, his two favourite surfaces, are probably his to lose. Can Roger beat the greatest clay-court player of all time, Nadal, at Roland Garros though? It will be difficult but Roger is peaking and Rafa's muscularly physical style of play has taken its toll, so a more equal combat than in the past cannot be ruled out. It is also possible that Rafa will be eliminated in the early rounds so that Roger will have to overcome mere clay mortals such as Murray and Djokovic.

Of Roger's ascendant phase, I recall David Foster Wallace who wrote memorably that to see 'power and aggression made vulnerable to beauty is to feel inspired and [in a fleeting, mortal way] reconciled'. (Although, to be honest, that description seems exactly wrong when thinking about who succumbed to whom in the Roger–Rafa duels.) Of his decline, Brian Phillips wrote that seeing Roger miss was like watching 'beauty succumb to death'.

An exegesis of Roger's third, resurgent phase awaits a David Foster Wallace or Brian Phillips. But its title, evoking Frank Kermode and Julian Barnes, readily suggests itself: 'Sense of an Ending, Indefinitely Postponed'.

Tennis Fandom in
the Federer–Nadal Era

When Steven Pinker waxes eloquent about living in humanity's Golden Age, Walter Benjamin's 'every document of civilization is also a document of barbarity' comes back as haunting riposte. But no Benjamin can qualify the assertion that the last fifteen years have been the chosen era in human history to be a tennis fan. We, the todayers, are truly blessed to bear witness to the divine talents of, and scarcely human displays put on by, Roger Federer and his bromance buddy, rival, nemesis and plausible co-claimant to GOAT ('greatest of all time') status, Rafael Nadal.

Paradoxically, though, what Roger gives his flock of tennis watchers with one hand, he partially takes away from the other, a point brought home by the wreck wreaked by Rafael Nadal at the 2018 French Open.

All comparisons are odious but inter-temporal comparisons of sporting prowess and achievements are, in addition, indefensible. The sport changes, settings are altered (old versus new grass at Wimbledon), technology intervenes (rackets and strings), human physiology improves (Rod Laver's forearm versus Rafa's bulging biceps), and training, fitness and management methods evolve radically (the solitary circuiteers of the 1970s are replaced today by players with their harems of coaches, analysts, physios, professional soothers and handholders, not to mention psychotic parents).

But if you have lived long enough, spectated seriously for forty-plus years, observing roughly three to four generations of players, and been borne up and dragged down with every fortune of your idol of the time, you have sort of earned a right: to make comparisons across time based less on objective statistics and more on the reactions of a fan aficionado. And for someone my age, that right stems from having caught in my teens the end of the great Rosewall–Laver–Newcombe era, and then being fully involved in the eras of Connors–Borg–McEnroe–Lendl, Becker–Sampras, and now, Federer–Nadal. That span, and allowing a bit of condescension towards the past, nearly covers all relevant tennis history, give or take a Tilden, Budge, von Cramm, Gonzales or the French Musketeer.

Having clarified terms and perspectives and drawn all the caveats, it is time to substantiate the Pinkerian claim as applied to tennis. This is the 'golden age' because never in tennis history has two insanely gifted players played at the same time, and played such unusual and contrasting styles of tennis. So, it is not just that Roger and Rafa are GOATs, they are GOATs in their own, distinctive and inimitable ways. All the clichés about the contrasting twosome are, of course, true: the serve–volleyer and the baseliner, the swift executioner and the attrition practitioner, the ballerina and the bull, the floater and the pounder, the one not breaking a sweat after five hours of toil while the other is all straining effort. The odds are low of there ever being another era of two great players but those odds lengthen into nullity of the two being as different as Roger and Rafa.

There is a twist in the tale. We are privileged to have had these two maestros, and yet the most flawlessly efficient tennis of any one season in nearly all of tennis history happened arguably in our times in the form of, yes, Novak Djokovic in 2011. Uncharitable though it may be, Novak is not the GOAT, nor terribly distinctive, and yet he, not Roger or Rafa, gave us the winningest season of dominant tennis. Of the three, it was Novak who came closest to winning the Grand Slam (in 2011) and only the forgotten wiles and clutch serving of Roger came in the way at the French Open. He, not Roger or Rafa, held all four Grand Slam titles at once. And the most competitively thrilling, high-octane tennis that we have seen were the Novak–Rafa contests at the Australian and French opens, eclipsing on that specific metric even the Roger–Rafa encounters at Wimbledon and the Australian Open.

In short, we have been privileged to see the prodigious and diverse talents of Roger and Rafa, and for one season, also the ruthless dominance of Novak Djokovic. When has that ever happened before?

But why is Roger the giver also a spoiler? Here I speak as a besotted believer. Over the years, we have been so enthralled and so wanting the best for him that secretly we have wished Rafa failure so as to not undermine Roger's GOAT status. Deep in our hearts we know that that status is forever asterisked because in their head-to-heads, Rafa has been dominant, often embarrassingly so.

But our fandom has extracted a subtle cost. It is not just that zealotry has made us ill-wishers of Rafa so that Roger can reign supreme; it has come in the way of fully and objectively revelling as fans in Rafa's incomparable greatness. As Roger cultists—overrating his niceness while under-acknowledging Rafa's—we have paid a cost as tennis fans. Think of it: where are the paeans to Rafa, where is the prose poetry to describe his tennis, where is his David Foster Wallace? That omission is telling because it is becoming increasingly clear—and the latest French Open (2018) confirms it beyond doubt—that Rafa belongs in the pantheon of tennis gods alongside Roger.

Who has so dominated one surface like Rafa while always contending on others? Who has produced that vicious kicker spin where the ball, as heavy as Rafa's drenched T-shirt, apparently sailing long comes thudding down in defiance of gravity only to rear venomously high for the opponent? Who has practised the clichéd coach's exhortation to play with 'give-it-all' intensity at every point, whether in training or tournament, satellite or Grand Slam? Who has that inside-out forehand from midcourt that can be dispatched with late deceit? Who can hit that slap-slam forehand-masquerading-as-backhand and find shallow angles from locations closer to adjoining courts? Whose defence and commitment to retrieval can unleash the demons in your mind even before you have tread foot on the tennis court? Who had any business to enjoy a tennis longevity so incommensurate with the destructive demands placed on his body? Who, oh who, is the most clutch player in history, not just imperturbable under tension but ratcheting up the dial—serving harder and acuter, hitting more viciously, returning more confidently, flirting more brazenly with the lines—on crucial points?

How often have we seen Roger's break points remain maddeningly unconverted into games, sets, matches and more Grand Slam victories? And let us not forget that seventeen and counting for Rafa is not that far away from Roger's twenty Grand Slam titles. Our Roger-rooting has unconsciously blinded us to Rafa, to savour all this distinctive magnificence.

The Swiss has swanned around the tennis court Nureyev-like for nearly two decades. But it is time for us Federistas to render our long overdue apologies and begin genuflecting at the altar of the Matador from Majorca. Doubly blessed and doubly blissed have we been to be alive in the Roger–Rafa tennis era. And, oh my god, it is not over yet.

Notes

Chapter 1: Igniting Ideas for India

1.1: Precocious Development

1. GST implementation began on 1 July 2017.

1.3: From Socialism with Limited Entry to Capitalism without Exit: The Chakravyuha Challenge

1. This was written with Rangeet Ghosh and Rohit Lamba.

1.4: The Big Puzzle of India: Diverging Regional Economic Development despite Equalizing Forces

1. This was written with Josh Felman, Rangeet Ghosh, Gayathri Raj, Sutirtha Roy and Navneeraj Sharma.

Chapter 2: Money and Cash

2.2: Government's Capital in RBI: Prudence or Paranoia?

1. This piece was written with Abhishek Anand, Josh Felman, Rangeet Ghosh and Navneeraj Sharma.

2. Revaluation gains occur, for example, when the exchange rate depreciates, increasing the local currency value of the foreign exchange reserves.

3. One counter to this argument is that from a consolidated balance sheet perspective, any excess capital in the central bank will already be reflected as lower net government debt, which should benefit the government via lower borrowing costs. But in practice this never happens. Even rating agencies do not include the central banks' capital in assessing the government's fiscal position. So, deploying excess capital outside the central bank's balance sheet might create clear additional benefits.

Chapter 3: The Great Structural Transformation (GST)

3.1: The Goods and Services Tax: One India, One Market

1. This piece, written with Dr Hasmukh Adhia, the revenue secretary, soon after the passage of the Constitutional Amendment Bill, was a celebration of the achievement and delineation of its benefits.

3.2: The GST's Last and Critical Lap

1. This was written in early 2017 just before the GST Council was deciding on the entire rate structure for the GST.

3.3: Black Money's Next Frontier: Bringing Land and Real Estate into a Transformational GST

1. As of October 2018, LARE continues to be outside the GST.

3.4: Why, How and When Electricity Must Come into the GST

1. This was written with Navneeraj Sharma.

3.5: A Buoyant Force: Understanding GST Revenue Performance

1. This was written with Kapil Patidar in June 2018.

Chapter 4: Climate Change and the Environment

4.1: India's Approach to Paris

1. https://www.ft.com/content/1b5e1776-df23-11e0-9af3-00144feabdc0.

4.2: Combating Carbon Imperialism

1. This piece appeared as the COP-21 negotiations were being finalized in December 2015.

4.3: Renewables May Be the Future, But Are They the Present?:
Coal, Energy and Development in India

1. Chandra, Rohit. *Adaptive State Capitalism in the Indian Coal Industry*. Harvard University. PhD dissertation, 2018.
2. Friedman, Lisa. 'Coal-fired Power in India May Cause More Than 100,000 Premature Deaths Annually'. *Scientific American*, 11 March 2013, https://www.scientificamerican.com/article/coal-fired-power-in-india-may-cause-more-than-100000-premature-deaths-annually/. A 2017 IMF study based on Leileveld and others in *Nature* (2015) has a different set of estimates which are not strictly comparable. All these estimates are contingent on the tricky issue of valuing human life.
3. Nordhaus, William D. 'Revisiting the Social Cost of Carbon'. *Proceedings of the National Academy of Sciences* (2017): 201609244.
4. Bhatnagar, Gaurav Vivek. 'Water Scarcity behind Decline in Thermal Power Generation in India', 16 March 2017, https://thewire.in/116859/water-scarcity-behind-decline-thermal-power-generation-india/.
5. Bennet, James. 'Bill Gates: "We Need An Energy Miracle"'. *Atlantic*, 17 August 2017, https://www.theatlantic.com/magazine/archive/2015/11/we-need-an-energy-miracle/407881/.
6. For a counter-view, see Sharan Poovanna's article in *LiveMint*, 'How the World's Largest Solar Park Is Shaping Up In Karnataka', 6 March 2017, http://www.livemint.com/Industry/

UEJYwZQT5m3wNvGupBShZJ/How-the-worlds-largest-solar-park-is-shaping-up-in-Karnatak.html.

7. There is a view that at least in rural India, decentralized solar is the way forward. Another view is that every Indian—rural or urban—must be on the grid to receive uninterrupted, high-quality power. Until such time as decentralized power can match this, calls for decentralization carry the whiff of 'carbon imperialism'. In any case, India has settled this for the moment by choosing to electrify every village by 2018.

8. Renewable generation has fiscal and promotional incentives such as capital and/or interest subsidies, tax holidays on earnings for ten years, generation-based incentives, accelerated depreciation, viability gap funding, financing rooftop solar as part of home loans, concessional customs duties, preferences for power generated from renewables, 25 per cent capital subsidy for solar equipment production and implicit subsidies on the land provided for siting of solar plants.

9. Gowrisankaran, Gautam, Stanley S. Reynolds and Mario Samano. 'Intermittency and the Value of Renewable Energy'. *Journal of Political Economy*, 2017.

10. The US experience may not travel easily to India in one sense because land costs—very low in the Arizona region—are potentially greater in India.

11. *The Economist*. 'Support for Bavaria's Long-dominant CSU Falls to Its Lowest Level since 1950', 2017, https://www.economist.com/news/briefing/21717365-wind-and-solar-energy-aredisrupting-century-old-model-providing-electricity-what-will.

4.4: Cooperative and Competitive Federalism to Further Reforms: The Case of the Power Sector

1. See a paper by Raj Chetty, Adam Looney and Kory Kroft, titled 'Salience and Taxation: Theory and Evidence', in *American Economic Review* (2009), https://are.berkeley.edu/SGDC/Chetty_Looney_Kroft_AER_2010.pdf.

2. See 'Powering "One India"', http://indiabudget.nic.in/budget2016-2017/es2015-16/echapvol1-11.pdf.

Chapter 5: Agriculture

5.1: Transforming Indian Agriculture: By Loving Some Agriculture Less and the Rest More

1. Speech delivered at the National Academy of Agricultural Sciences, New Delhi on 5 June 2017.
2. The data is based on the Agricultural Situation and Assessment Survey for 2012–13.

Chapter 6: The State's Relationship with the Individual

6.2: Transforming the Fight against Poverty in India

1. This piece originally appeared in the *New York Times*, 22 July 2015.

6.4: Universal Basic Income from a Gandhian Perspective

1. This piece is based on a speech delivered at Sabarmati Ashram on Gandhi Jayanti, 2 October 2016.
2. *Young India*, 1925, http://www.gandhiserve.org/cwmg/VOL032. PDF, p. 284.

Chapter 7: Speaking Truth to Power

7.0: Speaking Truth to Power: Being Karna and Arjuna

1. The primary balance is the difference between revenue and non-interest expenditure. It is the part of the budget that the government can control (as opposed to interest obligations, which must always be met in full). Moreover, if the primary deficit is placed on an appropriate path, debt and, consequently, interest expenditures will gradually decline.

7.3: FRBM: A Dissent Note Outlining an Alternative Fiscal Architecture

1. A similar flow failure, stemming from a large increase in the fiscal deficit, led to the 1991 balance-of-payments crisis. The

pattern in Figure 1 holds broadly at the general government level as well.

2. It is worth noting that while the international consensus is moving towards providing greater scope for counter-cyclical policy (Furman, J., 2016, 'The New View of Fiscal Policy and Its Application', VOXEU.ORG, 2 November 2016), the Indian experience highlights the need to judiciously circumscribe counter-cyclical policy.

3. Recall that the condition for a declining debt path is for the primary balance (pb) to be greater than $[(r-g)^*d]/[1+g]$, where 'r' is the nominal cost of borrowing, 'g' the nominal growth rate, and 'd' the debt–GDP ratio.

4. Any fiscal windfall from demonetization—either in the form of unreturned high denomination notes or tax revenues under the Pradhan Mantri Garib Kalyan Yojana—should not affect the path of consolidation going forward as it is one-off in nature.

5. See the chapter in the committee's report on 'State-level Fiscal Responsibility Legislation', Table 5.

6. Ignoring valuation changes and the assumption of debts from other branches of government.

7.4: Fiscal Federalism in India: An Analytical Framework and Vision

1. This is an abbreviated version of the Business Standard Public Lecture that I gave in Mumbai on 17 July 2018. The longer technical version will be published in the *Economic& Political Weekly*.

References

This book is about my analysis and ideas. They can never be static; they must necessarily evolve as facts, evidence and circumstances change. Mine have too. Some of the reflections here are based on, and elaborations, adaptations and evolutions of, my earlier writings. Even though almost nothing here is reproduced verbatim from before, it is not only appropriate but essential that I acknowledge the first incarnations of these ideas—the places, dates and fellow contributors. Sections without such references imply that they are new material, having never appeared before in any public forum.

Section 1.1 is based on an extended conversation with Prof. Karthik Muralidharan on 20 July 2015 in New Delhi on the occasion of the 6th annual IGC-ISI India Development Policy Conference.

Section 1.2 is an edited version of a piece that appeared in Project Syndicate on 8 February 2018 under the title 'India's Path from Crony Socialism to Stigmatized Capitalism'.

Section 1.4 is an edited version of a piece—co-authored with Navneeraj Sharma and Gayathri Raj—that appeared in the *Hindu* on 21 February 2017.

Section 1.5 is an abbreviated version of a piece that appeared in the *Business Standard* on 1 February 2017. It was co-authored with Josh Felman, Rangeet Ghosh, Gayathri Raj, Sutirtha Roy and Navneeraj Sharma.

Section 2.1 is based on a piece—co-authored with Josh Felman, Rangeet Ghosh and Zubair Noqvi—that appeared in the *Indian Express* on 8 February 2017.

Section 3.1 is a reworked version of a piece—co-authored with Dr Hasmukh Adhia—that appeared in the *Hindu* on 19 July 2016.

Section 3.2 is an elaborated version of a piece that appeared in a number of newspapers on 4 April 2017.

Section 3.3 draws upon a piece that appeared in the *Indian Express* and *Financial Express* on 3 March 2017.

Section 3.4 is based on a piece—co-authored with Navneeraj Sharma—that appeared in the *Indian Express* and *Financial Express* on 7 December 2017.

Section 3.5 is an edited version of a piece—co-authored with Kapil Patidar—that appeared in the *Indian Express* and *Financial Express* on 20 June 2018.

Section 4.2 is an expanded version of a piece that appeared in the *Financial Times* on 26 November 2015.

Section 4.3 is based on TERI's 16th Darbari Seth Memorial Lecture that I delivered in New Delhi on 17 August 2017.

Section 4.4 is a reworked version of a piece—co-authored with Rangeet Ghosh, Sutirtha Roy and Navneeraj Sharma—delivered as a public lecture at the Hindu Centre for Politics and Public Policy in Chennai on 7 November 2017.

Section 5.1 is a reworked version of a piece delivered as the annual lecture at the National Academy of Agricultural Sciences in New Delhi on 5 June 2017.

Section 5.2 is an adapted version of a piece that appeared in the *Indian Express* and *Financial Express* on 9 November 2016.

Section 5.3 is an edited version of a piece that appeared in the *Indian Express* and *Financial Express* on 11 July 2018.

Section 6.2 is an edited version of a piece—co-authored with Siddharth George—that appeared in the *New York Times* on 22 July 2015.

Section 6.3 is an adapted version of a piece—co-authored with Siddharth George—that appeared in the *Indian Express* and *Financial Express* on 2 April 2016.

Section 6.4 was first delivered as a public lecture at Sabarmati Ashram on 2 October 2016.

Section 7.1 is an edited version of the 6th V.K.R.V. Rao Memorial Lecture delivered in Bengaluru on 11 May 2017.

Section 7.2 is an elaborated version of a piece—co-authored with Josh Felman—that appeared in *LiveMint* on 1 February 2017.

Section 7.4 is based on a Business Standard public lecture delivered in Mumbai on 20 July 2017. An edited version appeared in the *Business Standard* on 21 July 2017.

Section 8.1 is an edited and elaborated version of NCAER's Annual India Policy Forum Lecture delivered in New Delhi on 12 July 2016.

Section 8.2 is a reworked version of a piece that appeared in the Project Syndicate on 22 February 2017.

Section 8.3 is an edited version of an obituary that appeared in the *Indian Express* and Financial Express on 28 February 2017.

Section 8.4 is an edited version of a piece that appeared in the *Business Standard* on 22 April 2017.

Section 8.5 is an edited version of a piece that appeared in the *Business Standard* on 16 June 2018.